BABY NAMES 2021

Eleanor Turner

white
LADDER

First published in Great Britain in 2020 by White Ladder
An Hachette UK company

1

Copyright © Eleanor Turner 2020

A CIP catalogue record for this title is available from the British Library

Trade Paperback ISBN 9781910336625

Typeset in Zapf Humanist BT by Hewer Text UK Ltd, Edinburgh
Printed and bound in Great Britain by Clays Ltd, Elocraf S.p.A.

Hodder & Stoughton policy is to use papers that are natural, renewable
and recyclable products and made from wood grown in sustainable
forests. The logging and manufacturing processes are expected to
conform to the environmental regulations of the country of origin.

Hodder & Stoughton Ltd
Carmelite House
50 Victoria Embankment
London EC4Y 0DZ

www.hodder.co.uk

Contents

Author's note

Baby names vary widely in spelling and pronunciation. To simplify things, this book usually lists each name only once: under the most common initial and spelling. If a name has an alternative spelling with a different initial, it may also be listed under that letter.

Information relating to statistics and trends in baby names is based on the most recent data at the time of writing.

Acknowledgements

Many thanks as always to Beth Bishop at Crimson Publishing: your good humour and patience has helped this series endure to its eleventh edition. Thank you for sticking with me through it all.

My husband Mike has always been my biggest cheerleader and advocate, and writing this edition during the Covid-19 lockdown, surrounded by children and with nowhere quiet to escape to, has proved quite the challenge. Thank you for everything you do, particularly bringing me snacks and caffeine.

And finally, everything I do and everything I write about in this book is because of my children. If I have one hope, it's that they don't grow up hating their names . . . because that would be mortifying as a baby names expert. Owen Henri, Jasper Hugh, Josie May and Felix Brian: you are fantastic little people and I love each of you more and more every day. Now go and put some clothes on – I don't care if there is a pandemic and we're not leaving the house for a month. Love, Mama.

Introduction

Goodness me – what a year we've just had! 2020 was a year of chaos and uncertainty, and for those who had a baby I imagine it was also filled with worry and trepidation. It made for unforgettable global headlines as society was turned on its head, and we narrowed down what was truly important to each of us and how to protect it.

In the middle of all the fear, though, babies continued to be born and names were joyfully and carefully chosen for each new life. It made for some interesting developing trends, as you'll go on to learn about in this book. My wish for you if you are expecting a baby in 2021 is a calmer, simpler year ahead and a return to normal life. I hope it also comes with a renewed sense of optimism for the next generation about to be born: may they arrive into a world with love, peace . . . and practically perfect names.

Inside *Baby Names 2021* you'll find out:

- Why nicknames are out and vintage names are back in

- What the science says about baby naming

- What babies are being called in different countries around the world

- Where to register your baby's name

- . . . and what to do if you change your mind!

All the weird, wonderful, trendy and sciency trivia in this book is backed up by the most recent data from the Office of National Statistics, and includes all kinds of interesting titbits collected throughout the previous year. The goal is to make the decision over what to name your new baby as fun and easy as possible; so grab a pencil and a cuppa, dip in, and find some names you like. Use the plentiful suggestions and lists we've given you to find out whether one of them is your baby's future name.

Good luck!

Eleanor Turner

Part one

Naming your baby

1 Current baby-naming trends

'Every Tom, Dick, and Harry is called Arthur' Sam Goldwyn, film producer

While I think it's fair to say that 2020 was a bit of a rough ride, there were still plenty of causes for celebration. Babies continued to be born, names were lovingly chosen for them, and millions of people decided 'Netflix and chill' could be both a euphemism and an instruction on how to pass the time during a lockdown.

Last year was somewhat of a turning point for the human race. We all learned how valuable and short life can be, promising to slow down, see more of each other, and return to a simpler way of life once the global pandemic was over. And, true to form, this approach was immediately reflected in the curious world of baby names.

In the UK, this meant a few different trends emerged, including the return of short-and-sweet names, classic names from yesteryear, and even some musical and literary names. The joy of wrapping yourself in a fuzzy blanket with a new film or favourite book has never been more inspirational.

The UK Top 10 for both boys and girls for 2020 lined up like this:

The Top 10

Boys	Girls
1. Oliver	1. Olivia
2. George	2. Amelia
3. Harry	3. Ava
4. Noah	4. Isla
5. Jack	5. Emily
6. Leo	6. Mia
7. Arthur	7. Isabella
8. Muhammad	8. Sophia
9. Oscar	9. Ella
10. Charlie	10. Grace

Twins Oliver and Olivia continued to hold the top spots, and while there were only two new additions (Grace and Arthur), there was a lot of shuffling in the ranks elsewhere. Names that moved up included George, Leo and Muhammad for the boys, and Ava, Mia and Sophia for the girls; while Harry, Oscar and Charlie slipped on the boys' chart, and Isla and Isabella fell in the girls'.

But what's astounding is that nearly all the names in the Top 10 sound suspiciously the same. Notice a theme in the list for girls? There are eight names that sound strikingly alike: Amelia, Ava, Ella, Isabella, Isla, Mia, Olivia and Sophia. Consider how remarkable that is, for there to be only two names among the most popular in the country that don't end in —a. Now, I'm not saying we're in danger of becoming clones of each other, but we do clearly enjoy familiarity (and names that end in —a).

The boys are a little more varied in spelling and sound, but what's striking about their list is that it's dominated by the classics like Arthur, George and Noah. Simple, old-fashioned and perfect for the babies of our newly changed world.

Muhammad: #1 in 2030?

This spelling of Muhammad was the eighth most popular name for baby boys in 2020, jumping an impressive thirty spots in the last decade. However, there are many ways to spell this popular and symbolic Islamic name, such as Mohammed, Mohammad and Mohamed, and if all the various spellings were combined it would have been in first place! As it currently stands, Muhammad by itself could be in first place by 2030 if an additional two thousand babies are given that spelling each year. There may be a few reasons for the push up the charts, including a growth in the UK's overall Muslim population, an increase in the number of Muslim families choosing Muhammad over other religious names and celebrities such as boxer Amir Khan choosing it for their own babies.

The theory behind the names

So why do we do it? Why do we find ourselves naming our children the same as everyone else, and why do names in general come in cycles of popularity? Also, why do we humans choose names for our babies that are a reflection of the times we live in?

If you recall, 2020 was one of the strangest years to be alive in modern history. The world took a deep breath and paused life for a moment as we collectively agreed to socially distance ourselves in order to stop the spread of the coronavirus that caused a disease called Covid-19. It was an unprecedented and sudden stop to life as we knew it, and will go down in the annals of history as one of those 'where were you when . . .?' events we talk about with our grandchildren.

Current events have ways of infiltrating our psyche, and the pandemic was no different. Forcing us to spend time with our immediate family, locked down and appreciating how precious life and good health is made a lot of us stop and take stock. It also meant a lot of babymakin' went on (right?!) Of course, a natural consequence of a changed outlook, restricted social movement and more screen time was a pared-down approach to naming babies born during the lockdown. It meant returning to simpler, easy-to-spell names, or names we'd seen on the telly. Our lives were simpler and more focused, and therefore so were the names we gave our children. More on this trend on page 17.

> While most of us wanted to forget about the pandemic of 2020 entirely, others took the more . . . permanent approach of memorialising the event. India was the first country to announce babies born with virus-themed names, when boy and girl twins Covid and Corona were born in March of that year.

Of note, another interesting pattern that emerged during the lockdown was the number of parents giving their children inspirational names, or names with strong meanings. According to website ChannelMum, visitors confessed to choosing names such as Hope, Bravery, Hero and even Florence, after nursing legend Florence Nightingale. Florence moved up another few places to fourteenth place, Hope popped into the Top 150, and Hero was up in both the boys' and the girls' charts in 2020. Conversely, parents also admitted to moving away from names that sounded even remotely similar to coronavirus or Covid-19: Corina, Rona and even Lockie, (from 'lockdown') were all down last year.

> 'Alexa . . . tell me about baby names . . .' Our love for technology has even forced changes in the names we give to our children. The name Alexa has more than halved in popularity since 2017, when Amazon first introduced its virtual assistant into our homes, moving from 181st place to a lowly 380th.

Baby-naming trends

What else is going on in baby names at the moment? Well, there are some larger trends that have been going on for the last decade or so that don't show any sign of slowing down.

One of these ongoing patterns is that there are fewer babies being given the same name and a greater number of baby names being registered. In 2020 there were 319,492 baby girls included in the dataset and 337,584 boys. Of these, there were 27,946 different names registered for baby boys and 34,783 for baby girls. The Office for National Statistics (ONS) counts each spelling as a separate entry, even if it's essentially the same name; for example, Lily is counted separately from Lilly, Lillie and Lili, and the spelling with the most registrations reaches a higher place on the charts. Hyphenated names are also separated: Lily-Mae, Lily-May and Lily-Mai are all counted as individual names in the UK's official statistics (see page 20 for more on hyphenated names).

This is not how all countries create their baby name statistics. Australia, for example, used to tally names by sound, not spelling, which meant that way back in 2018 the popular boys' names Jackson/Jaxon/Jaxson appeared in shared ninth place, and Sophia/Sofia sat in shared seventh place for girls. However, in 2019, McCrindle, the agency that collates this data Down Under, decided to switch up their methodology and began isolating names by spelling, which meant that by 2020 Jackson fell to 47th place and Sophia plonked down to 21st, which was quite a tumble from grace for both of them. Another fun fact about Australia: it's also the country that allowed the names Hippo, Google, Burger and Hurricane to be registered for babies. Strewth!

Australia's Top 10

Boys		Girls	
1. Oliver	6. Thomas	1. Charlotte	6. Isla
2. Jack	7. Leo	2. Olivia	7. Grace
3. William	8. Lucas	3. Amelia	8. Harper
4. Noah	9. James	4. Ava	9. Chloe
5. Henry	10. Liam	5. Mia	10. William

Anyway, enough about our Aussie cousins; back to the UK. Other patterns to have emerged in the last year include an increase in nature-themed names. High climbers for girls included Willow, Rosie, Summer, Luna, Violet and Rose; and for boys the name Jasper jumped an impressive thirteen spots in a single year to appear in the Top 100 for the first time. Long names are also on the rise for boys, with Sebastian, Frederick, Theodore and Dominic all storming up the charts. Interestingly, it was the opposite for girls: the trendy choice for bundles of pink in 2020 was short, simple names such as Ava, Ayla, Esme and Zoe.

Master Archie

Did you notice that Harry and Meghan did something rather clever with their son's name, Archie Harrison? Archie is a shortened version of Archibald, which sounds a bit stuffy for a modern royal, so they went for a more popular (currently ranked 16th) and more relaxed version . . . just like the couple themselves. In addition, the middle name Harrison literally means 'son of Harry', and blends both Meghan's American roots with Harry's British ones as it's popular in both countries. The name Harrison is currently ranked 115th in the USA and 34th here in the UK. However, watch out for Archie's parents' names to take a nosedive in the ranks: now the couple has emigrated to Canada, their influence on UK baby names may start to wane.

Another solid trend for 2020 was the number of parents eagerly taking inspiration from their box-set binges during the pandemic. In particular, those of us who prioritised staring into the blue eyes of Cillian Murphy in *Peaky Blinders* rediscovered the classic names Arthur and Ada, both of which had massive surges in popularity, appearing in the Top 100 for the first time ever. For the record, the name Cillian also climbed the charts, jumping seventy spots in a single year to now appear in the Top 250. For more on big-screen inspiration, turn to page 35.

> According to naming website Nameberry, the reason we love names beginning with A is because we associate the first letter of the alphabet with being important. Absolutely amazing!

Biggest winners and losers

After more than a decade of writing the *Baby Names* book I've learned a thing or two. And one of those things is if a name is suddenly staggeringly popular one year and appears in our biggest winners club, it will gain traction and continue to grow in popularity the following year. So really we shouldn't be surprised that several of our big hitters are back in the game for 2020: Bonnie, Hallie, Hunter, Ezra and Roman.

Biggest Winners

Boys	Girls
1. Hunter	1. Margot
2. Grayson	2. Ada
3. Ezra	3. Delilah
4. Finn	4. Mila
5. Jesse	5. Hallie
6. Sonny	6. Bonnie
7. Dominic	7. Summer
8. Rowan	8. Ivy
9. Roman	9. Ayla
10. Jasper/Louis	10. Aurora

Like last year, we are still majorly into baby girl names that end in 'ah' sounds. Flip back to the Top 10 on page 5 and you'll see what I mean, and then take a gander at the Biggest Winners table for 2020: Ada, Delilah, Mila, Summer, Ayla, Aurora . . . 'ah', 'ah', 'ah'. Interestingly, though, Bonnie and Hallie were both on this list last year, and neither follows this trend. However, a few years back parents of little girls adored picking names ending in —y and —ie, so this older trend might be making a comeback. The new addition of Ivy certainly suggests that's the case.

Boys are more complicated. Hunter, Ezra and Jasper all sound alike – but we also have a really broad range of new sounds too. Jesse and Sonny are both big hitters, while Roman and Rowan could practically be twins, but generally there doesn't seem to be one overarching trend at all for boys. Other than Hunter of course, which was the highest-climbing name in 2019 as well as 2020. A decade ago only fifty-two baby boys were called Hunter, and yet now it's the 44th most popular name in the UK. Amazing.

Turning to some of the other high climbers from 2020, it's delightfully obvious that we are once again in love with vintage names that have been plucked from the pages of a well-thumbed history book. Ada, Ezra, Jasper, Margot and of course Roman all fit this theme beautifully, and support the idea that the classics are very much back in style. In fact, we predicted the name Ada would be a big climber in our 2019 edition, due to the rollover effect of the 100th anniversary of women's suffrage (marked in 2018 in the UK and 2020 in the USA). Ada Lovelace, a pioneer for early women's rights and all-round mathematical cleverclogs, is just the inspirational namesake we need for little girls everywhere. And popular actor Margot Robbie has been a big influence too, with her frankly disturbing yet unmissable portrayal of DC Comics villain Harley Quinn. For boys, Hunter is a very old surname whose use as a forename has been a more modern trend, while Rowan is a traditional Gaelic name meaning 'little red one'. All timeless, and all rising through the ranks.

One final note on our ascending favourites: Summer is a bit of a surprise this year. In 2019 and 2018 she appeared on our Biggest Losers list, so any baby names expert worth their salt would have predicted a further stumble down the charts in 2020 for this sunshine name . . . ahem . . . And yet here we are! Summer has actually been steadily falling since a peak of 23rd place in 2008, so to see her popping back up is a bit of a turn up for the books. Stay tuned to see if it's a seasonal blip or if Summer really is here to stay this time.

Let's switch now to address the Biggest Losers list, and what have we here? Harvey, Jake, Luke, Matthew and Ollie were all on last year's lists of plummeting names, and Darcie's alternative spelling of Darcey appeared there too. Ollie and Jake are likely not as popular due to the nation's slight pendulum swing back to full, traditional names instead of nicknames, but I really can't explain Matthew or Martha. Back when we started keeping baby name records electronically in 1996, Matthew was the sixth most popular name for boys, but has dropped so far down the charts that only 757 babies were called that last year. It's such a classic that it will probably make a comeback in the next few years, but for now it joins lowly Martha on the list of less-loved names.

> Less than one per cent of the UK's population changes their name by deed poll every year. According to the UK's largest deed poll service, recent name changes include Donald Duck, Ting A Long, Huggy Bear and Jellyfish McSaveloy.

Biggest Losers

Boys	Girls
1. Luke	1. Martha
2. Riley	2. Sara
3. Matthew	3. Darcie
4. Jenson	4. Lucy
5. Harvey	5. Jessica
6. Harley	6. Daisy
7. Jake	7. Ellie
8. Toby	8. Jasmine
9. Ollie	9. Anna
10. Zachary	10. Lola

Another name to have hit the skids is Anna. A beneficiary of the *Frozen* effect, Anna and her sister Elsa saw extraordinary increases in popularity in 2014 and 2015 after the release of the first film, but that effect seems to have worn off (for now). Anna tumbled far enough to make our Biggest Losers list in 2020, and Elsa has gone from a peak of 104th place in 2014 to just 437th. *Frozen 2* was released so late in the year in 2019 that it didn't have much time to have an impact on the data for 2020, so we may see some improvement in the fortunes of these names next year instead.

Regional flavours and flairs

As with a fine Cornish pasty or tasty haggis, different regions in the UK come with variations in flavour. Take baby names as another example. You'll find that, across the UK, each nation favours different names. Parents in England are more likely than those in any other region to name their child Muhammad; Welsh parents choose Alfie and Theo more frequently than the English; and Scottish parents like Lewis and Harris far more than both the English and the Welsh combined.

England's Top 10

Boys

1. Oliver	6. Leo
2. George	7. Arthur
3. Harry	8. Muhammad
4. Noah	9. Oscar
5. Jack	10. Charlie

Girls

1. Olivia	6. Mia
2. Amelia	7. Isabella
3. Ava	8. Sophia
3. Isla	9. Grace
5. Emily	10. Ella

Wales' Top 10

Boys

1. Oliver	6. Theo
2. Noah	7. Jack
3. Jacob	8. Alfie
4. George	9. Charlie
5. Oscar	10. Leo

Girls

1. Olivia	6. Mia
2. Ava	7. Elsie
3. Amelia	8. Lily
4. Ella	9. Emily
5. Isla	10. Freya

Scotland's Top 10

Boys

1. Jack	6. Noah		
2. Oliver	7. Lewis		
3. James	8. Leo		
4. Charlie	9. Rory		
5. Harris	10. Alfie		

Girls

1. Olivia	6. Amelia
2. Emily	7. Ava
3. Isla	8. Grace
4. Sophie	9. Freya
5. Ella	10. Charlotte

Northern Ireland's Top 10

Boys

1. James	6. Jacob
1. Noah	7. Oliver
3. Jack	8. Harry
4. Charlie	9. Thomas
5. Daniel	10. Leo

Girls

1. Grace	6. Amelia
2. Emily	7. Isla
3. Olivia	8. Anna
4. Sophie	9. Lily
5. Ella	10. Lucy

When it comes to girls' names, all four regions agree that Amelia, Ella, Emily, Isla and Olivia are excellent choices, as they appear in every single list, but disagree on some others. English parents overwhelmingly liked Sophia, for example, while those in Scotland and Northern Ireland preferred Sophie. In fact, the name Sophia slid down a slippery thirteen spots in Wales in 2020, as it used to be in seventh place! Whatever did poor Sophia do to the Welsh, I wonder? Mamau a tadau Cymraeg (Welsh mums and dads, for those of us not from the Land of Song) did however join Scottish ones in their love for Freya, and parents in Northern Ireland stood contrarily against the rest of the UK in their opinion of Anna (see page 13 for more on this *Frozen* name).

A couple of our regional lists this year have shared rankings, which is always intriguing. The reason for this is simple: with smaller datasets it only takes a handful of parents choosing the same name for there to be joint winners. In Scotland, 260 parents chose Amelia and another 260 chose Ava, creating a tie for sixth place. By comparison, Mia was sixth in England and was the favourite name of 2,362 parents. Even more astonishing, Northern Ireland had a tie for first place in 2020! James and Noah share the top of the podium with 217 baby boys apiece.

> The Deadspin tournament 'Name of the Year' pronounced Pope Thrower the winner of its annual competition last year, making it the second time in the competition's history a Pope has won. (Pope McCorkle III took the crown in 2016.) Mr Thrower beat out popular competitors Jizyah Shorts, Chastity Gooch-Fant and Storm Duck for the title.

Elsewhere, we see the reason why Arthur popped into the national Top 10 (see page 5): streaking up an impressive twelve places, Arthur has pushed Muhammad down a spot in England's individual rankings and is likely to stick around for a while more. In Scotland and Northern Ireland, Jack, James and Noah are the runaway hits for boys' names – names that have appeared all over the UK's Top 10 for years. In fact, Jack reigned supreme for a whopping sixteen years before being toppled by Oliver and Harry a few years ago. While its popularity has dominated for the last twelve years in Scotland, it's unlikely to return to glory in the rest of the UK soon as it has been losing ground for years; there were 202 fewer babies called Jack in 2020 than in the year before, but 600 from the year before that, so it's a lot of ground to make up.

There are quite a few names to appear in all four lists for the boys: Charlie, Jack, Leo, Noah and Oliver, which explains why they all appear in the nation's overall Top 10. And they all sound rather lovely in any regional accent, don't they? Interestingly, Muhammad was top in the North West, Yorkshire and the Humber, West Midlands and London regions, but only ranks eighth in the nation. However, given it climbed two spots in 2020 and came top in so many regions, it may yet keep climbing.

> The Cornish language is undergoing a revival, and so are its traditional names. Locryn, the name of a legendary British king, is once again in the charts, as is Demelza for little girls.

Verifiably vintage

Earlier in this chapter I mentioned that the biggest news story of 2020, the global pandemic of coronavirus Covid-19, had had an impact in more ways than we can count – including on the world of baby names.

Babies born in 2020 entered a world completely changed from what came before. Their parents likely birthed them in circumstances they had never imagined during their pregnancy: in many large cities across the world, women were told they had to labour alone, without a birth partner or their family close at hand. The risk of contracting one of the most contagious viruses seen since the Spanish Flu pandemic of 1918 was too great to chance it, and to protect our smallest infants everyone deemed non-essential was asked to stay away. It seemed unfathomable before the outbreak, and just as unfathomable once it was all over.

At the time of writing, the world was just starting to emerge from the global lockdown that grounded planes and parted loved ones. I hope you're safe now and excited to become a parent, free from the fear that gripped us all in 2020. I truly do.

> One glorious distraction from the pandemic came in the form of cult documentary series *Tiger King*. It spurred memes galore . . . and also inspired some baby names. In 2020 there were 17 babies called Tiger, 151 called Joe, but not a single one named Carole. (Or Sardine.)

But of course, thousands of babies were born during the crisis, and had to wait to meet their extended family. To appreciate the impact this had on the rippling waves of baby names, we need to explore the mindset of the parents who brought new life into the world just as we worked to protect life as we knew it.

Pregnant women in 2020 went through the ringer. It's a lot to be asked to birth alone, and to bring your baby home to an empty house because visitors are being told to stay away. No baby shower, no colleagues to bring you tea, no friends to help do the washing while you settle down to breastfeed (again). The chaos and the anxiety and the endless hours spent in your own home with your own company . . . it's a daunting prospect that many parents had to face on their own.

Is it really a surprise that parents in this situation decided en masse to simplify one of the foundation stones of their new baby's life: their name? Because that's exactly what happened.

By far and away the biggest trend to hit the world of baby names in 2020 was to pare down the extras. We removed the erroneous ys and xs from our spelling; gone are the weird but wonderful attempts at plunking two names together that we sort of liked, to create a brand new one that nobody ever really liked; and trending down were the 'tacky' names of the last decade. It was helped by the cancellation and postponement of many sporting events, concert tours and film and TV recordings – which meant pop culture was a lot less influential than in previous years.

Instead, we returned to simple, vintage, elegant names from history and from around the world, finding joy again in the traditional names that we'd once forgotten. Ivy, Harriet and Violet are back; and Mackenzie, Kayleen and Abbigail (yes, that's a real spelling for six baby girls in the UK) are all fading away. Parents of baby boys were equally enthusiastic about making things uncomplicated: Isaac, Albert and Theodore are rising in the ranks again, whereas Kaidan, Sylwester (again, a real spelling for real children), and Xzavier are all falling out of fashion. The old is new again, much to our collective relief.

Because really, simple is beautiful. And that's how we want the world to look again in 2021.

> A quick peek at the birth announcement sections of *The Times* and the *Telegraph* in 2020 provided the following collection of names. They might not be simple, but my goodness are they wonderful: Maximilian Roland Roger (all first names); Theodore Edmund Oliver (known as Teddy); Minnie Merry Melissa; and Tabitha Jane (sibling to Jemima Juliette and Xanthe Joy).

No longer forgotten

Other names of times gone by, such as Alexander, Florence, Penelope and Muhammad, have maintained their place in popularity, ranking within the Top 100 lists and joining such stalwarts as Beatrice, Eleanor, George and Jack. However, their typical nickname counterparts have recently started to head down the charts, including Alexei, Georgie, Jackie and Mo, for boys; and Bea, Ellie, Flora and Penny for girls. We went through several years of really embracing nicknames-as-first-names here in the UK, but it's too soon to tell if the trend is truly over. The return to simple, traditional names seen during the pandemic may yet be a blip, and parents of 2021 might be eager to pick up the nicknames trend where it left us back in 2019. Only time will tell. For more on nicknames turn to page 50.

Finally, what can you do if you want to give your little one a more traditional name, but don't want to saddle them with something that everyone else in their nursery class will also have? Well, how about resurrecting a really long-forgotten name? What about the Medieval options of Ulric, or Isolde; the Roman names Aquilia and Decimus; or perhaps the Ancient Mayan choices of Itzel or Aapo? Tradition doesn't have to mean boring, you know.

Spelling options for traditional names

Boys		Girls	
You like …	**Try …**	**You like …**	**Try …**
Benjamin	Bennie	Charlotte	Lottie
Daniel	Danny	Jessica	Jessie
Joseph	Josef	Lucy	Lucie
Thomas	Tomaz	Molly	Mollie
William	Willem	Robin	Robyn

Heavenly hyphenation

Let's explore some other ways to include a traditional name while making it your own. While it's a trend that's on the decline, still one of the most common ways parents add twists is by hyphenating names. There are over one thousand names with a hyphen in the most recent combined list of boys' and girls' names.

Popular endings include: -Rose, -May/-Mae and -Leigh/-Lee, which make names such as Amelia-Rose, Lily-Mae, Ava-Leigh and Ellie-May. In fact, if you add all the spelling variations together, names that end in -Rose would be in the Top 50 and those that include -May or -Mae would be around position 100. The highest-ranking hyphenated girl's name is Amelia-Rose, in position 254.

Boys are not exempt from this rule either, as it has become fashionable to add -James or -Lee to the end of a baby boy's name. In 2020 there were also a significant number of boys given the suffix –Junior, after their fathers. The highest-ranking hyphenated boys' name is Tommy-Lee (in position 767).

French law prohibits all names other than those on an approved list, and those that are deemed contrary to the interests of the child. Napoleon Bonaparte came up with the unusual law in 1803, and also decreed you couldn't name swine Napoleon. Which makes George Orwell's dictator pig in *Animal Farm* the literary equivalent of a giant middle finger, I suppose?

Perfect prophecies

In the last edition of this annual book we predicted that floral and nature names would be big in 2020 for little girls. We expected to see lots of names such as Willow, Rose, Violet and Ivy because they had already started growing the year before. Well, I'm delighted to say that yes, floral names were huge in 2020, and not just among those at the top of the charts. Other, more unusual names to have found a new lease of life included Orchid, Petal, Bloom and Birdy – none of which appeared in the data for 2019, but have suddenly sprung to the surface now. Options for boys in 2020 included Rocky, Robin, Ocean and Woody.

In a similar vein, we also predicted that jewel-themed names would become trendy and – being careful not to pat ourselves too strenuously on the back – we were right on this one, too. Onyx crept up the charts for both boys and girls, while Jasper has skyrocketed into the Top 100 for the first time ever. I will concede that Ruby is on a bit of a downward

Some of Britain's quirky baby names in 2020

Boys	Girls
Bamber	Arrow
Crew	Excellent
Dodge	Hendrix
Falcon	Kirby
Hannibal	Lettice
Juke	Lyric
Marvellous	Promise
Peace	Sunshine
Prosper	Tuba
Sailor	Zixi

slide, from a peak position of number one in 2007 to a lowly 32nd place in 2020, but an impressive 1,500 babies were still given that name. Other options for this trend include Diamond, Garnet and Jet.

Finally, when predicting trends for 2020 it looked as though feminist names would spring up. Names such as Emmeline, Ada, Nancy, Rosa and Frida were considered likely to grow in popularity thanks to a roll-over effect from the 100th anniversary of women's suffrage in the UK in 2018 and in the USA in 2020 . . . and, by golly gosh, we were right! We even called out Ada specifically, foretelling that it would appear in the Top 100, and wouldn't you know it? It not only appeared in the top 100, but it jumped the highest of any name there: from 114th place in 2019 to an impressive 65th in 2020. Other feminist names to march to the top were Emmeline (up 85 spots), Sylvia (up 81 spots) and Millicent (up 41 spots). Well done, sisters! (And well done us.)

 # This year's predictions

So, what goodies will the *Baby Names* fairy bring in 2021? (Because I bet there is such a fairy and that she's got a great first name.) Well, it will certainly be interesting to see if the trend for simple, traditional names seen in 2020 will continue, or if the reversal back to normal life and travel will encourage parents to pick more free-thinking names. Pop culture will of course have an impact on our choices, as well as any political goings-on, so let's take a look at some of the other latest and greatest ways to name a baby this year:

- Foreign flora and fauna. While it's true that floral names have been a hit in 2020, the lifted travel restrictions in 2021 might lead us to choose nature-themed names in other languages from around the world. Watch out for Zahra (Arabic for 'flower'), Parna (Gujarati for 'leaf'), and Latica (Croatian for 'petal') to all jump up the charts.

- Jewels and gemstones will shine. Just like the theme above, this one sees new parents sticking with an old 2020 trend but adding a foreign translation. If you love gemstone names like Onyx, Garnet and Ruby, how about Hirkani (Sanskrit for 'like a diamond'), Poho (Hawaiian for 'gemstone'), or even just simple Margaret (Greek for 'pearl')?

- Simple, vintage and traditional names. Covered extensively in Chapter 1, this trend has every chance of sticking around. Nicknames-as-names are on the decline, as are names with unusual spellings – or, frankly, just made up. Watch for Eleanor, Felicity, Gabriel and Ralph.

- Children's books names. It's natural for parents to think about their own childhood when preparing for a new baby, and it often gets us remembering fondly the characters from our favourite children's books. I always wanted to name my daughter Darrell, from Enid Blyton's terrific *Malory Towers* series, but my husband never shared my enthusiasm unfortunately. Sigh. However, there might be the perfect name for your baby just hanging out on the nursery bookshelf, so let's see if 2021 brings us more Charlottes (from *Charlotte's Web*), Winnies (from *Winnie The Pooh*), Alices (from *Alice's Adventures in Wonderland*), and Maxes (from *Where the Wild Things Are*).

> Iceland is so strict about its baby-naming laws that it has a committee that votes on whether to permit new additions to the approved list of names each year. There are only about 4,000 names on the list, and just three of them appear on both the boys and girls lists: the rest are strictly segregated. Names added to the list in 2020 included Systa and Sólúlfur, and rejected names included Zion and Alex.

Predicted 2021 Top 10

Boys	Girls
1. Oliver	1. Olivia
2. George	2. Amelia
3. Noah	3. Ava
4. Harry	4. Emily
5. Leo	5. Isla
6. Arthur	6. Mia
7. Muhammad	7. Sophia
8. Jack	8. Grace
9. Thomas	9. Isabella
10. Archie	10. Charlotte

Finally, I'm going out on a limb here, but I'm also predicting Great Depression and Great Recession names will cycle around again. This one's a smidge controversial, but history has proved time and again that economics plays a part in what we name our children. As the world's economy ground to a sudden halt in 2020, there were echoes of the Great Depression (1929 until the late 1930s) as well as the Great Recession (2005–9). Now, with millions still affected by the global slowdown last year, it's fair to say our interest in the names that were popular in those times might be piqued – especially as we are drawing closer to it being a century since the Great Depression, and therefore being able to apply the cyclical 100-year-rule. Names from the Great Depression include Betty, Charles, Mary and Robert; and Grace, Emily, Harry and Jack from the Great Recession.

Goings on in 2021

As the pandemic was unfolding, it was hard to keep track of all the events that were cancelled in 2020. However, many of them were simply postponed until 2021, so we will still have ample opportunity this year to see how they can have an impact on baby names. For that reason, 2021 is predicted to be a bit of a stonker. Between the Summer Olympics, Euro 2021, the Women's Rugby World Cup and goodness knows what in Europe's political landscape, it is going to be a hectic twelve months. And the fallout will naturally affect baby names, because let's face it: pretty much everything else does.

Athletes who perform well at 2021's major sporting events will no doubt become inspirational for new parents.

The Summer Olympic and Paralympic Games will finally take place in Tokyo and we will no doubt see the champions' names fly up the charts. The success of Great Britain's Olympic team in 2016 led to an increase in babies being born with the names Laura (after cyclist Laura Trott), Alistair (after triathlete Alastair Brownlee), Jade (after taekwondo-ka Jade Jones) and, of course, Mohamed (after athletics legend Sir Mo Farah). However, two years after each Olympics the names all dropped down again – proof that sporting events really do have an impact, even if it is only temporary.

UEFA Euro 2021 is also finally being held in a dozen different European cities this summer, and, as footballers have a strong tradition of influencing baby names, this event will provide inspiration to many. After the 2018 FIFA World Cup, Neymar and Luis Suárez saw their names create waves on and off the pitch. Neymar jumped a staggering 2,300 places in three years, and Luis moved up 30 spots to the Top 350. With the Women's Rugby World Cup happening in 2021, it will be interesting to see which girls' names move up in the charts in response to this.

> According to American media outlet ABC News, the smash hit musical *Hamilton*, based on the life of US Founding Father Alexander Hamilton, continues to give rise to an increase in the number of babies given the name. This follows the trend of naming babies after US historical figures, such as Lincoln and Madison.

In terms of politics, politicians have an up and down relationship with baby name trends. During Barack Obama's term as US President his name never moved up more than a few places, but after the Presidential Election in 2016 the name Donald moved up 500 places in a single year here in the UK. Interestingly, in the run up to the 2020 Presidential Election, Donald took a dive in the US charts and landed somewhere around position 550. At the time of writing the 2020 elections hadn't happened yet, so it will be fascinating to see whether this decline in his name's popularity will also be a reflection of how voters act. American baby name statistics are seeing a slight lean towards more Southern-US-style names due to Trump's large voting bloc there, and some of those names and style of names are catching on here too. Suggestions include Brayden, Kynslee, McKenna and Royan.

Also worth noting is that while Barack never trended either here or across the pond, the names of his daughters, Sasha and Malia, actually did, as did the children of David Cameron during his term as the nation's leader – particularly Florence. Boris Johnson's new son Wilfred also has a trendy name: it was up 20 places in 2020 and now sits in the Top 150. The name Boris, however, was only given to 47 babies last year.

But what of Brexit? At the time of writing we are still waiting to assess the political and economic impact of Brexit in Britain, but 2020 will surely be a game-changer regardless. My guess is that with the opening up of travel once again we will see a pleasant mixture of continental names and names that are inspired by Great Britain. That could include regal names; geographical names such as London, Preston, Elan or Iona; or names from British folklore such as Robin, Britannia, Arthur or Bran.

By Royal Decree

Did you know that the Queen gets a say in what new princes and princesses are called? In 1988, Princess Beatrice was going to be called Annabel but the Queen dismissed it as 'too yuppie', according to the *Sun*. She suggested the more traditional Beatrice and it stuck. Maybe she had the final say in Prince George's name – George was her father's name, after all – but probably not in Prince Harry's son Archie's. As Archie has not been given a royal title, it's not quite as important that his name 'fits the bill', so to speak.

3 The world of celebrity babies

Celebrities are nothing if not trendsetters. From your regular old-school actors and singers to the newest waves of Instagram influencers and YouTube stars, it's never been more important for celebrities to curate a brand for themselves – and three million of their closest friends and followers. Recently this has spilled over into the world of celebrity baby names, with a whole host of stars expressing profound personal meanings behind the names they picked. It's become crucial to celeb branding to assign value to every product they endorse on social media . . . so why would baby names be any different?

Now, please note that this observation is not coated in cynicism. As an author and researcher of baby names, I personally love this concept! In fact, you'll see it mentioned several times elsewhere in this book: to give your child a name with personal meaning and connection is a really worthwhile endeavour. The fact that celebrities are joining in the movement is wonderful! Although true to form, there are always some celebrities who take it a little too far – looking at you, Elon Musk – and that's why we love them, right?

> There was a sharp uptick in the numbers of babies called Kobe in 2020 in both the UK and the USA charts, after the death of American basketball legend Kobe Bryant.

Let's start with Raddix, the name selected by Cameron Diaz and Benji Madden for their newborn daughter in 2020. Diaz and Madden shared with friends that they created the name from two of their favourite words: 'rad' and 'dix', with dix apparently being a translation of 'new beginning' in a philosophical belief system shared by the couple. So there you go – if you're truly stuck for a name, just follow their lead and make one up! In 2021 anything goes.

Moving on to Lucy Mecklenburgh and Ryan Thomas, this celebrity duo picked the first name Roman for their little boy, and combined it with the middle name Ravello. According to sources Ravello is the Italian town where the couple got engaged, and Roman means 'from Rome', so the Italian theme is strong with this one. Maybe his first word will be *'ciao'*?

> British model Iskra Lawrence announced her daughter's name in 2020 by casually dropping just the initials A. M. P. into a Twitter post. Unfortunately it meant fans of the couple started calling their baby Amp, which seems to have stuck. What an electric nickname.

One of the more unusual names on the list is Slash Electric Alexander, the moniker awarded to the son of model Amber Rose. Explaining that their son 'is a rockstar', Amber Rose's partner Alexander 'AE' Edwards commented that his baby boy also shares his name. I suppose if you're going to go with something like Slash Electric for a first name, balancing it with the more modest Alexander helps keeps things palatable.

Another unusual choice is Birdie, from David and Georgia Tennant, who are also parents to Ty, Olive, Wilfred and Doris. Birdie's name was accidentally dropped by the couple's eldest son Ty, when he gave a shout out to each of his siblings during an appearance on *Lorraine*. Coincidentally, Birdie is also the name American singer Jessica Simpson gave to her daughter in 2019, and was given to sixteen other baby girls in the UK in 2020.

Keeping with the nature theme, other names that celebrate flora and fauna include Winter Mercy, Alanis Morissette's third baby, and Coco Knox, singer Ronan Keating's newest addition. The singer's wife, Storm Keating, shared the news about their pregnancy in 2019, confessing that she had already picked out 'a non-traditional' name for the baby ahead of the birth.

Keeping Mum

While most celebrities embrace living in the public eye, there are definitely those who want to protect their children by keeping them far away from it. That often starts on day one, with stars such as *TOWIE's* Amy Childs pledging to keep her newborn son's name quiet in 2018 before accidentally announcing it in 2020 as Rich. She managed an impressive eighteen months of secrecy, but that pales in comparison to music mogul Pharrell Williams. The names of his triplets born in 2017 have never been made public, much to the chagrin of this name-obsessed author. Come on . . . how many times do you get to write about celebrity baby trios? Spill the beans, Pharrell!

American comedian Amy Schumer legally changed her infant son's name in 2020 from Gene Attell Fischer to Gene David Fischer, after 'helpful' online commentators pointed out that Gene Attell sounded a lot like 'genital'. Oops. Attell was chosen as a tribute to a family friend, so Amy and her husband Chris Fischer switched their little boy's name to the friend's first name of David instead.

My long-held theory behind unusual celebrity choices is that being a celebrity often demands a unique name, so that people know instantly to whom that news headline or BAFTA award belongs. Celebrities are probably just being smart in this regard: give a baby a unique name from birth and you've already started their brand. Job done.

However, there are some completely normal names on the list this year too, such as Isaiah, Maven, Max and Muhammad to name just a few. Enrique Iglesias and Anna Kournikova chose the eternal favourite Mary for their baby girl, nicknaming her the Russian version Masha in homage to Kournikova's heritage; and Boris Johnson and Carrie Symonds chose Wilfred Lawrie Nicholas after two family members and the NHS doctors who saved the Prime Minister's life during his hospitalisation with Covid-19.

So what is this particular batch of celeb babies to do with their normal, more conventional names? I would argue that these saner choices are reflective of the greater general trend of parents moving back towards older, more traditional names. Although the thought has simultaneously occurred to me that perhaps our perception is just skewed, and maybe Alanis Morissette's choice of Winter Mercy for a baby boy doesn't seem half as bonkers as it should, because we've had decades to get used to celeb offspring: think sixteen-year-old Apple Martin, twenty-four-year-old Heavenly Hiraani Tiger Lily Hutchence Geldof and seventeen-year-old Daisy Boo Pamela Oliver.

Finally . . . it would be remiss of us not to mention the most talked-about name choice of all from 2020. Tesla founder Elon Musk and his partner, the musician Grimes, were caught in the middle of some of the madness when rumours abounded that they were naming their unborn child Influenza Musk, in keeping with the global pandemic theme. However, this was only a prequel to the main event, when it was announced they'd actually chosen X Æ A-12.

New Arrivals

A. M. P. (Iskra Lawrence and Philip Payne)
Birdie (David Tennant and Georgia Tennant)
Coco Knox (Ronan Keating and Storm Keating)
Ella (Ola Jordan and James Jordan)
Ilana (Iveta Lukosiute and Jenya Raytses)
Isaiah (Christina Milian and Matt Pokora)
Lyra (Michael Sheen and Anna Lundberg)
Mary/Masha (Enrique Iglesias and Anna Kournikova)
Maven (Rachel Riley and Pasha Kovalev)
Max Valentine (Natalie Imbruglia)
Muhammad Zaviyar (Amir Khan and Faryal Makhdoom)
Raddix (Cameron Diaz and Benji Madden)
Roman Ravello (Lucy Mecklenburgh and Ryan Thomas)
Sienna Grace (Millie Mackintosh and Hugo Taylor)
Slash Electric Alexander (Amber Rose and Alexander Edwards)
Wilfred Lawrie Nicholas (Boris Johnson and Carrie Symonds)
Winter Mercy (Alanis Morissette and Mario Treadway)
X Æ A-12 (Elon Musk and Grimes)

The couple explained it was a combination of letters and sounds related to love, artificial intelligence and an airplane model. As you do. However, as Californian baby name law prohibits the registration of names that use characters other than the standard 26 characters of the English alphabet, it's likely the couple's child won't be saddled with this choice for long.

Upcoming arrivals

Celebrity couples expecting new arrivals include Katy Perry and Orlando Bloom, Dermot O'Leary and Dee Koppang, and Rochelle and Marvin Humes. If history is anything to go by, the names these couples pick will be highly scrutinised and influential on the rest of us. And frankly, I'm

---

Bumps Ahead

Katy Perry and Orlando Bloom
Vogue Williams and Spencer Matthews
Dermot O'Leary and Dee Koppang
Alec Baldwin and Hilaria Baldwin
Michelle Williams and Thomas Kail
Sophie Turner and Joe Jonas
Ciara and Russell Wilson
Felicity Jones and Charles Guard
Kevin Hart and Eniko Hart
Michelle Hardwick and Kate Brooks
Rochelle Humes and Marvin Humes

---

expecting big things. Come on Alec and Hilaria Baldwin: this is baby number five for you and I'm expecting big, bonkers things this time around.

4 On-screen inspo

The impact of characters in movies, books and TV programmes is always huge on baby names. We've seen some predictable trends, such as *Star Wars*, Marvel films and anything produced by Disney, but also some unexpected ones. So, think of your Netflix and Disney+ binges as technically research. Winning!

In an unprecedented twist of fate, many blockbuster films set to release in 2020 had to push back their premiere dates as cinemas closed their doors during the pandemic. There was therefore less of an impact on baby names from the entertainment industry last year than in years past, but 2021 looks set to make up for it in droves. As an example, *Trolls World Tour* released straight to streaming services, and the name Poppy, which had bounced up to eighth place in 2016 after the first film's release, actually slid down a few spots in 2020. We're left wondering if this would have been different if the film had gone to cinemas instead.

> Did you know Chandler used to be one of the highest-climbing names in the UK in the 1990s, thanks to *Friends*? At a peak of position 342, since the series ended in 2004 there have been next to no babies born with the name. However, with a reunion special planned to celebrate the series' 25th anniversary, exciting things could happen again for Mr Bing!

Mulan, Disney's live-action update of the 1998 cartoon, was one such movie to be affected by the coronavirus outbreak, when its release date was pushed back from spring to summer. However, the star of the film, Liu Yifei, did see her name appear in our charts for the first time since 2017. Another casualty to the cause was *Black Widow*, which moved from spring to autumn. Natasha, the real name of the titular character, was in freefall in the UK until 2020, when it suddenly spiked. Perhaps studios should pay attention to its audience and release more female-led superhero movies . . . huh, Marvel? Finally, *Wonder Woman 1984* was an extraordinary film that followed the enduring adventures of Diana Prince, an Amazonian princess who once again saves the world. Diana, a name that has been slowly increasing in popularity since the 1997 death of Princess Diana, saw a new spike in 2020 to regain its place in the Top 300.

Influences on boy names kicked off with *Top Gun: Maverick*, the sequel to 1986's original *Top Gun*. The name Maverick jumped an impressive 200 spots to land in the mid-500s, and Miles – the name of actor Miles Teller – is now in position 170. *The Way Back*, a Ben Affleck drama about a man named Jack, was also released to critical acclaim. Jack has been consistently amongst the Top 10 for decades, with as many as two per cent of all baby boys born in the UK given the name back in the 1990s. 2020 saw the name stabilise after a brief decline, which may be thanks to the film. And finally, *No Time to Die*, the final James Bond movie for star Daniel Craig, was released just as 2020 ended. Both James and Daniel remain hugely popular in the UK, but fewer babies are being given the names every year. It will be interesting to see if the names perk up again in 2021 as the film came out a little too late in the year to have much of an impact on trends.

> *Star Wars: The Rise of Skywalker* was released on streaming platform Disney+ in 2020. Surprisingly, the name Kylo has seen amazing growth, jumping 1,500 places since the character

of Kylo Ren first appeared on screen in 2015 – this is highly unusual as, historically, baddies have the opposite effect on the baby name charts! *The Mandalorian*'s second season also had an impact on the name Pedro, after star Pedro Pascal, which moved up nearly eighty places in 2020.

Other big movies in 2020 included the remake of Leonard Bernstein's *West Side Story*. Directed by Steven Spielberg, this mammoth musical blockbuster brought 1950s New York back to life, and with it a whole host of wonderful names. Names to attract our interest included Valentina, Riff and Anita – played by original 1961 cast member Rita Moreno. Moreno's birth name is Rosa Delores Alverío Marcano, but she was nicknamed Rosita at a young age. When Hollywood beckoned she shortened it to Rita and adopted her stepfather's last name to become the legend she is today. Impressively, all three of her names are currently trending: Rosa, Rosita and, of course, Rita.

Popular recent TV shows include *The Crown*, *Killing Eve*, *Fleabag* and *Liar*. No doubt *The Crown* has provided huge inspiration for parents, who may well now consider the names George, Elizabeth, Philip, Margaret or Charles. The fourth series brought us Margaret Thatcher and of course Lady Diana Spencer, and is another explanation for why the name Diana is currently trending again.

Killing Eve, everyone's favourite show about the cat-and-mouse game between a serial killer and the officer hired to catch her, had a third series in 2020. The name Eve has started to move up the charts again after a decade of decline, but unfortunately – or fortunately – there wasn't a single baby named Villanelle last year. Head writer for *Killing Eve*, Phoebe Waller-Bridge, also created and starred in the tragicomedy *Fleabag*, where the lead character curiously doesn't have a name. The name Phoebe has stayed pretty consistently in the Top 25 for a number of years, and last year it hung out in 21st place.

It took almost 20 years, but a Vietnamese teenager was able to successfully change his name to Mai Hoang Long, meaning Golden Dragon, after a lifetime of ridicule. His father, forced to pay a fine for the birth of his fifth child, originally named his newborn son Mai Phat Sau Nghin Ruoi – which translates to Fined Six Thousand And Five Hundred.

Liar haunted our living rooms early in the year, and with it came a host of new parents naming their baby boys after co-star Welsh actor Ioan Gruffudd. His name, the Welsh version of John, moved up forty places in 2020 following the broadcast of the second series of this thriller drama. Another name of note is Martin (Freeman, from *Breeders*), which rose thirty-five spots last year.

And finally, *Twilight* was back! Do you remember how mad we all went for the name Bella back in the day, watching it soar from a lowly 260th place to the Top 50 in only five years? Well, after the 2020 release of Stefanie Meyer's fourth book, *Midnight Sun*, everyone's ears perked up again over the names Bella, Edward and Jacob. Stay tuned to see how they impact 2021 data, as the book came out mid-year and didn't have much time to truly make its mark.

Banned Names Around the World

@ – China
Chow Tow (meaning 'smelly head') – Malaysia
Lucifer – Germany
Messiah – New Zealand
Mona Lisa – Portugal
Monkey – Denmark
0 – Sweden
Osama Bin Laden – Germany
Stompy – Germany

Did you know the artist Pablo Picasso was actually born Pablo Diego José Francisco de Paula Juan Nepomuceno María de los Remedios Cipriano de la Santísima Trinidad Ruiz y Picasso? That would have been one hell of a signature to fit at the bottom of a painting.

So what's next?

The year 2021 is going to be pretty interesting for film and television. In addition to the planned releases, there are dozens of mega hits that were originally due to be released in 2020 that never made it (thank you *again*, pandemic . . . sigh . . .) Included in the line-up are a third *Fantastic Beasts* film starring Eddie Redmayne; *Cruella*, a prequel to *101 Dalmations*; *Jungle Cruise*, a family action adventure based on the Disneyland ride; Marvel's *Thor: Love and Thunder*; and the much-anticipated *Avatar 2* and *The Matrix 4*.

Names that are featured in these films stand a good chance of influencing baby names if past trends are repeated. *Avatar 2*, for example, will almost definitely spike interest in the name Zoe again, given the popularity of lead actress Zoe Saldana. After the release of the original *Avatar* in 2009, the name Zoe peaked in popularity, but it's been going downhill ever since. It's entirely possible the sequel will introduce a new generation to names such as Neytiri and Jake, although the likelihood of anyone being named Na'vi is perhaps a bit of a stretch.

Big Screen Baby Names

Boys	Girls
Daniel	Diana
Ioan	Elizabeth
James	Eve
Keanu	Natasha
Martin	Phoebe
Maverick	Rita
Miles	Rosita
Neo	Valentina
Phillip	Yifei

Most excitingly, for those of us old enough to remember the initial trilogy, *Matrix 4* will be on the big screen in 2021. The popularity of the name Keanu has risen dramatically since the announcement of the fourth instalment, jumping nearly 500 spots last year. And the name Neo, which didn't exist on the charts prior to the first film's release in 1999, has become so popular it broke into the Top 300 in 2003 when the last film came out. Following the same trend, it's expected that both names will spike again in 20201.

As for the influence the telly could wield on our collective baby-naming psyche in 2021, *Intelligence* is a good place to start. This comedy series starring Nick Mohammed and David Schwimmer was new in 2020, but with a second series being shown in 2021 we can expect it to keep influencing the name Mohammed. This particular spelling is currently 32nd and gathering steam. Another traditionally Muslim name that will be impacted by TV in 2021 is Mobeen. The comedy series *Man Like Mobeen* was first broadcast in 2017, and the name immediately doubled in popularity. With the fourth series predicted for next year, watch out for this name to keep on climbing.

And finally, we can't finish this chapter without another hat tip to *Peaky Blinders*. Like many other programmes, filming had to be delayed for the pandemic, but that hasn't stopped the show from being a heavy influence on baby names such as Ada, Arthur and Cillian. For a more detailed look at what happened to names from the show in 2020, turn to page 10.

Old Hollywood Names

Boys	Girls
Cary	Audrey
Clark	Ava
Clint	Doris
James	Grace
Jimmy	Elizabeth
Oliver	Ingrid
Marlon	Judy
Rock	Vivien

5 How to choose a name

Your baby-naming checklist

Naming a baby should be, above all, a fun experience. I encourage you to think carefully about your final decision because it does have real-life implications, but there's no reason why careful consideration cannot be combined with enjoyment. Here are some nice ideas to get the old brain cells working.

- Fall in love with the name(s) you've chosen. Pick a name that makes you smile, because if you love it, hopefully your child will too.

- Try it out. While you're pregnant, talk to your baby using their name to see if they respond. You can also try writing names down, practising a few signatures, or saying one out loud enough times to see if you ever get sick of it.

- Don't listen to other people. Sometimes family and friends offer well-meaning baby-naming advice, which may not always be welcome. If you've got your heart set on a name, keep it a secret until after the birth to avoid any unnecessary criticism.

- Don't steal ideas! One survey found that friends stealing baby names was a legitimate reason for the break down of adult friendships.

- Find a name with meaning. Choosing a name that is rooted in history or folklore might just inspire your little one to be as great as their namesake. There's research to suggest this inspirational rub-off effect has real legs, so even if you pick a name out of the air, consider making something up to tell them later!

  > Norwegians and the Portuguese are only allowed to use names that appear on an approved list, which has led to parents being fined and even jailed for breaking the law! Banned names in Norway include Gesher (meaning bridge), and anything that could be mistaken for a surname.

- Have fun. Picking out names should be fun. Laughing at the ones you'd never dream of choosing can really help you to narrow it down to the ones you would.

- Expand your mind. Be brave and bold if that's what you want, but just in case you get it massively wrong (definitely a possibility, let's face it) you might want to give them a simpler middle name so they can jump ship to that instead.

  > According to the BBC, non-British names are mispronounced more often in places of work, leading to embarrassing situations such as reporter Dhruti Shah being called Dorito, or IT professional Nana Mardo acquiring the nickname Nandos. Suggested solutions? Spell it out for people or rhyme it with something else to make it easy to remember.

- What if you can't agree? This is probably the trickiest problem to solve. Research a number of names that you and your partner both like, and make a point of

Posh Names

Algernon	Araminta
Aubyn	Blanche
Cosmo	Jori
Horace	Milicent
Merlin	Octavia
Tybalt	Tansy
Zebedee	Tuppence

discussing them long before the baby is due. The delivery room is *not* the place for these discussions.

- Compromise is key. Pick two middle names so that you each have one in there that you love, or you could each have five names that you're allowed to veto – but no more. Whichever way you go about it, it's important that you eventually agree on the name you are giving your baby, even if it means losing out on the one you've had your heart set on for a while.

- Finally: keep reading and re-reading this book – the answer is in here.

Think to the future

Let's go back to the future. Will the name you've chosen stand the test of time? Will names popular in 2021 remain popular in 2051? Will your son or daughter be able to enter a room and give a confident presentation with an awkward or unpronounceable name? Heck, can they survive the playgrounds of primary and secondary school with a name that could be embarrassing?

Buzzfeed.com recently ran an article on funny names of real people who worked in retail. Serving us in supermarkets and shops around the world are Porsche Keys, Crystal Metz and Harry Bush, among others. Imagine one of those names coming over the intercom when you're shopping? A few of the stories also came from people who explained the reasons their parents gave them unusual names: one was named after a football stadium, one after their grandmother's cat and another after a female IRA terrorist. At least they have origin stories, I guess!

At the same time, another article appeared listing all the reasons why having an unusual name was a pain, such as never being able to find your name on novelty souvenirs, and other people giving you 'fun' nicknames because they can't be bothered with your actual name. Pretty annoying, huh?

> Word of caution when considering the name of your second or third child. If your first child is called Sam, don't do what one family almost did and name your daughter Ella. Sam-and-Ella sounds a little too close to Salmonella for comfort!

Stereotypes: true or false?

'With a name like yours, you might be any shape, almost.' *Through the Looking-Glass*, Lewis Carroll

Will the name you choose actually affect your child's life? Will it have an impact on the person they become, or how they see the world? Will names that seem clever mean that your child will be brainier? Will names with positive meanings make your child into a happier person? The answer is . . . possibly.

Anthroponomastics is the term used for the study of personal names, and it's a field that continues to intrigue and amaze us. For example, a study conducted by the Hebrew University of Jerusalem in 2017 found that we subconsciously act like stereotypes of our names, and that other people can pretty accurately guess what our names are as a result. They asked students to guess the names of faces they were shown, and the students were able to correctly match them twice as often as expected. So if you're choosing a name traditionally associated with a particular personality trait, it might be time to find out what the stereotype is. (But you can probably relax: Herbert was the

Emotional Names

Destiny	Joy
Happy	Peace
Heaven	Serenity
Hope	Unique
Innocence	Unity

name suggested to be most associated with a dimwit and only fifty baby boys were given that in 2020, so odds are you're safe.)

One thing you should consider is how your child's name will be perceived by the outside world. There's no getting around the fact that judgements are passed on names, even before meeting a person, in situations such as job interviews or at school.

Recently, teachers across the country were asked to decide from a list of names which children were more likely to be badly behaved than others. Topping the 'naughty' charts were Callum and Jack for boys, and Chelsea and Courtney for girls. On the other hand, the names in the 'clever' category were Alexander and Christopher for boys, and Elizabeth and Charlotte for girls.

Teachers were also asked to pick names that they felt were given to popular children and these included Jack, Daniel, Emma and Hannah – which means that little boys named Jack are naughty but popular!

A study by the University of Hertfordshire asked members of the opposite sex to rate names according to attractiveness, luck and success. The top names were James and Elizabeth, which authors concluded was a result of them being traditionally royal names, and therefore aspirational and associated with intelligence and success. However, the lowest-ranked name for sexiness was George, which is also traditionally royal . . . and I'm fairly certain fans of George Clooney would dispute the results anyway.

An article from the BBC *Science Focus* magazine noted that there are also people who have entered (or fallen into) professions that match their name. The phenomenon, called 'nominative determinism', helps explain world-class athletes such as Usain Bolt, dentists such as Dennis Smiler from Los Angeles, and one of the academic researchers for the article itself being called Richard Wiseman. So that might be a cool trick to consider for your child's future: pick a first name that encourages them to be successful in their career endeavours, or a superstar athlete. No pressure at all.

> How about a name without vowels? In 2020, Flynn, Fynn, Kym, Lynn, Wynn, Sky, Syd and Vy all made their way onto the Births Register.

Names that mean 'clever'		Names that sound 'clever'	
Abner	Shanahan	Alastair	Gabriel
Cassidy	Todd	Charles	Harriet
Haley	Ulysses	Christian	Sophia
Penelope	Washington	Elizabeth	Spencer
Portia	Wylie	Frances	William

Quirky names

While there are drawbacks to having an obviously out-there name, being different has advantages too. For one thing, other people will never forget your child's name, which means they won't be easily forgotten either. But does a quirky name demand a quirky personality? If you don't think your genes could stand up to a name such as Satchel or Kerensa, perhaps it's time to think of one that's a little more run of the mill.

> The only names you can't change your name to by UK Deed Poll are those that indicate rank or title (such as Sir or Lord) and those that are deemed blasphemous – including Jesus and Satan. You also can't use numbers or symbols . . . so Sir Duke 1976 is a no-go. New Zealand has a similar law, but also puts a limit of one hundred characters for the overall name.

A survey carried out by the National Centre for Social Research found that the more unusual the name, the less likely a candidate is to be called for a job interview. Whether or not this fact would affect a child's development and future career is yet to be determined, but it is something to consider. Along the same lines, an American study found that African-American girls given names such as Ebony tended to be more successful in later life and finish university, but the name was rarer among working-class black families. As a result, young women called Ebony were held in higher regard as adults regardless of their socioeconomic standings, and more likely to be called back for job interviews, because an assumption was being made about their name right from the start.

> ## Controversial names adopted by real people
>
> | | |
> |---|---|
> | Adolf Hitler | Jezebel |
> | Beelzebub | Jihad |
> | Desdemona | Mussolini |
> | Hannibal | Stalin |
> | Himmler | Voldemort |

There is other new research that says that as many as one in seven parents regrets their choice of baby name. Website Channelmum carried out a member survey in 2019, and found that a staggering twenty-eight per cent of respondents admitted to telling their child they regret the choice, and more than one in ten said their child confessed that they hated their own name. Two of the most common reasons given were that the name suddenly became extremely popular, or that a celebrity chose the same one, and sadly nearly one in five members said they had felt pressured into using the name by a relative or other person. Which just underscores my most important rule about naming your own baby: you HAVE to love it! Love it and you won't regret it; feel apathetic about it, and you'll almost certainly look back with remorse.

When it comes to the name Lucifer, America and Germany think differently. While German officials once intervened in a request to name a child after Satan, in the USA twenty-four babies were recorded as receiving that moniker in 2018.

New Zealand's Top 10		Top 10 Māori Names	
Boys	**Girls**	**Boys**	**Girls**
1. Oliver	1. Amelia	1. Nikau	1. Mia
2. Noah	2. Charlotte	2. Mikaere	2. Aria
3. Leo	3. Isla	3. Ari	3. Maia
4. Jack	4. Olivia	4. Manaia	4. Ariana
5. Lucas	5. Ruby	5. Mateo	5. Nina
6. George	6. Sophie	6. Te Ariki	6. Manaia
7. James	7. Harper	7. Taika	7. Kaia
8. William	8. Mila	8. Ariki	8. Aroha
9. Thomas	9. Willow	9. Kauri	9. Tui
10. Charlie	10. Ava	10. Rawiri	10. Ataahua

Sex and gender

How do we define what makes a name masculine or feminine? Well, it may be connected to the sounds that the letters create when spoken. Harder-sounding combinations (-ter, -it, -ld, -id) tend to be found in masculine names, whereas softer-sounding combinations (-ie, -ay, -la) are generally associated with feminine names. You therefore end up with Sophie, Joanie and Bella versus Harold, Walter and David.

If you're planning on choosing a feminine-sounding name, approach with caution: research suggests that girls who are given particularly girly names – think Tiana, Kayla and Isabella – are much more likely to misbehave when they reach school age. These girls were also far less likely to choose subjects such as maths and science at school, while their sisters with more masculine names – for example, Morgan, Alexis and Ashley – were encouraged to excel in these courses. Which is fascinating and scary in equal measure.

> ## Popular Gender-neutral Names
>
> | | |
> |---|---|
> | Ashley | Robin |
> | Sam | Charlie |
> | Riley | Morgan |
> | Jamie | Alex |
> | Kai | Andy |
> | Bobby | Fran |

Nowadays, names are becoming more androgynous and many appear in both boys' and girls' lists, including Hayden, Riley, Madison and, of course, Alex – some form of which appears in the Top 100 for both boys and girls every year. Therefore, if you want a more gender-neutral name for your new arrival, you won't be alone. Interestingly, a study by the University of Illinois found that boys with androgynous names (the example given was Ashley) tend to act up and do worse in high school exams. The theory was that they get teased and compared to girls with the same name, so their academic progress stalls. I'd love to know how this compares to UK examinations.

But what about your own gender? A study by Bounty found that mothers tend to win the argument over who gets to pick the final name of a newborn, with forty per cent of mums ignoring the choices selected by dads and ten per cent of dads simply backing down. However, a further forty per cent of couples don't make the final decision until after the baby is born, and a third will argue about it before settling. Now, I'm not saying that the person who grows the baby and goes through the process of removing said baby from her own body should get final say, but . . . actually, that is exactly what I'm saying.

> A naming taboo in Imperial China prevented the masses from naming their babies after the reigning emperor.

Nicknames

'Nicknames are fond names. We do not give them to people we dislike.'
Edna Ferber

Nicknames are unavoidable. They can range from the common – such as Mike from Michael or Sam from Samantha – to the trendy, funny or downright insulting. As we saw earlier, for years there was trend of parents using simplified or shortened versions of their baby's full name and getting rid of the longer name altogether, and it's only been in the last year or so that the trend has slowed down. However, if you're going to stick with a longer name like the new parents of 2020 did, make sure that you'll be happy with any nicknames that emerge.

You can pre-empt problem nicknames to some extent by saying the name you've chosen out loud and trying to find rhymes for it. This is a clever way to avoid playground chants and nursery rhyme-type insults, such as Andy Pandy or Looby Lou. A word of caution though: it's inevitable that children will find a way to poke fun at literally anything, however carefully you plan, so maybe mothers should worry less about their children's classmates, and more about what to do when their child discovers mum rhymes with bum.

Using family names

This is a huge trend at the moment. It is very en vogue to choose a name from a grandparent or parent and then to make sure everyone else knows the reason you chose it!

Some families have a strong tradition of using names that come from the family tree and therefore there are instances where it's a given that you will name your baby boy Augustine VIII – it's not an option, it's a rule. Admittedly, this doesn't seem to happen very often in the UK, but it is something to consider if it is one of your family's traditions. There are pros and cons with using family names.

- **Pro:** your child will feel part of a strong tradition, which will create a sense of familial security.

- **Pro:** if you're struggling to select a name, this is an easy solution.

- **Con:** you might not actually like the name that's being passed down.

- **Con:** it could be that the cultural associations with that name have changed in your lifetime and it is no longer appropriate.

How about a compromise? You could use the family name as a middle name or refer to your baby by a nickname instead. You could also suggest using a name from the other parent's family: if the first name comes from your side, try finding a name you like from the other side for a middle name.

Whether or not you decide to use a family name, remember that this is your baby. Just as your parents got to decide what they named you, you get to decide this. If family and friends are disappointed, rest assured that once the baby is here, all they will see is how she has her grandmother's nose or he has his grandfather's ears, and the name will become far less important.

Spellings and pronunciation

Once you've finally agreed on a name, it's time to think about how you want it to be spelled and pronounced. Some parents love experimenting with unusual variations of traditional names, while others prefer names to be instantly recognisable. The only advice here is to

Bizarre US Baby Names

Boys	Girls
Arrow	Footi
Chap	Kizzy
D'Artagnan	Madonna
Miggy	Psalm
Quest	Swayze

use caution in your experiments so your kid isn't saddled with an unfortunate name that neither they nor anyone else knows is supposed to be pronounced 'Lucy'.

One couple changed their daughter's name by deed poll in 2019 because other people couldn't pronounce it properly. Baby Lana, who has a Croatian mother and British father, was supposed to have a name to rhyme with Anna, but the spelling was officially changed to Lanna after months of correcting strangers and family members alike.

Try to avoid making a common name too long or too unusual in its spelling, as this will be the first thing your child learns how to write. They will also be subjected to constantly correcting others during their lifetime, as people misspell or mispronounce their name in ever more frustrating ways. Substituting the odd 'i' for a 'y' isn't too bad, but turning the name Felicity into Philleysatee doesn't do anyone any favours.

A Swedish couple were banned from naming their child Brfxxccxxmnpccccllllmmnprxvclmnckssqlbbllll6, which they claimed was pronounced Albin. The law in Sweden also bans religious names that could cause offence, such as Allah and Jesus.

Middle names

Giving your child a middle name is pretty standard practice. In fact, it's fairly uncommon not to do so, although the use of second and third names only became popular around the turn of the twentieth century. Before then, giving a child a middle name was seen as a status symbol;

it was only really used when a man married a higher-class woman and they wanted to keep the woman's maiden name as a reminder of that child's heritage.

Historical Names

Boys		Girls	
1921	*2001*	*1921*	*2001*
1. John	1. Jack	1. Mary	1. Chloe
2. Robert	2. Thomas	2. Dorothy	2. Emily
3. William	3. Joshua	3. Helen	3. Megan
4. James	4. James	4. Margaret	4. Jessica
5. Charles	5. Daniel	5. Ruth	5. Sophie
6. George	6. Harry	6. Virginia	6. Charlotte
7. Joseph	7. Samuel	7. Mildred	7. Lauren
8. Edward	8. Joseph	8. Betty	8. Hannah
9. Frank	9. Matthew	9. Frances	9. Lucy
10. Richard	10. Lewis	10. Elizabeth	10. Olivia

Since the 1900s middle names have become pretty much the norm for everyone. A recent study by Netmums found that three quarters of parents chose a single middle name for the baby, and one in six parents chose two or more.

In Spanish cultures, middle names are often the mother's surname or other name, to preserve the matriarchal lineage. Similarly, parents where one has chosen not to take the other's surname or who are not married may choose to give their child one surname as a middle name and one as a surname so that both parents are represented. However, be aware that doing either of these things can create some strange name combinations

– as Richard Tiffany Gere, Billie Paul Piper and Courtney Bass Cox can testify. Other traditions may use an old family name, passed down to each first-born son or daughter, to encourage a sense of family pride and history.

Speaking of history . . .

Historian George Redmonds collated all the names of every adult living in England between 1377 and 1381, according to poll-tax records of the time. Times don't change much, do they?

Men	Women
1. John	1. Alice
2. William	2. Agnes
3. Thomas	3. Joan
4. Richard	4. Matilda
5. Robert	5. Isabel
6. Henry	6. Margaret
7. Roger	7. Emme
8. Walter	8. Marg
9. Adam	9. Margery
10. Nicholas	10. Ellen

If you are choosing a middle name, here are some common trends to help you narrow it down.

- Names from the family tree. Parents frequently look back to their own lineage for interesting, unusual or influential names, and it is becoming increasingly popular to use a mother's surname as a middle name.

- Opposite-length names. Generally, if the first name has only one or two syllables (Owen, Steven, Yasmin, Zoe) then the middle name could have two, three, or even four syllables (Owen Jonathan, Steven Michael, Yasmin Samantha, Zoe Jessica). And vice versa, so if the first name is three or four syllables long (Anthony, Jennifer, Nicholas,

Rosemary) the middle name may be only one or two (Anthony Kevin, Jennifer Ruth, Nicholas John, Rosemary Dawn).

> The shortest baby names are only two letters long (Al, Ed, Jo and Ty) but the longest could be any length imaginable. Popular eleven-letter names include Bartholomew, Christopher, Constantine and Maximillian.

Long, Longer and Longest

How about trying to beat the record for the world's longest name? A woman from Hartlepool claims to have the longest name in the world, after changing it by deed poll. She went from Dawn McManus to Red Dreams (to raise money for her charity of the same name, set up after the death of her son) with no fewer than 159 middle names, including Wacky, Strange, Lunar, Sheep and Coalition! She beat the previous record-holder by a mile; he had won the title in 2011 with Barnaby Marmaduke Aloysius Benjy Cobweb Dartagnan Egbert Felix Gaspar Humbert Ignatius Jayden Kasper Leroy Maximilian Neddy Obiajulu Pepin Quilliam Rosencrantz Sexton Teddy Upwood Vivatma Wayland Xylon Yardley Zachary Usansky. However, the official title as kept by the Guinness Book of Records only recognises names on birth certificates. That honour belongs to Rhoshandiatellyneshiaunneveshenk Koyaanisquatsiuth Williams from Texas.

- Unusual names. Parents are beginning to choose more unusual middle names, which makes sense if they're sticking to tradition for the first name. They're using the middle name to show some individuality and creativity. So you might well come across Elizabeth Bronte, Katherine Keilyn or Thomas Titan.

Some famous examples of multiple middle names include British musician Brian Eno, whose full name is actually Brian Peter George St John le Baptiste de la Salle Eno, and Canadian actor Kiefer Sutherland, who has shortened his name considerably from Kiefer William Frederick Dempsey George Rufus Sutherland. The Royal Family also likes to give an abundance of middle names: Prince Charles's full name is Charles Philip Arthur George Mountbatten-Windsor and Prince William is William Arthur Philip Louis Mountbatten-Windsor. The newest member of the royal family is, of course, Archie Harrison Mountbatten-Windsor. This was a surprise to many, as the couple chose not to use a family name and just one middle name.

Many people choose to go by their middle name instead of their first name, so it could be seen as a safety net if you're worried your child won't like their name. For example, Alyson Hannigan and Alexis Denisof have given their daughters – Satyana Marie and Keeva Jane – more traditional middle names as a way of balancing their unusual first names, thus providing them options when they grow up.

Celebrities who go by middle names

Antonio Banderas (José Antonio Dominguez Banderas)
Ashton Kutcher (Christopher Ashton Kutcher)
Bob Marley (Nesta Robert Marley)
Brad Pitt (William Bradley Pitt)
Brooke Shields (Christa Brooke Camille Shields)
Dakota Fanning (Hannah Dakota Fanning)
Evangeline Lilly (Nicole Evangeline Lilly)
Hugh Laurie (James Hugh Calum Laurie)
Kelsey Grammer (Allen Kelsey Grammer)
Reese Witherspoon (Laura Jean Reese Witherspoon)
Rihanna (Robyn Rihanna Fenty)
Will Ferrell (John William Ferrell)

Initials

What surname will your baby have? Does its first letter already lend itself to amusing acronyms or initialisms? And would choosing certain first names only exacerbate the problem? My brother-in-law was going to be called Andrew Steven Schmitt before he was born, until his parents realised at the last minute what his initials would spell . . .

It's worth taking the time to think about the acronyms or initialisms formed by initials in the real world too, such as how names are displayed on credit cards or imagining your child's name written out on a form. Nobody should have to go through life known as S Lugg because their parents didn't think that far ahead.

> Across the UK, there are people whose initials spell out three-letter words – from RAT and FAG to FAB or POP – and some are better than others, so do check!

Amusing initialisms given to real people

David Vernon Durante – DVD
George Barry Holmes – GBH
Jake Clive Baxter – JCB
Neil Harvey Smith – NHS
Patricia Mary Simpson – PMS
Sally Theresa Donaghue – STD
Samuel Alan Spencer – SAS

Your surname

Tied to your child's potential new initials is their new surname. Whether they are receiving their name from their mother, father or a hyphenated combination of both, matching their first name to their surname is key. Try writing down all the names you like alongside your child's surname and have someone else read them out loud. This second pair of eyes and ears might just spot something that you didn't.

The age of the internet has given parents a wonderful new weapon in their baby-naming arsenal: the search engine. Before you settle on anything final, try searching for any examples of the complete first name, middle name and surname of your new baby. You may find out that your baby has an axe-murderer namesake or, like one of my former colleagues, the same name as a well-known porn star.

There is also the possibility of your child having a spoonerism made out of their name, where the first letters or syllables get swapped around to form new words. Named after the Reverend Dr William Archibald Spooner (1844–1930), a spoonerism can be created out of almost anything to make clever, amusing or downright inappropriate phrases instead.

An unfortunate example of this would be Angelina Jolie and Brad Pitt's daughter Shiloh, whom they named Shiloh Jolie-Pitt – thus avoiding the inevitable Shiloh Pitt spoonerism.

Naming twins, triplets and more

Ah, multiples. One of those beautiful little gifts of nature and science that strikes a unique combination of terror and infatuation into the heart of any parent. If you have discovered you are expecting multiples, congratulations! When it comes to baby names, naming multiples needn't be any different from naming one child . . . unless you want it to be. You could stick to the same process as everyone else by picking a unique name for each child. Or . . . you could be awesome.

Some parents do like to use a pattern, such as going down the alphabet (think Alastair, Benjamin,

Unfortunate first name/ surname combinations

Anna Sasin	Jenny Taylor
Barb Dwyer	Justin Thyme
Barry Code	Mary Christmas
Ben Dover	Oliver Sutton
Duane Pipe	Paige Turner
Grace Land	Russell Sprout
Harry Rump	Stan Still
Hazel Nutt	Teresa Green

Christopher and David) or doing what the famous Phoenix acting clan did and give each child a name to do with nature: River, Rain, Leaf (now Joaquin), Liberty and Summer.

Others choose matching initials (Cash and Cainen; Stella and Sophia), or names that mean the same – such as Bernard and Brian, both of which mean strong; or Lucy and Helen, which both mean light. You could use two Roman deities, such as Jupiter and Juno, or monarchs of England, such as Elizabeth and Victoria, or Henry and Arthur.

Twin names with the same meaning

Bernard and Brian (strong)
Daphne and Laura (laurel)
Deborah and Melissa (bee)
Dorcas and Tabitha (gazelle)
Elijah and Joel (God)
Eve and Zoe (life)
Irene and Salome (peace)
Lucius and Uri (light)
Lucy and Helen (light)
Sarah and Almira (princess)

The possibilities for triplets go even further. Think of the fun you could have! You could have a row of beautiful flowers such as Daisy, Violet and Lily; or a collection of Shakespearean heroes such as Beatrice, Helena and Antonio. Be bold with a set of House of Stark kids from *Game of Thrones* (Brandon, Robb and Arya), or be fabulous with some baby girls from *Clueless* (Cher, Tai and Dionne) – as if!

The official Guinness World Record for the most siblings baptised with the same initial is held by a Canadian family, who had ten sons and six daughters all given names beginning with the letter E. However, the unofficial challenger to this would be the notorious Duggar family from the USA, whose nineteen children all have names starting with J.

Celebrity twin names

Alexander and Ella (Amal and George Clooney)
Boo and Walt (Chris Evans and Natasha Shishmanian)
Esther and Stella (Madonna)
Eva and Mateo (Cristiano Ronaldo and Georgina Rodriguez)
Matteo and Valentino (Ricky Martin)
Myla Rose and Charlene Riva *and* Leo and Lenny (two sets for Roger and Mirka Federer!)
Nicholas and Lucy (Anna Kournikova and Enrique Iglesias)
Ottilie and Delilah (Clemmie and Simon Hooper)
Rumi and Sir (Beyoncé and Jay Z)
Zeppelin and Arrow (Jensen Ackles and Danneel Harris)

The UK's biggest family belongs to Sue and Noel Ratford, the stars of *21 Kids and Counting*. While each child has their own unique name, there are a couple of themes: all the girls have names ending in an –ie sound (Sophie, Chloe, Millie, Katie, Ellie, Aimee, Tillie, Hallie, Phoebe, Bonnie and newest arrival Heidie). The boys however, have short punchy names: Chris, Jack, Daniel, James, Josh, Max, Oscar, Casper, Archie and Alfie.

There are a few pretty simple things to keep in mind when naming twins or multiples.

- Don't use very long names. You will often find yourself needing to write both names down, or calling both children for dinner, so use shorter versions of the names you like to save yourself time and effort, such as Max for Maximilian, or Eve for Evangeline.

- Don't get too complicated. Stick with traditional spellings if possible, like Cameron instead of Kammeryn and Elizabeth instead of Alyzybeth.

- Don't forget that your babies are still individuals. If you use names that sound so similar you often mix them up, your children may get frustrated as they get older and other people confuse them. Instead, keep those nearly identical names you love as middle names and use this opportunity to explore more individual first names to match your babies' unique personalities.

Names for triplets

Aidan, Diana and Nadia (anagrams)
Amber, Jade and Ruby (jewels)
Amy, May and Mya (anagrams)
Ava, Eva and Iva (similar)
Daisy, Lily and Rose (flowers)
Ginger, Saffron and Rosemary (herbs)
Jay, Raven and Robin (birds)
Olive, Violet and Sage (colours)
River, Rain and Summer (nature)

Registering a baby's name

There are slightly different guidelines for registering births and names depending on where you live in the UK.

In England, Wales and Northern Ireland a birth must be recorded within forty-two days of delivery, and if not done at the hospital it requires a visit to a register office. The birth certificate will be written in English if a child is born in England or Northern Ireland, and can be in both English and Welsh if they are born in Wales.

If the birth is recorded at the hospital or registered in the same district, birth certificates are usually issued straight away, but if you end up going to a different area office, the certificate may be sent to you after a few days. This is important when applying for Child Benefit or registering your baby with a doctor, as you will need a copy of the short birth certificate to apply.

If the parents of a newborn are a heterosexual couple and married, either parent can register a birth. However, if the parents are not married there are several ways to ensure that both names are put on the birth certificate, including both parents being physically present at the registration or one parent submitting a declaration form in lieu of their presence. It's worth remembering that if the father's details were not recorded on the original certificate or if the natural parents have married since the registration, a new birth certificate will have to be generated.

If the parents are same-sex female and married or in a civil partnership, either parent can register the birth and both can be named on the birth certificate. However, if the parents aren't married or in a civil partnership, they will need a court order (or one of several other documentation options, such as a parenthood agreement) to be able to add both names. For same-sex male couples, a parental order must be granted before the birth can be registered, no matter what the married status.

> While German law prohibits invented and androgynous names, the UK has some of the most liberal rules in the world on naming a baby. Only names that are deemed to be offensive make it onto the banned list here.

If neither parent can be present to register a birth, someone who was present at the birth or someone who is now responsible for the child can also carry out the duty.

After the registration, the parents or those with parental responsibility also have the option of requesting a naming ceremony. These non-religious ceremonies are conducted by local authorities and can be a nice replacement for a baptism or christening, as adults outside the family can be nominated to act in secular roles similar to godparents. A birth certificate is also needed for this event to take place.

In Scotland, births need to be registered within twenty-one days, and this can take place in any district. As well as either married parent being allowed to register the birth, their relatives may also do this duty. If the parents are not married, the father may register the birth only if the mother is also present, or a declaration form is submitted or a court agrees that he has parental responsibility. Parents of newborns in Scotland should take a card given to them at the hospital and a copy of their marriage certificate to the birth registration.

If you are a British national and your baby is born abroad, you will have to register the birth in that country, following the appropriate rules and

Registering a Birth

Information you'll need to register a birth
Place and date of your baby's birth
Name, surname and sex of your baby
Places and dates of birth for both parents
The date of the marriage or civil partnership of the parents (if applicable)
Jobs of both parents
Former names of both parents (maiden name or deed poll, if applicable)

What to bring
Form of ID: a birth certificate, driving licence, or passport
Marriage certificate (Scotland)
Your baby's NHS personal health record or 'red book'
Proof of paternity (if applicable)

Useful websites
England and Wales: www.gov.uk
Northern Ireland: www.nidirect.gov.uk
Scotland: www.nrscotland.gov.uk

regulations. You should also register it at the local British Embassy or Consulate, or with UK authorities when you are back home, in order to obtain a British birth certificate, proof that the baby is a British citizen by birth, and to have the birth registered with the UK General Register Office. The name you choose won't be included in the official UK statistics, but it will instead be part of the statistics for the country where your baby was born . . . which is kind of cool!

Changing your mind

If you later decide that you want to change details on a birth certificate there are procedures in place, although this can be a time-consuming process. In fact, even if the name was copied down incorrectly and is now misspelled, the burden is on the parents to prove it wasn't intentional.

Documents showing the correct spelling at the time of the birth must be produced – and those can be tricky to find.

If you've just changed your mind about your baby's name, you only have about twelve months to act before it becomes an even bigger headache. Visit www.gov.uk/change-name-deed-poll/change-a-childs-name for instructions on what to do, and remember that it can only be done once. The original name will still appear on the new birth certificate, with the new name listed underneath.

> One family in the USA changed their daughter's name when she was three months old, from Ottilie to Margot. Their reason? Ottilie is a German name, and when it's pronounced in Europe it comes with hard T sounds (Ott-ti-lee). But due to the slacker T sounds of many regional accents in the USA, their poor daughter's name ended up sounding like Oddly . . . oddly enough.

Changing the surname of your baby is only possible in two cases: either if the spelling is incorrect or if the details of the parents are being changed (such as the inclusion of the father or the parents now being married). A fee is usually incurred if a new certificate is required.

If you are in any way unsure about the choice you're about to make, keep in mind how difficult it may be for you to change your child's birth certificate at a later stage. On the bright side, though, bear in mind that if something unexpected happens and you need to make the change, it is possible.

South Africa's Top 10

Boys	Girls
1. Enzokuhle	1. Enzokuhle
2. Lethabo	2. Melokuhle
3. Melokuhle	3. Amahle
4. Lubanzi	4. Ohhule
5. Junior	5. Lethabo
6. Siyabonga	6. Omphile
7. Bokamosa	7. Lesedi
8. Omphile	8. Rethabile
9. Amogelang	9. Amogelang
10. Thato	10. Onthatile

Part two

Boys' names A–Z

Baby names vary widely in spelling and pronunciation. To simplify things, this book usually lists each name only once: under the most common initial and spelling. If a name has an alternative spelling with a different initial, it may be listed under that letter also.

 Boys' names

Aaron

Hebrew, meaning 'mountain of strength'. In the Bible, Aaron was the older brother of Moses and the first high priest of Israel.

Abasi

Egyptian Arabic, meaning 'male'; Swahili, meaning 'stern'.

Abdiel

Hebrew, meaning 'servant of God'. Also the name of an important seraph in Milton's *Paradise Lost*.

Abdul

Arabic, meaning 'servant'. Often followed by a suffix indicating who Abdul is the servant of (e.g. Abdul-Basit, 'servant of the creator').

Abdullah
(alt. Abd-Allah, Abdallah, Abdollah)

Arabic, meaning 'servant of God'.

Abdur Rahman

Arabic, meaning 'one who serves a merciful man'.

Abel

Hebrew, meaning 'breath' or 'breathing spirit'. Associated with the biblical son of Adam and Eve, who was killed by his brother Cain.

Abelard

German, meaning 'resolute'.

Aberforth

Gaelic, meaning 'mouth of the river Forth'. The name of Dumbledore's younger brother in J.K. Rowling's *Harry Potter* books.

Abhik
(alt. Abheek)

Sanskrit, meaning 'fearless'. Popular name for boys in India.

Abhishek

Sanskrit, meaning 'bath for a deity' or 'anointing'. Abhishek Bachchan is currently one of Bollywood's highest-paid and most popular actors.

Abner

Hebrew, meaning 'father of light'. Abner was the commander of Saul's army in the Bible.

Abraham

(alt. Abram; abbrev. Abe)

Hebrew, meaning 'father of the multitude'. Famous Abrahams include President Abraham Lincoln and Abraham Van Helsing – the vampire hunter and doctor in Bram Stoker's *Dracula*.

Absalom

(alt. Absalon)

Hebrew, meaning 'father/leader of peace'. The name of King David's favourite son in the Bible, and one of Chaucer's curly-haired characters in *The Canterbury Tales*.

Acacio

Greek, meaning 'thorny tree' or 'honourable'. Now widely used in Spain.

Ace

Latin, meaning 'unit'. Also used in English to mean 'number one' or 'the best'.

Achilles

Greek, mythological hero of the Trojan war, whose heel was his only weak spot.

Achim

Hebrew, meaning 'God will establish'; Polish, meaning 'the Lord exalts'. Also, in Germany, a shortened version of the name 'Joachim'.

Ackerley

Old English, meaning 'oak meadow'.

Adam

(alt. Adão (Portuguese))

Hebrew, meaning 'man' or 'earth'. In the Bible the Creation story names Adam as the first man on earth.

Addison

Old English, meaning 'son of Adam'. Also used as a female name in the USA.

Ade

Yoruba, meaning 'peak' or 'royal'; a common name in Nigeria.

Adelard

French or German, meaning 'brave' or 'noble'.

Adelbert

(alt. Adalberto)

Old German form of Albert. Popularity decreased in the 19th century, when Albert became more commonly used.

Adetokunbo

Yoruba, meaning 'the crown came from over the sea'.

Adin

Hebrew, meaning 'slender' or 'voluptuous'. Also Swahili, meaning 'ornamental'.

Aditya

Sanskrit, meaning 'belonging to the sun'. In Hindi, Aditya means 'sun god'. Aditya refers to the offspring of Aditi, the mother of the Gods.

Adlai

Hebrew, meaning 'God is just', or sometimes 'ornamental'.

Adler

Old German, meaning 'eagle'.

Adley

English, meaning 'son of Adam'.

Admon

Hebrew, variant of Adam meaning 'earth'. Also the name of a red peony.

Adolph
(alt. Adolf)

Old German, meaning 'noble majestic wolf'. Once popular before World War II, this name has now become deeply unpopular due to its association with Adolf Hitler, and several European nations have actually banned its use.

Adonis

Phoenician, meaning 'Lord'. Adonis was the god of beauty and desire in Greek mythology.

Adrian

Latin, meaning 'from Hadria', a town in northern Italy.

Adriel

Hebrew, meaning 'of God's flock'. Adriel was one of Saul's sons-in-law in the Bible.

Adyn
(alt. Ade)

Irish, meaning 'manly'. Also the name of a UK men's streetwear company.

Aeneas

Greek/Latin, meaning 'to praise'. Name of the hero who founded Rome in Virgil's Aeneid.

Aero

Greek, meaning 'air'.

Aeson
(alt. Aesion)

Greek, father of Jason in ancient Greek mythology.

Afonso

Portuguese, meaning 'eager noble warrior'.

Agamemnon

Greek, meaning 'leader of the assembly'. Figure in mythology, commanded the Greeks at the siege of Troy.

Agathon

Greek, meaning 'good' or 'superior'. The name of a tragic poet in ancient Greece.

Agustin

Latin/Spanish, meaning 'venerated'.

Ahab

Hebrew, meaning 'father's brother'. Name of the obsessed captain in Moby-Dick.

Ahijah

Hebrew, meaning 'brother of God' or 'friend of God'.

Ahmad
(alt. Ahmed)
Arabic/Turkish, meaning 'worthy of praise'. Ahmad is also one of the prophet Muhammad's many given names.

Aidan
(alt. Aiden, Aodhán)
Gaelic, meaning 'little fire'. Derives from Aodh, which is the name of a Celtic sun god.

Aidric
Old English, meaning 'oaken'. St Aidric was a bishop and court diplomat in the ninth century.

Ainsley
Old English, meaning 'meadow' or 'clearing'. Also a girls' name. Ainsley Harriott is a well-known TV chef.

Airyck
Old Norse, from Eric, meaning 'eternal ruler'.

Ajani
Swahili, meaning 'he fights for what he is'; Sanskrit, meaning 'of noble birth'.

Ajax
Greek, meaning 'mourner of the Earth'. A Greek hero from the siege of Troy.

Ajay
Hindi, meaning 'unconquerable'. One of the most popular names in India.

Ajit
Sanskrit, meaning 'invincible'. Alternative name for both Shiva and Vishnu in Hindu mythology.

Akeem
Arabic, meaning 'wise or insightful'. Popular name throughout Africa, particularly in Nigeria.

Akio
Japanese, meaning 'bright man'. Akio Morita was one of the co-founders of the electronics company Sony.

Akira
Japanese, meaning 'intelligent'. Name of a hugely influential animated Japanese film.

Akiva
Hebrew, meaning 'to protect' or 'to shelter'.

Akon
American, meaning 'flower'. Made popular by the rapper.

Aladdin
Arabic, meaning 'servant of Allah'. From the medieval story in *1001 Arabian Nights*.

Alan
(alt. Allan, Allen, Allyn, Alun)
Gaelic or old French, meaning 'rock'. Alan is one of the oldest names still in popular use in the UK, and its roots can be traced back to the Norman invasion in the 11th century.

Alaric
(alt. Aleric)

Old German, meaning 'noble regal ruler'. King Alaric I of the Visigoths played a key role in the downfall of the Roman Empire.

Alastair
(alt. Alasdair, Alastor, Alistair, Allister; abbrev. Ali, Allie)

Greek/Gaelic, meaning 'defending men'. Famous Alastairs include comedian and TV presenter Alistair McGowan, English cricketer Alastair Cook and Ali G, whose 'real name' is Alistair.

Alban

Latin, meaning 'from Alba'. Also the name of St Alban, the first British Christian martyr.

Alberic

Germanic, meaning 'Elfin king'.

Albert
(abbrev. Albie, Bert, Bertie)

Old German, meaning 'noble, bright, famous'. Probably most commonly associated with Prince Albert, Queen Victoria's husband, who died in 1861.

Albin

Latin, variant of Albus, meaning 'white'. Popular in some areas including Scandinavia, Slovenia, Germany and Poland.

Less common three-syllable names

Alastair	Elijah
Barnaby	Lancelot
Dominic	Roberto
Dorian	Theodore

Albus

Latin, meaning 'white'. Made famous by Albus Dumbledore, the headmaster of Hogwarts in J.K. Rowling's *Harry Potter* books.

Alcaeus

Greek, meaning 'strength'. Alcaeus of Mytilene was an influential ancient Greek poet.

Alden

Old English, meaning 'old friend'. More commonly used as a given name in the USA.

Aldis

English, meaning 'battle-seasoned'.

Aldo
(alt. Aldous)

Latin, meaning 'the tall one'. Aldo is the main gorilla character in the *Planet of the Apes* movie series.

Aldric

English, meaning 'old king'.

Aled

Welsh, meaning 'child' or 'offspring'. Aled Jones is a Welsh singer and TV presenter, who shot to fame as a choirboy with *Walking in the Air*.

Aleph
(alt. Alef)

Hebrew, meaning 'first letter of the alphabet', or 'leader'.

Aleron
(alt. Aileron, Alerun, Ailerun, Alejandro)

Latin, meaning 'child with wings'.

Alessio
(alt. Alejo)

Italian, meaning 'defender'.

Alexander
(alt. Alexandro, Alessandro, Alejandro; abbrev. Alec, Alex, Alexei, Sandy, Xander)

Greek, meaning 'defender of mankind'. Alexander the Great was an undefeated fourth-century king whose empire stretched from Greece to modern Pakistan.

Alfonso
(alt. Alonso, Alonzo)

Germanic/Spanish, meaning 'noble and prompt, ready to struggle'. Associated with *Gravity* director Alfonso Cuarón Orozco, and actor Alfonso Ribeiro.

Alford

Old English, meaning 'old river/ford'.

Alfred
(abbrev. Alf, Alfie)

English, meaning 'elf' or 'magical counsel'. Alfred the Great was a ninth-century king of England who defended the Anglo-Saxons against Viking invasion. *Alfie* is the name of a successful 1966 film starring Michael Caine.

Algernon

French, meaning 'with a moustache'. A popular name among the nobility in 18th- and 19th-century England.

Alois

German, meaning 'famous warrior'.

Alok

Sanskrit, meaning 'cry of triumph'. Also the name of a style of singing in Javanese gamelan.

Alon

Hebrew, meaning 'oak tree'.

Aloysius

Old German, meaning 'fame and war'. Also the name of an Italian saint.

Alpha

First letter of the Greek alphabet.

Alphaeus

Hebrew, meaning 'changing'. Alphaeus is mentioned in the Bible as being the father of two of the twelve Apostles, Matthew and James.

Alpin

Gaelic, meaning 'related to the Alps'. The House of Alpin refers to a dynasty of Scottish kings.

Altair

Arabic, meaning 'flying' or 'bird'. Altair is one of the brightest stars seen in the night sky from Earth.

Alter
(alt. Altar)

Yiddish, meaning 'old man'.

Alton

Old English, meaning 'old town'.

Alva

Latin, meaning 'white'. Used more commonly for girls than boys.

Alvin
(alt. Alvie)

English, meaning 'friend of elves'. Alvin and the Chipmunks are a cartoon singing group, first created in 1958 and still featuring in films today.

Alwyn

Welsh, meaning 'wise friend'. May also come from the River Alwen in Wales.

Amachi

Swahili, meaning 'who knows what God has brought us through this child'.

Amadeus

Latin, meaning 'God's love'. One of the given names of the composer Wolfgang Amadeus Mozart.

Amadi

Igbo, meaning 'appeared destined to die at birth'. Often given to babies who unexpectedly survive against the odds.

Amado

Spanish, meaning 'God's love'.

Amador

Spanish, meaning 'one who loves'.

Amari

Hebrew, meaning 'given by God'. Can be a boys' or girls' name.

Amarion

Arabic, meaning 'populous, flushing'.

Amasa

Hebrew, meaning 'burden'.

Ambrose

Greek, meaning 'undying, immortal'.

Americo

Germanic, meaning 'ever powerful in battle'. Popular in the 19th century, this is now an infrequently used baby name.

Amias
(alt. Amyas)

Latin, meaning 'loved'.

Amil

Sanskrit, meaning 'unavailable'. Popular name for boys in India.

Amir
(alt. Emir)

Arabic, meaning 'chieftain' or 'commander'. Emir or Amir is a title for a high-ranking sheikh, used in many Muslim communities.

Amit

Hindi, meaning 'infinite'. One of the 108 names for the Hindu God Shri Ganesha.

Ammon

Hebrew, meaning 'the hidden one'. The Ammonites were an ancient tribe of people mentioned in the Bible.

Amory

German/English, meaning 'work' and 'power'. Its popularity has waned since the 19th century, when it was a common name.

Amos

Hebrew, meaning 'encumbered' or 'burdened'. St Amos wrote the Book of Amos in the eighth century, which is part of the Hebrew Bible.

Anacletus

Latin, meaning 'called back' or 'invoked'. Pope Anacletus was the third pope in history, and served during the first century.

Anakin

American, meaning 'warrior'. Made famous by Anakin Skywalker in the *Star Wars* films.

Ananias

Greek/Italian, meaning 'answered by the Lord'. Ananias Dare was the first baby born to English parents in North America, making him the first-ever 'modern' American.

Anastasius
(alt. Anastasios)

Greek, meaning 'resurrection'. Popular name for popes, emperors, and saints – there are nearly 20 St Anastasiuses on record.

Anatole
(alt. Anatolius)

French, meaning 'sunrise'. Monsieur Anatole was an influential 19th-century French composer, ballet dancer and ballet master.

Anders

Scandinavian, meaning 'lion man'. A popular name for boys in Sweden.

Anderson

English, meaning 'male'.

Andrew
(alt. Andreas)

Greek, meaning 'man' or 'warrior'. One of the Top 10 names for baby boys during the 1980s and '90s.

Androcles

Greek, meaning 'glory of a warrior'. *Androcles and the Lion* was a well-known folktale of the second century, made famous in the 20th century by George Bernard Shaw's play of the same title.

Angel
(alt. Angelo)
Greek, meaning 'messenger'. Angels appear throughout the Bible and modern culture, and the name Angel is often used in Spanish-speaking cultures as a name for both boys and girls.

Angus
Gaelic, meaning 'one choice'. An ancient name especially popular in Scotland.

Anil
Sanskrit, meaning 'air' or 'wind'. Anil Gupta is the producer (and for some the creator) of many leading television comedies, including *Goodness Gracious Me*, *The Kumars at No. 42* and *The Office*.

Anselm
German, meaning 'helmet of God'. St Anselm was an archbishop of Canterbury and influential figure in the Christian religion.

Anson
English, meaning 'son of Agnes'. Most commonly used in the USA.

Anthony
(alt. Antony; abbrev. Ant, Tony)
English, meaning 'invaluable grace'. *Antony and Cleopatra* is a Shakespearean play depicting the romance between the Roman general Mark Antony and Queen Cleopatra of Egypt.

Antipas
Latin, meaning 'for all or against all'. Herod Antipas was the leader mentioned in the Bible as being responsible for the executions of John the Baptist and Jesus.

Antwan
(alt. Antoine)
Old English, meaning 'flower'. Older and more unusual spelling of Antoine.

Apollo
Greek, meaning 'to destroy'. Greek god of poetry, music and the sun.

Apostolos
Greek, meaning 'apostle'. The Apostolos book is a text believed to have been written by one of the twelve disciples of Jesus.

Ara
Arabic, meaning 'brings rain'.

Aragorn
Literary, a character in J.R.R. Tolkien's *The Lord of the Rings* trilogy.

Aram
Hebrew, meaning 'royal highness'. Aram is an ancient region in modern-day Syria, mentioned in the Bible.

Aramis
Latin, meaning 'swordsman'. Aramis is one of the three musketeers in Alexandre Dumas's eponymous novel.

Arcadio

Greek/Spanish, from a place in ancient Greece. The word 'Arcadia' (meaning paradise) comes from this.

Archibald
(abbrev. Archie)

Old German, meaning 'genuine, bold, brave'. A popular name in Scotland. Archie is the son of Prince Harry and Meghan Markle.

Ardell

Latin, meaning 'eager, burning with enthusiasm'.

Arden

Celtic, meaning 'high'. A very early English motor car.

Ares

Greek, meaning 'ruin'. Son of Zeus and Hera, and the Greek god of war.

Ari

Hebrew, meaning 'lion' or 'eagle'. Can also be used in Hebrew to refer to an important or honourable man.

Arias

Germanic, meaning 'lion'.

Aric

English, meaning 'merciful ruler'. Alternative spelling of Eric.

Ariel

Hebrew, meaning 'lion of God'. One of the archangels, the angel of healing and new beginnings.

Arild

Old Norse, meaning 'battle commander'. Arild Andersen is an internationally popular Norwegian jazz musician.

Aris

Greek, meaning 'best figure'. Popular name in both ancient and modern Greece.

Ariston

Greek, meaning 'the best'. Ariston of Athens was the philosopher Plato's father.

Aristotle

Greek, meaning 'best'. Also an ancient Greek philosopher.

Arjun

Sanskrit, meaning 'bright and shining'. Name is derived from Arjuna, an ancient and legendary archer.

Arkady

Greek, a region of central Greece. Popular name for boys throughout Eastern Europe.

Arlan

Gaelic, meaning 'pledge' or 'oath'.

Arlie

Old English place name, meaning 'eagle wood'. Sometimes used as a shortened form of Arlan.

Arliss
(alt. Arlis)

Hebrew, meaning 'pledge'.

Arlo

Spanish, meaning 'barberry tree'. Can also be linked back to the Old Norse word for 'army of troops'.

Armand
(alt. Armani)

Old German, meaning 'soldier'. Armand van Helden is a top American DJ and producer of electronic house music. Armani is the name of an Italian fashion house after designer Georgio Armani.

Arnaldo

Spanish, meaning 'eagle power'.

Arnav

Hindi, meaning 'the sea'. Can be pronounced as 'Arnav' or 'Arnaf'.

Arnold
(abbrev. Arnie)

Old German, meaning 'eagle ruler'. Also the name of actor, former bodybuilder and US politician Arnold Schwarzenegger.

Arrow

English, from the common word denoting weaponry.

Art

Irish, name of a warrior in Irish mythology, Art Oenfer (Art the Lonely). Also a shortened form of Arthur.

Arthur
(alt. Art, Arte, Artie, Artis)

Celtic, probably from 'artos', meaning 'bear'. Made famous by the tales of King Arthur and the Knights of the Round Table.

Arvel

From the Welsh 'Arwel', meaning 'wept over'. Used in literature for mythical characters – for example, Arvel Crynyd in *Star Wars*, and Arvel the Swift in *The Elder Scrolls V: Skyrim*.

Arvid

Old Norse, meaning 'eagle in the woods'. Commonly used in Scandinavia.

Arvind
(alt. Aravind)

Sanskrit, meaning 'red lotus'. May also be derived from the word for 'white lotus', upon which the Hindu goddess Lakshmi sits.

Arvo

Finnish, meaning 'value' or 'worth'.

Asa

Hebrew, meaning 'doctor' or 'healer'.

Asante

Asante, meaning 'thank you'. Also refers to the language of the Ashanti people.

Asher

Hebrew, meaning 'fortunate' or 'lucky'. One of the 12 sons of Jacob in the Bible, and one of the brothers who sells Joseph into slavery in the story of Joseph and his multi-coloured coat.

Ashley

Old English, meaning 'ash meadow'. The name of several football players, including Ashley Cole and Ashley Young.

Ashok

Sanskrit, meaning 'not causing sorrow'. Popular in India and Sri Lanka.

Ashton

English, meaning 'settlement in the ash-tree grove'. Name has been popularised due to the American actor Ashton Kutcher.

Aslan

Turkish, meaning 'lion'. Strongly associated with the lion Aslan in C.S. Lewis's *The Lion, the Witch and the Wardrobe*.

Asriel

Hebrew, meaning 'help of God'. Lord Asriel is an important character in Philip Pullman's *His Dark Materials* trilogy.

Astrophel

Latin, meaning 'star lover'. *Astrophel and Stella* is the name of a group of sonnets by Philip Sidney, written in the 1590s, and the first time the name is recorded as being used.

Athanasios

(abbrev. Thanasis, Thanos)

Greek, meaning 'eternal life'.

Atílio

Portuguese, meaning 'father'. Can also be lengthened to Attilius.

Atlas

Greek, meaning 'to carry'. In Greek mythology Atlas was a Titan forced to carry the weight of the heavens.

Atlee

Hebrew, meaning 'God is just'.

Atticus

Latin, meaning 'from Athens'. Atticus Finch is one of the main characters in Harper Lee's influential novels *To Kill A Mockingbird* and *Go Set a Watchman*.

Auberon

Old German, meaning 'royal bear'. Also the name for a fairy king. It is the French spelling for Oberon.

Aubrey

French, meaning 'elf ruler'. Popular for boys during the Middle Ages; now more usually given to girls.

Auden

Old English, meaning 'old friend'. W.H. Auden is considered one of the most influential 20th-century poets.

Audie

Old English, meaning 'noble strength'. Audie L. Murphy was one of the most decorated and honoured American soldiers of World War II.

Augustus

(alt. Augustas)

Latin, meaning 'venerated'. The first Roman emperor. Also a character in Roald Dahl's *Charlie and the Chocolate Factory*.

Aurelien

French, meaning 'golden'. Also the name of a Roman emperor.

Austin

Latin, meaning 'venerated'. Austin Healey played rugby union for England. Also the name of a classic car.

Avery
(alt. Avrie, Averey, Averie)

English, meaning 'wise ruler'. Can also be derived from the name Alfred, or the ancient English word for elf.

Avi

Hebrew, meaning 'father of a multitude of nations'. Name of an author of popular children's and teens' fiction.

Awnan

Irish, meaning 'little Adam'.

Axel
(alt. Aksel, Axl)

German and Scandinavian, a form of the Hebrew Absalom, meaning 'father of peace'. Its name day is 23 March, and babies with this name are sometimes celebrated in Nordic countries on this day. Made famous by Guns 'n' Roses front man Axl Rose.

Ayers
(alt. Ayer, Aires, Aire)

English, meaning 'heir to a fortune'.

Azarel
(alt. Azaryah)

Hebrew, meaning 'helped by God'. Also the name of an evil spirit in the Bible.

Azriel

Hebrew, meaning 'God is my help'. Name is often used to describe the angel of death in many religions, including Christianity and Judaism.

Azuko

Igbo, meaning 'past glory'. Most commonly found in Japan.

Boys' names

Baden

German, meaning 'battle'. Also the name of a city in Switzerland known for its hot springs.

Bailey

English, meaning 'bailiff'.

Baird

Scottish, meaning 'poet' or 'one who sings ballads'. John Logie Baird was a Scottish engineer credited with inventing the world's first working television.

Bakari

Swahili, meaning 'hope' or 'promise'.

Baker

English, from the word 'baker'.

Baldwin

Old French, meaning 'bold, brave friend'. The Baldwin family is a well-known acting dynasty in Hollywood, with brothers Alec, Stephen, William, and Daniel.

Balin

Old English. Balin was one of the Knights of the Round Table.

Balthazar

Babylonian, meaning 'protect the King'. A name commonly attributed to one of the Three Wise Men in the Christian Nativity story.

Balwinder
(alt. Balvinder)

Hindi, meaning 'merciful, compassionate'. Balwinder Singh Sandhu is a well-known former Indian Test cricketer.

Bannon

Irish, meaning 'descendant of O'Banain'. Also a river in Wales.

Barack

Contraction of the Swahili name Baruch and the Hebrew name Mubarak. Made popular by the 44th US President, Barack Obama.

Barclay
Old English, meaning 'birch tree meadow'.

Barker
Old English, meaning 'shepherd'.

Barnaby
(abbrev. Barney)
Greek, meaning 'son of consolation'. *Barnaby Rudge* is a novel by Charles Dickens.

Barnard
English, meaning 'strong as a bear'.

Baron
(alt. Barron)
Old English, meaning 'young warrior'. Baron is a title given to men of nobility.

Barrett
English, meaning 'strong as a bear'.

Barry
(abbrev. Baz)
Irish Gaelic, meaning 'fair haired'. Famous Barrys include Barry Humphries, best known as the comedian behind Dame Edna Everage. Also Baz Luhrmann, the Australian film director.

Bartholomew
(abbrev. Bart)
Hebrew, meaning 'son of the farmer'. The name of one of Jesus' apostles. Bart is the name of the eldest child of the cartoon family the Simpsons.

Barton
Old English, meaning 'barley settlement'. One of the more popular names of towns in England, with at least 25 on record.

Baruch
Hebrew, meaning 'blessed'. Also a term for a Jewish blessing.

Barzillai
Hebrew, meaning 'made of iron'. Found in the Bible, Barzillai supposedly teaches youngsters not to be afraid of old age.

Bashir
Arabic, meaning 'well educated' and 'wise'.

Basil
Greek, meaning 'royal, kingly'. Basil is the lead character in the TV comedy *Fawlty Towers*. Also the name of a herb.

Basim
Arabic, meaning 'smile'.

Bastien
Greek, meaning 'revered'. Bastien Pagez was one of the most important servants to Mary, Queen of Scots.

Baxter
Old English, meaning 'baker'.

Bay
From the bay tree or the indentation in the coastline. Also a girls' name.

Bayard

French, meaning 'auburn haired'. Bayard Rustin was one of Martin Luther King Jr's mentors and advisors during the American Civil Rights movement.

Bayo
(alt. Baio)

Swahili, meaning 'to find joy'.

Bayre

American, meaning 'beautiful'.

Beau

French, meaning 'handsome'. Beau Bridges is an American actor. Beau Brummell was a fashionable figure in Regency England and friend of the future King George IV. Beau was not the given name of either man, but an adopted name.

Beck

Old Norse, meaning 'stream'.

Beckett

Old English, meaning 'beehive' or 'bee cottage'. Associated with the Irish writer Samuel Beckett.

Beckham

English, meaning 'homestead by the stream'. Made famous by David and Victoria Beckham.

Béla

Hungarian, meaning 'within'. Famously associated with the actor Bela Lugosi.

Belarius

Shakespearean, meaning 'a banished lord'. From Shakespeare's play Cymbeline.

Benedict
(abbrev. Ben)

Latin, meaning 'blessed'. Benedict Cumberbatch is a succsssful actor and the star of the TV series Sherlock. Ben Ainslie is the most successful Olympic sailor ever.

Benicio

Spanish, meaning 'benevolent'. Benicio del Toro is an Oscar-winning actor from Puerto Rico.

Benjamin
(abbrev. Ben, Benjie, Bennie, Benny)

Hebrew, meaning 'son of the south'. Benjamin Franklin, American inventor and discoverer of electricity was one of the Founding Fathers of the United States. Ben Affleck, actor, and Ben Fogle, adventurer and TV personality, are both Benjamins.

Bennett

French/Latin vernacular form of Benedict, meaning 'blessed'.

Benoit

French form of Benedict, meaning 'blessed'.

Benson

English, meaning 'son of Ben'. Also linked to the village of Benson in Oxfordshire.

Bentley

Old English, meaning 'bent grass meadow'. Usually associated with the British luxury car company.

Benton

Old English, meaning 'town in the bent grass'. Derived from the towns of Long Benton and Little Benton in Northumberland.

Beriah

Hebrew, meaning 'in fellowship' or 'in envy'. Beriah was a son of Asher in the Bible.

Bernard

(abbrev. Bernie)

Germanic, meaning 'strong, brave bear'.

Berry

Old English, meaning 'berry'.

Berton

Old English, meaning 'bright settlement'. Guitartist Berton Averre was part of the band The Knack, known for its hit 'My Sharona'.

Bertrand

(alt. Bertram; abbrev. Bert, Bertie)

Old English, meaning 'illustrious'. Bertrand Russell was a British philosopher and social critic. Bertram (Bertie) Wooster was one of P.G. Wodehouse's most beloved characters.

Bevan

Welsh, meaning 'son of Evan'.

Bilal

Arabic, meaning 'wetting, refreshing'. Popular in many Muslim communities.

Bill

(alt. Billy)

English, from William, meaning 'strong protector'.

Birch

Old English, meaning 'bright' or 'shining'. Also a type of tree.

Birger

Norwegian, meaning 'rescue'.

Bishop

Old English, meaning 'bishop'.

Bjorn

Old Norse, meaning 'bear'. Bjorn Ulvaeus was one of the founding members of Swedish pop supergroup ABBA, and is still a prolific songwriter with partner Benny Andersson.

Blaine

Irish Gaelic, meaning 'yellow'.

Blair

Scottish Gaelic, meaning 'plain'. Can be used as a boys' or a girls' name.

Blaise

French, meaning 'lisp' or 'stutter'. St Blaise was an Armenian bishop who was beaten and beheaded for his faith. Also commonly used as a girls' name.

Blake
Old English, meaning 'dark, black'.

Blas
(alt. Blaze)
German, meaning 'firebrand'. Also a mountain in the Alps.

Bo
Scandinavian, short form of Robert, meaning 'bright fame'. Rock and roll pioneer and musician Ellas Otha Bates was known by his stage name Bo Diddly.

Boaz
Hebrew, meaning 'swiftness' or 'strength'. Found in the Bible, in the Book of Ruth.

Bob
(alt. Bobby)
Old German, from Robert, meaning 'bright fame'.

Boden
(alt. Bodie)
Scandinavian, meaning 'shelter'. In some translations Boden also means 'messenger'.

Bogumil
Slavic, meaning 'God's favour'. Usually associated with Bogomil Cove in the Shetland Islands.

Bolívar
Spanish, meaning 'the bank of the river'. Simón Bolívar was a leader in Latin America's struggle for independence from Spain. The bolívar is the currency of Venezuela.

Bond
Old English, meaning 'peasant farmer'. Usually associated with novel and film character James Bond.

Boris
Slavic, meaning 'battle glory'. Boris Johnson is a politican and former Mayor of London.

Bosten
English, meaning 'town by the woods'.

Botolf
English, meaning 'wolf'. St Botwulf of Thorney is the patron saint of travellers and farming.

Bowen
Welsh, meaning 'son of Owen'. The Bowen knot is a common heraldic symbol, and looks like a square with loops at each corner.

Bowie
Gaelic, meaning 'long double-edged sword'.

Boyd
Scottish Gaelic, meaning 'yellow'. Famous Boyds include English historian Boyd Hilton, designer and star of *American Hot Rod* Boyd Coddington and cricketer Boyd Rankin.

Bradley
(abbrev. Brad)
Old English, meaning 'broad' or 'wide'. Brad Pitt is one of America's most famous modern actors. Cyclist

Sir Bradley Wiggins is the winner of multiple Olympic medals and the Tour de France.

Brady
Irish, meaning 'large-chested'.

Bradyn
(alt. Braden, Brayden)
Gaelic, meaning 'descendant of Bradan'.

Bram
Gaelic, meaning 'raven'.

Brandon
(alt. Bran)
Old English, meaning 'gorse'. Brandon Stark is a character in the TV series *Game of Thrones*.

Brandt
(alt. Brant)
Old English, meaning 'beacon'.

Brannon
Gaelic, meaning 'raven'. Brannon Braga is a TV producer.

Branson
English, meaning 'son of Brand'. Sir Richard Branson is an entrepreneur and adventurer, the founder of the Virgin Group of companies.

Braulio
Spanish, meaning 'shining'.

Brendan
Gaelic, meaning 'prince'. Actor Brendan Fraser is known for his role in *The Mummy* film series.

Brennan
Gaelic, meaning 'teardrop'. The Brennan family are Ireland's most successful musical family, selling over 100 million records worldwide.

Brenton
English, from Brent, meaning 'hill'. Actor Brenton Thwaites is known for his role in soap opera *Home and Away*.

Brett
English, meaning 'a brewer'. Singer Brett Michaels is the lead singer of rock group Poison.

Brewster
(alt. Brew, Brewer)
English, meaning 'a brewer'.

Brian
(alt. Bryan, Bryant)
Gaelic, meaning 'high' or 'noble'. Famous Brians include physicist and TV star Professor Brian Cox, actor Brian Blessed and Queen guitar legend Brian May.

Brice
(alt. Bryce)
Latin, meaning 'speckled'.

Brier
French, meaning 'heather'.

Brock
Old English dialect, meaning 'badger'.

Broderick
English, meaning 'ruler'.

Brody

Gaelic, meaning both 'ditch' and 'brother'. It can be used for girls but more commonly for boys.

Brogan

Irish, meaning 'sturdy shoe'. A very old name, being mentioned in texts from the ninth century.

Bronwyn

Welsh, meaning 'white breasted'. More commonly used as a girls' name.

Brook

English, meaning 'stream'.

Brooklyn

From the name of the New York borough. Commonly associated with David and Victoria Beckham's eldest child.

Bruce

Scottish, meaning 'high' or 'noble'. Television presenter the late Sir Bruce Forsyth holds the Guinness World Record for the longest television career for a male entertainer.

Bruno

Germanic, meaning 'brown'. Bruno Tonioli is a judge on *Strictly Come Dancing*, and its American counterpart *Dancing With The Stars*.

Brutus

Latin, meaning 'dim-wit'. The name of Julius Caesar's assassin.

Bryant

English variant of Brian, meaning 'high' or 'noble'.

Bryden
(alt. Brydon)

Irish, meaning 'strong one'.

Bryn

Welsh, meaning 'mount' or 'hill'.

Bryson
(alt. Bryce, Brycen)

Welsh, meaning 'descendant of Brice'.

Bubba

American, meaning 'boy'. Associated with the character Bubba in *Forrest Gump*.

Buck

American, meaning 'goat' or 'deer', specifically a male deer.

Buddy
(abbrev. Bud)

American, meaning 'friend'.

Burdett

Middle English, meaning 'bird'.

Burgess
(alt. Burges, Burgiss, Berje)

English, meaning 'business'.

Burke

French, meaning 'fortified settlement'.

Burl

French, meaning 'knotty wood'.

Buzz

American, shortened form of Busby, meaning 'village in the thicket'. The US astronaut Buzz Aldrin was the second person to set foot on the moon.

Byron

Old English, meaning 'barn'. Made famous by the poet Lord Byron.

Boys' names

Cabot
Old English, meaning 'to sail'.

Cadby
(alt. Cadbey, Cadbee, Cadbie)
English, meaning 'soldiers' colony'.

Cade
(alt. Caben, Caden)
English, meaning 'round, lumpy'. A character in the novel *Gone With The Wind*.

Cadence
Latin, meaning 'with rhythm'. Can be used as a girls' or a boys' name.

Cadogan
Welsh, meaning 'battle glory and honour'. Sir Cadogan is a knight who constantly challenged Gryffindors to duels in J.K. Rowling's *Harry Potter* books.

Caedmon
Celtic, meaning 'wise warrior'. An early English poet.

Caelan
Gaelic, meaning 'slender'.

Caerwyn
(alt. Carwyn, Gerwyn)
Welsh, meaning 'white fort' or 'settlement'. Carwyn Jones is a former First Minister of Wales.

Caesar
Disputed origin. The Roman military leader and dictator Gaius Julius Caesar favoured the Moorish meaning 'elephant'.

Caetano
Portuguese, meaning 'from Gaeta, Italy'.

Cagney
Irish, meaning 'successor of the advocate'.

Caiden
Arabic, meaning 'companion'. A variant of the name Caden.

Caillou

French, meaning 'pebble'. Name of the main character in a Canadian children's cartoon.

Cain

Hebrew, meaning 'full of beauty'. Brother of Abel in the biblical Book of Genesis.

Cainan

Hebrew, meaning 'possessor' or 'purchaser'.

Cairo

Egypt's capital city. Located near Giza, home of the great pyramids.

Calder

Scottish, meaning 'rough waters'.

Caleb
(alt. Calen; abbrev. Cal)

Hebrew, meaning 'dog'. Caleb was one of 12 spies sent by Moses into Caanan.

Calhoun

Irish, meaning 'slight woods'.

Calix

Greek, meaning 'very handsome'.

Callahan

Irish, meaning 'contention' or 'strife'.

Callum
(alt. Calum)

Gaelic, meaning 'dove'. Often associated with St Columba, one of the Twelve Apostles of Ireland. The name has become popular outside of Scotland and Ireland in recent years.

Calvin
(alt. Kalvin)

French, meaning 'little bald one'. Name of popular fashion designer Calvin Klein.

Camden

Gaelic, meaning 'winding valley'. Also an area of north London.

Cameron

Scottish Gaelic, meaning 'crooked nose'. Name of a Scottish Clan.

Camillo

Latin, meaning 'free born' or 'noble'. A popular Italian name.

Campbell

Scottish Gaelic, meaning 'crooked mouth'. Was first used as a nickname.

Canaan

Hebrew, meaning 'to be humbled'. A region in the Middle East that existed during biblical times.

Candido

Latin, meaning 'candid' or 'honest'. Candido Jacuzzi is the inventor of the jacuzzi tub.

Canon
(alt. Cannon)

French, meaning 'of the church'.

Canton

French, meaning 'dweller of corner'.

Canute
(alt. Cnut, Cnute)
Scandinavian, meaning 'knot'. Name of an 11th-century King of England.

Cappy
Italian, meaning 'lucky'. A nickname for someone with the rank of Captain.

Carden
Old English, meaning 'wool carder'. Carding is the process of combing raw wool fibres to remove tangles and impurities.

Carey
Gaelic, meaning 'love'. Becoming more popular as a girls' as well as a boys' name.

Carl
(alt. Carlo, Carlos)
Old Norse, variant of Charles, meaning 'free man'.

Carlton
Old English, meaning 'free peasant settlement'.

Carmelo
Latin, meaning 'garden' or 'orchard'. Its variant, Carmel, refers to Mount Carmel in Israel, which in biblical times was known for its fruitfulness.

Carmen
Latin/Spanish, meaning 'song'. Name of one of the most famous French operas. Used for both boys and girls.

Carmine
Latin, meaning 'song'. Also a bright red pigment.

Carnell
English, meaning 'defender of the castle'.

Carson
(alt. Carsten)
Scottish, meaning 'marsh-dwellers'.

Carter
Old English, meaning 'transporter of goods'.

Cary
Old Celtic river name. Also means 'love'. Cary Grant was a legendary romantic lead actor in films; Cary Elwes is a British actor.

Case
(alt. Casey)
Irish Gaelic, meaning 'alert' or 'watchful'.

Casimer
Slavic, meaning 'famous destroyer of peace'.

Casper
Persian, meaning 'treasurer'. The name of a friendly ghost in a comic book.

Caspian
English, meaning 'of the Caspy people'. From the Caspian Sea. A literary character from the C.S. Lewis book *Prince Caspian*.

Cassidy

Irish, meaning 'clever' or 'curly haired'. Originated from the surname, Caiside.

Cassius
(alt. Cassio, Cason, Cash)

Latin, meaning 'empty, hollow'. A name popular during the Roman era. Cassius Clay was the original name of legendary American boxer Muhammad Ali.

Cathal

Celtic, meaning 'battle rule'.

Cato

Latin, meaning 'all-knowing'. Cato the Younger was a Roman politician who opposed Caesar.

Cecil

Latin, meaning 'blind'. Name of famous American movie director Cecil B. DeMille.

Cedar

English, from the name of an evergreen tree.

Cedric

Welsh, meaning 'spectacular bounty'. First appeared in Sir Walter Scott's 1819 novel, Ivanhoe.

Celesto
(alt. Celestino, Celindo)

Latin, meaning 'heaven sent'.

Chad
(alt. Chadrick)

Old English, meaning 'warlike, warrior'. Use of this name was rare until it sprang to popularity in the 1960s.

Chaim
(alt. Chayyim)

Hebrew, meaning 'life'.

Champion

English, meaning 'warrior'.

Chandler

Old English, meaning 'candle maker and seller'.

Charles
(abbrev. Chas, Charlie)

Old German, meaning 'free man'. Popularised by Charles the Great (a.k.a. Charlemagne). Prince Charles is heir to the throne of England. Charles Dickens is one of the finest and most enduringly popular English authors.

Chaska

Sioux, the name usually given to a first son.

Chauncey
(alt. Chance)

English, from the word 'chance' meaning 'good fortune'.

Che

Spanish, shortened form of José. Made famous by Che Guevara.

Chesley
Old English, meaning 'camp on the meadow'.

Chesney
English, meaning 'place to camp'. Also used as a girls' name.

Chester
Latin, meaning 'camp of soldiers'. The name of an English city.

Chilton
(alt. Chillron, Chilly, Chilt)
English, meaning 'tranquil'.

Chima
Old English, meaning 'hilly land'.

Christian
English. Christian Bale is an actor and Christian Louboutin is a famous shoe designer.

Christopher
(alt. Christophe; abbrev. Chris, Christy)
Greek, meaning 'Christ bearer'. Christopher Columbus was a famous explorer.

Cian
Irish, meaning 'ancient'. Father of Lug in Irish mythology.

Ciaran
Irish, meaning 'black'. Was the name of two Irish saints.

Cicero
Latin, meaning 'chickpea'. Famous Roman philosopher and orator.

Cimarron
City in western Kansas. Also the name of a novel by Edna Ferber.

Ciprian
Latin, meaning 'from Cyprus'. Popular in Romanian heritage.

Ciro
Spanish, meaning 'sun'. Name of an opera by Francesco Cavalli dating back to 1654.

Clancy
Old Irish, meaning 'red warrior'. Evolved from the surname Mac Fhlannchaidh.

Clarence
Latin, meaning 'one who lives near the river Clare'.

Clark
Latin, meaning 'clerk'. The human identity of the famed superhero Superman (Clark Kent).

Claude
(alt. Claudie, Claudio, Claudius)
Latin, meaning 'lame'. Has been in use since the Middle Ages.

Claus
Variant of Nicholas, meaning 'victorious'.

Clay
English, from the word 'clay'.

Clement
(alt. Clem)

Latin, meaning 'merciful'. Has been used as the name for 14 different popes.

Cleo

Greek, meaning 'glory'. Most commonly used as a name for girls, but also for boys.

Cletus

Greek, meaning 'illustrious'. Used to refer to the third pope, Anacletus.

Clifford
(alt. Clifton; abbrev. Cliff)

English, from the word 'cliff'.

Clint
(alt. Clinton)

Old English, meaning 'fenced settlement'. Name of famous actor/writer/director Clint Eastwood.

Clive

Old English, meaning 'cliff' or 'slope'. Famous Clives include actor Clive Owen and author and broadcaster Clive James.

Clyde

Scottish, from the river that passes through Glasgow. Name of famous American bank robber Clyde Barrow of the duo Bonnie and Clyde.

Coby
(alt. Cody, Colby)

Irish, meaning 'son of Oda'.

Cody

English, meaning 'pillow'. Also a girls' name.

Colden

Old English, meaning 'dark valley'.

Cole
(alt. Coley)

Old French, meaning 'coal black'.

Colin

Gaelic, meaning 'young creature'. Famous Colins include actor Colin Firth and champion rally driver Colin McRae.

Colson

Old English, meaning 'coal black'.

Colton

English, meaning 'swarthy'. Evolved from the Old English name, Cola.

Columbus

Latin, meaning 'dove'. Name of Italian explorer Christopher Columbus.

Colwyn

Welsh, from the river in Wales.

Conan

Gaelic, meaning 'wolf'. Middle name of 'Sherlock Holmes' author, Sir Arthur Conan Doyle.

Conley

Gaelic, meaning 'sensible'.

Connell
(alt. Connolly)
Irish, meaning 'high' or 'mighty'.

Connor
(alt. Conor, Conrad, Conroy)
Irish, meaning 'lover of hounds'. Evolved from the name Conchobhar (King of Ulster).

Constant
(alt. Constantine)
English. A name widely used by Christians as early as the 17th century.

Cooper
Old English, meaning 'barrel maker'.

Corban
Hebrew, meaning 'dedicated and belonging to God'.

Corbett
(alt. Corbin, Corby)
Norman French, meaning 'young crow'.

Cordell
Old English, meaning 'cord maker'.

Corey
(alt. Cory)
Gaelic, meaning 'hill hollow'. Thought to have originated from the Old Norse name Kori.

Corin
Latin, meaning 'spear'. A variant of the German given name Quirin.

Corliss
(alt. Corlis, Corlyss, Corlys)
English, meaning 'benevolent'.

Cormac
Gaelic, meaning 'impure son'. Name given to a third-century Irish king.

Cornelius
(alt. Cornell)
Latin, meaning 'horn'. The head of the Ministry of Magic (Cornelius Fudge) in J.K. Rowling's *Harry Potter* books.

Cortez
Spanish, meaning 'courteous'.

Corwin
Old English, meaning 'heart's friend' or 'companion'.

Cosimo
(alt. Cosme, Cosmo)
Italian, meaning 'order' or 'beauty'. Given name of Pope Innocent VII (1339–1406).

Coty
French, meaning 'riverbank'. Surname of people who lived near a coast.

Coulter
English, meaning 'young horse'.

Courtney
Old English, meaning 'domain of Curtis'. A given name that has been in use since the 17th century. Used for both boys and girls.

Covey
English, meaning 'flock of birds'.

Cowan
Gaelic, meaning 'hollow in the hill'.

Craig
Welsh, meaning 'rock'. Originally used as a surname by people who lived near a cliff. Craig David is a singer-songwriter and there are two famous sporting Craig Bellamys, one a Welsh footballer and the other an Australian rugby league star.

Crispin
Latin, meaning 'curly haired'. Name of a third-century saint, twin brother of St Crispinian. Patron saints of shoemakers.

Croix
French, meaning 'cross'.

Cruz
Spanish, meaning 'cross'. Made famous by David and Victoria Beckham's son.

Cullen
Gaelic, meaning 'handsome'. Made famous by the *Twilight* book series.

Curran
Gaelic, meaning 'dagger' or 'hero'.

Curtis
(alt. Curt)
Old French, meaning 'courteous'. Commonly used in the Middle Ages as a name of a courteous person.

Cutler
Old English, meaning 'knife maker'.

Cyprian
English, meaning 'from Cyprus'.

Cyril
Greek, meaning 'master' or 'Lord'. Name of St Cyril, one of the inventors of the Glagolitic alphabet, the precursor to the Cyrillic alphabet.

Cyrus
Persian, meaning 'Lord'. Cyrus the Great conquered Babylon in 539 BC.

Boys' names

Dabeel
(alt. Dabee, Dabie, Daby)
Sanskrit, meaning 'warrior'.

Daelan
English, meaning 'aware'. Also a girls' name.

Dafydd
(alt. Dai)
Welsh, meaning 'beloved'. Welsh version of David.

Daichi
Japanese, meaning 'great wisdom'.

Daire
(alt. Daer, Daere, Dair)
Irish, meaning 'wealthy'.

Daisuke
Japanese, meaning 'lionhearted'.

Dakari
Swahili, meaning 'happy'.

Dale
Old English, meaning 'valley'.

Dallin
English, meaning 'dweller in the valley'.

Dalton
English, meaning 'town in the valley'.

Daly
Gaelic, meaning 'assembly'.

Damarion
Greek, meaning 'gentle'.

Damian
(alt. Damien, Damon)
Greek, meaning 'to tame, subdue'. Name of a fourth-century patron saint of physicians. Damon Hill is British champion racing driver and Damon Albarn is a musician and the lead singer of Blur.

Dane

Old English, meaning 'from Denmark'.

Daniel
(alt. Dan, Danny)

Hebrew, meaning 'God is my judge'. Daniel was a prophet during biblical times. An enduringly popular name for boys.

Dante

Latin, meaning 'lasting'. Associated with the 13th-century Italian poet Dante Alighieri, author of *The Divine Comedy*.

Darby

Irish, meaning 'without envy'.

Darcy
(alt. Darcey)

Gaelic, meaning 'dark'. Associated with Jane Austen's Mr Darcy, and the parody of this character in *Bridget Jones' Diary*. A name more commonly used for girls in modern times.

Dario
(alt. Darius)

Greek, meaning 'kingly'. Associated with Dario Argento, an Italian film director.

Darnell

Old English, meaning 'the hidden spot'.

Darragh
(alt. Dara)

Irish, meaning 'dark oak'. A popular name in Ireland, now being seen across the UK.

Darrell
(alt. Daryl)

Old English, meaning 'open'. Originated from the Norman French surname d'Airelle.

Darren
(alt. Darrian)

Gaelic, meaning 'great'. Darren Aronofsky is an American film-maker. In the UK the name is well connected with sport, including cricketer Darren Gough.

Darrick

Old German, meaning 'power of the tribe'.

Darshan

Hindi, meaning 'vision'.

Darwin

Old English, meaning 'dear friend'. Often associated with the naturalist Charles Darwin.

Dash
(alt. Dashawn)

American, meaning 'enlightened one'. Associated with one of the characters in Disney Pixar's *The Incredibles*.

Famous male drummers

Dave (Grohl)	Phil (Collins)
John (Bonham)	Ringo (Starr – real name Richard Starkey)
Keith (Moon)	Stewart (Copeland)
Lars (Ulrich)	Tommy (Lee)
Mick (Fleetwood)	Travis (Barker)

Dashiell

French, meaning 'page boy'. Dashiell Hammett was an American author, famous for hard-boiled detective fiction.

Dason

Native American, meaning 'chief'.

David

(alt. Dave, Davey, Davie, Davin)

Hebrew, meaning 'beloved'. Associated with the King of Israel who killed Goliath the giant as a boy.

Davis

Old English, meaning 'son of David'.

Dawson

Old English, meaning 'son of David'. Associated with the main character in the TV show Dawson's Creek.

Dax

(alt. Daxton)

French, once a town in south-western France.

Dayal

Sanskrit, meaning 'kind'.

Dayton

Old English, meaning 'David's place'. A city in the US state of Ohio.

Dean

Old English, meaning 'valley'. Dean Koontz is an American author and Dean Martin was a hugely popular singer and entertainer, known as the 'King of Cool'.

Declan

Irish, meaning 'full of goodness'. Associated with St Declan, who was born in the fifth century.

Dedric

Old English, meaning 'gifted ruler'.

Deepak

(alt. Deepan)

Sanskrit, meaning 'illumination'. Associated with doctor and spiritual author Deepak Chopra.

Del

(alt. Delano, Delbert, Dell)

Old English, meaning 'bright shining one'. Associated with the main character in Only Fools and Horses.

Delaney
Irish, meaning 'dark challenge'.

Demetrius
Greek, meaning 'harvest lover'. Name of a fourth-century Greek sculptor.

Dempsey
Irish, meaning 'proud'.

Denham
(alt. Denholm)
Old English, meaning 'valley settlement'.

Dennis
(alt. Denis, Denny, Denton)
English, meaning 'follower of Dionysius'. Associated with the comic strip Dennis the Menace. Other famous Dennises include actors Dennis Hopper and Dennis Quaid and footballer Dennis Bergkamp.

Denzil
(alt. Densel, Denzel)
English, meaning 'fort'. Most commonly associated with Oscar-winning actor Denzel Washington.

Deon
Greek, meaning 'of Zeus'.

Derek
English, meaning 'power of the tribe'. Short form for the given name Diderik.

Dermot
Irish, meaning 'free man'. Dermot O'Leary is a prolific TV and radio presenter.

Desmond
Irish, meaning 'from south Munster'. Associated with South African social rights activist Archbishop Desmond Tutu.

Destin
French, meaning 'destiny'.

Deveraux
French, meaning 'from the town of Évreux'.

Devyn
(alt. Devin)
Irish, meaning 'poet'.

Dewey
Welsh, from Dewi (David). One of Disney character Donald Duck's three nephews.

Dexter
(alt. Dex)
Latin, meaning 'right-handed'.

Diallo
(alt. Dialo)
Swahili, meaning 'bold'.

Dick
(alt. Dickie, Dickon, Diccon)
From Richard, meaning 'powerful leader'. Dick is one of Enid Blyton's Famous Five and Dickon is a character in Frances Hodgson Burnett's The Secret Garden.

Didier

French, meaning 'much desired'. St Didier is a saint honoured in the Catholic Church. Famous Didiers include footballers Didier Deschamps and Didier Drogba.

Diego

Spanish, meaning 'supplanter'. Has been in use since the 11th century.

Dietrich

Old German, meaning 'power of the tribe'.

Diggory

English, meaning 'dyke'.

Dilbert

English, meaning 'day bright'. Popularised by the American comic strip of the same name.

Dimitri

(alt. Dimitrios, Dimitris)

Greek, meaning 'prince'. A popular name in Russia.

Dino

Diminutive of Dean, meaning 'valley'. Used as short form for names ending with -dino.

Dion

Greek, short form of Dionysius, the Greek god of wine. Dionysius was the son of Zeus and Semele.

Dirk

Variant of Derek, meaning 'power of the tribe'. A name also used to refer to a dagger.

Divakar

Sanskrit, meaning 'the sun'.

Dominic

Latin, meaning 'Lord'.

Donald

(alt. Don, Donal, Donaldo)

Gaelic, meaning 'great chief'. Famous Donalds include actor Donald Sutherland, businessman-turned-US President Donald Trump and ever-popular Disney character Donald Duck.

Donato

Italian, meaning 'gift'. Given name of Italian sculptor Donatello.

Donnell

(alt. Donnie, Donny)

Gaelic, meaning 'world fighter'.

Donovan

Gaelic, meaning 'dark-haired chief'. Associated with Australian singer and actor Jason Donovan.

Doran

Gaelic, meaning 'exile'.

Dorian

Greek, meaning 'descendant of Doris'. Name of the title character in Oscar Wilde's *The Picture of Dorian Gray*.

Douglas

(alt. Dougal, Dougie)

Scottish, meaning 'black river'. Douglas Adams was the author of *The Hitchhiker's Guide to the Galaxy*.

Doyle
Irish, meaning 'foreigner'.

Draco
(alt. Drake)
Latin, meaning 'dragon'. Made popular by the character Draco Malfoy in J.K. Rowling's Harry Potter books.

Drew
Shortened form of Andrew, meaning 'man' or 'warrior'.

Dryden
English, meaning 'dry town'.

Dudley
Old English, meaning 'people's field'. Also the name of Harry Potter's cousin.

Duff
Gaelic, meaning 'swarthy'.

Duke
Latin, meaning 'leader'. The title of a nobleman ruling over a duchy.

Duncan
Scottish, meaning 'dark warrior'. King Duncan is a character in Shakespeare's Macbeth.

Dustin
(alt. Dusty)
French, meaning 'brave warrior'. Popularised by American actor Dustin Hoffman.

Dwayne
(alt. Duwayne, Duane)
Irish Gaelic, meaning 'swarthy'.

Dwight
Flemish, meaning 'blond'. Associated with the 34th President of the United States, Dwight D. Eisenhower.

Dwyer
Gaelic, meaning 'dark wise one'.

Dyani
Native American, meaning 'eagle'.

Dylan
(alt. Dillon)
Welsh, meaning 'son of the sea'. Name of the famous Welsh poet Dylan Thomas.

 Boys' names

Eagan
Irish, meaning 'fiery'.

Eamon
(alt. Eamonn, Eames)
Irish, meaning 'wealthy protector'.

Earl
(alt. Earle, Errol)
English, meaning 'nobleman, warrior, prince'. Earl is a title of nobility, used since Anglo-Saxon times.

Ebenezer
(abbrev. Ebb)
Hebrew, meaning 'stone of help'. Ebenezer Scrooge is the main character in Charles Dickens' novel A Christmas Carol.

Edgar
(alt. Elgar)
Old English, meaning 'wealthy spear'. Poet and writer Edgar Allan Poe is known for works such as The Raven.

Edison
English, meaning 'son of Edward'. Thomas Edison was one of America's greatest inventors.

Edmund
(abbrev. Ed)
English, meaning 'wealthy protector'.

Edric
Old English, meaning 'rich and powerful'.

Edsel
Old German, meaning 'noble'. Henry Ford, the automobile magnate, named his son Edsel.

Edward
(alt. Eduardo; abbrev. Ed, Edd, Eddie, Eddy)
Old English, meaning 'wealthy guard'. Edward has become extremely popular since the release of the Twilight series.

Edwin
English, meaning 'wealthy friend'.

Efrain

Hebrew, meaning 'fruitful'. Normally used in Spanish-speaking cultures.

Egan

Irish, meaning 'fire'. Egan, derived from the name Aedhagan, is one of the oldest surnames in Europe.

Eilif

(alt. Elif, Eilyg, Elyf)

Norse, meaning 'immortal'. Eilif Paterssen was a Norwegian painter in the early 20th century.

Einar

Old Norse, meaning 'battle leader'. Still a popular name in Iceland.

Eladio

Greek, meaning 'Greek'. Related to the name Heladio.

Elam

Hebrew, meaning 'eternal'. Elam is mentioned in the Bible as being a son of Shem, and son of Noah.

Elan

French, meaning 'energy and enthusiasm'. Also the name of a river valley in Wales.

Elbert

Old English, meaning 'famous'. Variation of the name Albert.

Eldon

Old English, meaning 'Ella's hill'. Also refers to the town in County Durham, England.

Eldred

(alt. Eldridge)

Old English, meaning 'old venerable counsel'.

Elgin

Old English, meaning 'high minded'. Also refers to the town of the same name in Scotland.

Eli

(alt. Eliah)

Hebrew, meaning 'high'. Eli is a character in the Old Testament of the Bible.

Elias

(alt. Elijah, Elio)

Hebrew, meaning 'the Lord is my God'. Walt Disney's father was Elias Disney. Actor Elijah Wood played Frodo Baggins in the Lord of the Rings films.

Ellery

Old English, meaning 'elder tree'. Ellery Hanley is a former rugby league player and coach for Great Britain.

Elliott

English variant of Elio, meaning 'the Lord is my God'. Made popular by the lead character in the film E.T.

Ellis

Welsh, variant of Elio, meaning 'the Lord is my God'.

Ellison

English, meaning 'son of Ellis'.

Elmer

Old English, meaning 'noble'; Arabic, meaning 'aristocratic'. Elmer the elephant features in a number of

children's picture books by author
David McKee.

Elmo
(alt. Ellmo, Elmon)
Greek, meaning 'gregarious'.

Elmore
Old English, meaning from 'elm tree'
and 'moor'. Elmore Leonard was an
American author.

Elon
(alt. Alon)
Hebrew, meaning 'oak tree'. A very old
name, it is now not used much outside
of Hebrew-speaking communities.

Elroy
French, meaning 'king'.

Elton
Old English, meaning 'Ella's town'.
Singer and songwriter Sir Elton John's
real name is Reg Dwight.

Elvin
English, meaning 'elf-like'.

Elvis
Figure in Norse mythology. Made
famous by the singer Elvis Presley.

Emanuel
Hebrew, meaning 'God is with us'.
Features in hymns and carols.

Emeric
German, meaning 'work rule'.
St Emeric of Hungary was known for
a pure and pious life.

Emile
(alt. Emil, Emiliano, Emilio)
Latin, meaning 'eager'. Emile is Remy
the rat's older brother in Disney's
film *Ratatouille*.

Emlyn
Welsh. The name of a town,
Newcastle Emlyn, in west Wales.

Emmett
English, meaning 'universal'. Emmett
is a member of the Cullen family in
the *Twilight* series.

Emrys
Welsh, meaning 'immortal'. The
legendary magician Merlin is said
to have been given the name Emrys
at birth, and only later adopted his
more famous moniker.

Eneco
Spanish, meaning 'fiery one'.

Enoch
Hebrew, meaning 'dedicated'. Enoch
was the great-great-grandfather of
Noah in the Bible.

Enrico
(alt. Enrique)
Italian, form of Henry, meaning
'home ruler'. Extremely popular
name in Italy for boys.

Enzo
Italian, short for Lorenzo, meaning
'laurel'. Enzo Ferrari was the founder
of the Ferrari automobile company.

Eoghan
(alt. Eoin)
Irish form of Owen, meaning 'well
born' or 'noble'. Eoghan was an Irish

king in the fifth century. Eoin Colfer is the author of the young adult fiction series *Artemis Fowl*.

Ephron
(alt. Effron)
Hebrew, meaning 'dust'.

Erasmo
(alt. Erasmus)
Greek, meaning 'to love'. Erasmus was a Dutch humanist and theologian during the Renaissance period.

Eric
Old Norse, meaning 'ruler'. Often associated with singer and guitarist Eric Clapton.

Ernest
(alt. Ernesto, Ernie, Ernst)
Old German, meaning 'serious'. Author Ernest Hemingway is known for his influential novels *A Farewell to Arms* and *The Old Man and the Sea*.

Errol
English, meaning 'boar wolf'. Actor Errol Flynn is best known for his swashbuckler roles and the lead role in *The Adventures of Robin Hood*.

Erskine
Scottish, meaning 'high cliff'. Also a place in Scotland.

Erwin
Old English, meaning 'boar friend'.

Eryx
Greek, meaning 'boxer'. Sometimes used as an alternative spelling for Eric.

Ethan
(alt. Etienne)
Hebrew, meaning 'long lived'. Ethan Hawke is an Oscar-nominated actor.

Eugene
Greek, meaning 'well born'.

Evan
(alt. Ifan)
Welsh, meaning 'God is gracious'.

Evelyn
German, meaning 'hazelnut'. Evelyn Waugh is the author of *Brideshead Revisited*, *Decline and Fall* and *Scoop*.

Everard
(alt. Everett)
Old English, meaning 'strong boar'. Also the name of an old English ale.

Everly
(alt. Everleigh, Everley)
English, meaning 'grazing meadow'. Used as a name for boys and girls.

Ewan
(alt. Euan, Ewald, Ewen, Ewell)
Old English, from Owen, meaning 'well born' or 'noble'. Actor Ewan McGregor is known for his roles in *Trainspotting*, *Moulin Rouge* and *Star Wars*.

Exton
English, meaning 'on the River Exe'.

Ezra
Hebrew, meaning 'helper'. Ezra Pound was an American poet. George Ezra is a singer-songwriter.

Boys' names

Faber
(alt. Fabir)

Latin, meaning 'blacksmith'. Faber and Faber is a well-known UK publishing house.

Fabian
(alt. Fabien, Fabio)

Latin, meaning 'one who grows beans'. Also associated with the teen pop sensation Fabian in the 1950s and '60s.

Fabrice
(alt. Fabrizio)

Latin, meaning 'works with his hands'. Popular in France. Fabrice Muamba is a former football player who survived an on-pitch heart attack.

Faisal

Arabic, meaning 'resolute'. Faisal II was the last King of Iraq, whose reign ended during the revolution of 1958.

Falco
(alt. Falcon, Falconer, Falke, Faulkner)

Latin, meaning 'falconer'.

Faron

Spanish, meaning 'pharaoh'. Also derived from a Gaelic word for 'thunder'.

Farrell

Gaelic, meaning 'hero'.

Faustino

Latin, meaning 'fortunate'.

Fela
(alt. Felah, Fella, Fellah)

Swahili, meaning 'a man who is warlike'. The name of the famous Nigerian musician Fela Kuti.

Felipe
(alt. Filippo)

Spanish, meaning 'lover of horses'. Formula One driver Felipe Massa has driven for Ferrari and Williams.

Felix
(alt. Felice)

Italian/Latin, meaning 'happy'. Felix the Cat was a popular 20th-century cartoon character.

Fennel

Latin, name of a herb. More commonly used as a girls' name.

Ferdinand
(alt. Fernando)

Old German, meaning 'bold voyager'.

Fergus
(alt. Ferguson)

Gaelic, meaning 'supreme man'.

Ferris

Gaelic, meaning 'rock'. *Ferris Bueller's Day Off* was a runaway hit film during the 1980s.

Fiachra

Irish, meaning 'raven'. St Fiachra is the patron saint of gardeners.

Fidel

Latin, meaning 'faithful'. Fidel Castro was President of Cuba from 1976 to 2008.

Finbarr

Gaelic, meaning 'fair head'. St Finbarr is the patron saint of the City of Cork.

Finian
(alt. Finnian)

Gaelic, meaning 'fair'. St Finnian is an important Irish saint, and a founder of the theory of monasticism.

Finlay
(alt. Finley, Fynlee)

Gaelic, meaning 'fair-haired courageous one'.

Finn
(alt. Fynn)

Finnish, meaning 'from Finland'.

Finnegan

Gaelic, meaning 'fair'. Author James Joyce wrote *Finnegans Wake* as a complex work of comedy.

Fintan

Gaelic, meaning 'little fair one'. A seer in Irish mythology called Fintan supposedly saved one of Noah's granddaughters from the flood.

Fitzroy

English, meaning 'the king's son'. Usually associated with Vice-Admiral Robert Fitzroy, who accompanied Charles Darwin on his famous voyages.

Flavio

Latin, meaning 'yellow hair'. The opera *Flavio* was composed by Handel.

Florencio
(alt. Florentino)

Latin, meaning 'from Florence'.

Florian
(alt. Florin)

Slavic/Latin, meaning 'flower'. St Florian is the patron saint of chimney sweeps, soapmakers and firefighters.

Floyd
Welsh, meaning 'grey haired'.

Flynn
Gaelic, meaning 'with a ruddy complexion'.

Forbes
(alt. Forbs, Forb, Forbe)
Gaelic, meaning 'of the field'.

Forrest
(alt. Forest)
Old English, meaning 'dweller or worker of the forest'.

Fortunato
Italian, meaning 'lucky'.

Foster
Old English, meaning 'woodsman'.

Fotini
(alt. Fotis)
Greek, meaning 'light'.

Francis
(alt. Francesco, Francisco, Franco, François)
Latin, meaning 'from France'. After the election of Pope Francis, Francesco has become the most popular name for boys in Italy.

Frank
(alt. Frankie, Franklin, Franz)
Middle English, meaning 'free landholder'. Also a diminutive of Francis. Famous Franks include footballer Frank Lampard, crooner Frank Sinatra, and film director Frank Capra.

Fraser
(alt. Fraiser)
Scottish, meaning 'of the forest men'.

Frederick
(alt. Friedrich; abbrev. Freddie, Fred)
Old German, meaning 'peaceful ruler'. There is a spelling or pronunciation variation of Frederick in practically every European language.

Furman
Old German, meaning 'ferryman'.

Fyfe
(alt. Fife, Fyffes)
Scottish, meaning 'from Fifeshire'.

Boys' names

Gabino

Latin, meaning 'God is my strength'.

Gabriel
(abbrev. Gabe)

Hebrew, meaning 'hero of God'.
One of the archangels in the Bible.

Gael
(alt. Gale)

English, old reference to the Celts.
Gale is a character in the *Hunger Games* trilogy.

Gaius
(alt. Gaeus)

Latin, meaning 'rejoicing'. Julius Caesar's full name was Gaius Julius Caesar.

Galen

Greek, meaning 'healer'. Galen of Pergamon was a well-respected ancient Greco-Roman philosopher and physician.

Galileo

Italian, meaning 'from Galilee'.
Galileo Galilei was an important and influential physicist and astronomer during the Scientific Revolution.

Ganesh

Hindi, meaning 'lord of the horde'.
One of the Hindu deities.

Gannon

Irish, meaning 'fair skinned'.
Commonly used as a surname, particularly in Ireland.

Gareth
(alt. Garth, Garthe, Gart, Garte)

Welsh, meaning 'gentle'.

Garfield

Old English, meaning 'spear field'.
Also the name of the cartoon cat.

Garland

English, as in 'garland of flowers'.

Garnet

English, precious stone, red in colour. Occasionally used for boys, although not as frequently as for girls.

Garrett

Old German, meaning 'spear' or 'ruler'. Ireland's Garret the Great was known as 'the uncrowned King of Ireland' during his time of political power in the 15th century.

Gary
(alt. Garry, Geary)

Old English, meaning 'spear'. Some of Britain's best-loved Garys include Take That member Gary Barlow and football pundit Gary Lineker.

Gaspar
(alt. Gaspard)

Persian, meaning 'treasurer'.

Gaston

French, from the Gascony region in the south of France.

Gavin
(alt. Gawain)

Scottish/Welsh, meaning 'little falcon'.

Gene

Greek, shortened form of Eugene, meaning 'well born'. Famous Genes include actors Gene Kelly and Gene Hackman, and Kiss guitarist Gene Simmons.

Genkei

Japanese, meaning 'honoured'. One of Japan's most famous botanists is Genkei Masamune, who is credited with identifying hundreds of new species.

Gennaro

Italian, meaning 'of Janus'.

Geoffrey
(abbrev. Geoff)

Old German, meaning 'peace'.

George
(alt. Giorgio)

Greek, meaning 'farmer'. Chosen by the Duke and Duchess of Cambridge for their elder son who is third in line to the throne.

Gerald
(alt. Geraldo, Gerard, Gerardo, Gerhard; abbrev. Gerry)

Old German, meaning 'spear ruler'. Former President of the United States Gerald Ford is the only person to have served as both President and Vice President without being elected to either position, thanks to two infamous resignations before him.

Geronimo

Italian, meaning 'sacred name'. Originally the name of a prominent Apache Indian, this has now become a word for 'go-get-'em!'

Gert

Old German, meaning 'strong spear'.

Gervase

Old German, meaning 'with honour'. Gervase Phinn is a widely read author of several humorous books describing his life as a school inspector in Yorkshire.

Giacomo

Italian, meaning 'God's son'. Legendary womaniser Casanova's full name was Giacomo Girolamo Casanova.

Gibson

English, meaning 'son of Gilbert'.

Gideon

Hebrew, meaning 'tree cutter'. Gideon is a figure in the Bible.

Gilbert
(alt. Gilberto)

French, meaning 'bright promise'.

Giles

Greek, meaning 'small goat'.

Gino

Italian, meaning 'well born'.

Giovanni

Italian form of John, meaning 'God is gracious'.

Giri
(alt. Gririe, Giry, Girey)

Sanskrit, meaning 'from the mountain'.

Giulio

Italian, meaning 'youthful'. Composer Giulio Caccini was active during the Baroque era.

Giuseppe

Italian form of Joseph, meaning 'Jehovah increases'.

Glen
(alt. Glenn, Glyn)

English, from the word 'glen'.

Godfrey

German, meaning 'peace of God'.

Gordon

Gaelic, meaning 'large fortification'. Famous Gordons include chef Gordon Ramsay and former prime minister Gordon Brown.

Gottlieb

German, meaning 'good love'. One of Mozart's names at birth was Gottlieb; others included Johannes, Chrisostomus and Wolfgang.

Gower

Welsh, from the area of the Welsh coast, by the Bristol Channel.

Graeme
(alt. Graham)

English, meaning 'gravelled area'.

Grant

English, from the word 'grant'.

Granville

English, meaning 'gravelly town'. Probably the most famous Granville is the character portrayed by David Jason in sitcom *Open All Hours*.

Gray
(alt. Grey)
English, from the word 'grey'.

Grayson
English, meaning 'son of gray'. Grayson Perry is an artist who won the Turner Prize in 2003.

Green
English, from the word 'green'.

Gregory
(alt. Gregorio; abbrev. Greg, Greig)
English, from the word 'griffin'. Actor Gregory Peck was best known for his role in *To Kill A Mockingbird*.

Griffin
English. A griffin is a mythical creature with the body of a lion and the head and wings of an eagle.

Groves
English, meaning 'inhabits near grove of trees'.

Gruffudd
(alt. Griffith, Gruffydd; abbrev. Griff, Gruff)
Welsh, meaning 'strong prince'. It was a common name among medieval Welsh royalty.

Grylfi
(alt. Gylfie, Gylfee, Gylffi)
Scandinavian, meaning 'king'. Gylfi was the first Nordic king in Scandinavia.

Guido
Italian, meaning 'guide'.

Guillaume
French form of William, meaning 'strong protector'. William the Conqueror is known as Guillaume le Conquérant in France.

Gulliver
English, meaning 'glutton'. *Gulliver's Travels*, by Jonathan Swift, tells the story of a surgeon who sets sail for adventure.

Gunther
German, meaning 'warrior'.

Gurpreet
Sanskrit, meaning 'love of the teacher'. More commonly used in Punjabi-speaking communities.

Gustave
(abbrev. Gus)
Scandinavian, meaning 'royal staff'. Gustave Flaubert is the author of classics including *Madame Bovary*. Also the name given to a legendary crocodile in Burundi, whose length is said to be over 20ft and that has killed as many as 300 humans.

Guy
English. Guy Fawkes is the character most associated with the Gunpowder Plot of 1605, which was an attempt to blow up the Houses of Parliament.

Gwyn
Welsh, meaning 'white'. Commonly used as a name for girls as well as for boys.

Boys' names

Habib
Arabic, meaning 'beloved one'.

Hackett
(alt. Hacket, Hackit, Hackitt)
German, meaning 'small hacker'.

Haden
(alt. Haiden)
English, meaning 'hedged valley'.
Also a popular type of mango.

Hades
Greek, meaning 'sightless'. Name of
the god of the underworld in Greek
mythology.

Hadrian
From Hadria, a north Italian city.
Hadrian's Wall in northern England
is named after the Roman Emperor
Hadrian.

Hadwin
Old English, meaning 'friend in war'.

Hakeem
Arabic, meaning 'wise and insightful'.
Hakeem Lyon is a major character in
the musical epic drama *Empire*.

Hal
(alt. Hale, Hallie)
English, nickname for Henry,
meaning 'home ruler'. Used in this
context in Shakespeare's *Henry IV*
plays.

Halim
Arabic, meaning 'gentle'. Al-Halim is
one the names of God in Islam.

Hallam
Old English, meaning 'the valley'.

Hamid
Arabic, meaning 'praiseworthy'.
Hamid Karzai was the elected
president of Afghanistan from 2001
to 2014.

Hamilton
Old English, meaning 'flat-topped hill'.

Hamish

Scottish form of James, meaning 'he who supplants'.

Hamlet
(alt. Hamlett, Hammet, Hamnet)

German, meaning 'village'. A variation of the Danish Amleth, and often associated with Shakespeare's tragedy *Hamlet*.

Hampus

Swedish form of Homer, meaning 'pledge'. Hampus Lindholm is an international ice hockey player, originally from Sweden.

Hamza

Arabic, meaning 'lamb'. Also a letter in the Arabic alphabet.

Han
(alt. Hannes, Hans)

Scandinavian, meaning 'the Lord is gracious'.

Hanif
(alt. Haneef, Haneaf, Haneif)

Arabic, meaning 'devout'. In Islam it usually refers to people who submitted entirely to their religion.

Hank

German, form of Henry, meaning 'home ruler'.

Hansel

German, meaning 'the Lord is gracious'. One of the most famous Grimm fairy tales is the story of Hansel and Gretel.

Hardy

English, meaning 'tough'. Often associated with the author Thomas Hardy, comedic duo Laurel and Hardy and English actor Tom Hardy.

Harlan

English, meaning 'dweller by the boundary wood'. Harlan Coben is the author of several mystery novels.

Harland

Old English, meaning 'army land'. Fast food chain KFC was founded by Colonel Harland David Sanders. The *Titanic* was built at Belfast shipyard Harland and Wolff.

Harley

Old English, meaning 'hare meadow'.

Harmon

Old German, meaning 'soldier'.

Harold

Scandinavian, meaning 'army ruler'. The last Anglo-Saxon King of England was Harold II, whose reign ended after he lost the Battle of Hastings.

Harris

Old English, meaning 'home ruler'.

Harrison

Old English, meaning 'son of Harry' or 'son of Harris'. The middle name of Archie Mountbatten-Windsor.

Harry

Old German, form of Henry, meaning 'home ruler'. Famous Harrys include Harry Potter and One Direction singer Harry Styles.

Hart

Old English, meaning 'stag'.

Harvey

Old English, meaning 'strong and worthy'. The film *Harvey*, starring Jimmy Stewart and Josephine Hull, is about a man whose best friend is an enormous invisible rabbit.

Haskell

Hebrew, meaning 'intellect'.

Hassan

Arabic, meaning 'handsome'. Hassan Rouhani is the current President of Iran.

Haydn
(alt. Hayden, Haydon)

Old English, meaning 'hedged valley'. Franz Joseph Haydn, was one of the most influential and popular composers of the classical period.

Heart

English, from the word 'heart'.

Heath

English, meaning 'heath' or 'moor'. Heath Ledger was a prolific actor, known for his roles in *A Knight's Tale*, *10 Things I Hate About You* and *The Dark Knight*.

Heathcliff

English, meaning 'cliff near a heath'. Made famous by Emily Brontë's novel *Wuthering Heights*.

Heber

Hebrew, meaning 'partner'.

Hector

Greek, meaning 'steadfast'. A Trojan prince and historic fighter in ancient Greek mythology.

Henry
(alt. Henri, Hendrik, Hendrix)

Old German, meaning 'home ruler'. There have been eight Kings of England named Henry.

Henson

English, meaning 'son of Henry'.

Herbert
(alt. Heriberto; abbrev. Bert, Herb)

Old German, meaning 'illustrious warrior'. Herbert Hoover was a President of the United States and founder of the FBI.

Herman
(alt. Herminio, Hermon)

Old German, meaning 'soldier'.

Hermes

Greek, meaning 'messenger'. The messenger of the gods in Greek mythology.

Herschel
(alt. Hirsch)

Yiddish, meaning 'deer'.

Hezekiah

Hebrew, meaning 'God gives strength'. The 13th king of Judah was King Hezekiah.

Hideki

Japanese, meaning 'excellent trees'. The prime minister of Japan during World War II was Hideki Tojo.

Hideo

Japanese, meaning 'excellent name'. One of Japan's most prolific comedians is Hideo Higashikokubaru.

Hilario

Latin, meaning 'cheerful, happy'. Retired goalkeeper Henrique Hilario Meireles Sampaio is usually known just as Hilario.

Hilary
(alt. Hillary)

English, meaning 'cheerful'. Most used now as a girls' name although it can be used for boys, as with politician Hilary Benn.

Hildred

German, meaning 'battle counsellor'.

Hillel

Hebrew, meaning 'greatly praised'. Rabbi Hillel was an important leader in the Jewish faith.

Hilliard

Old German, meaning 'battle guard'.

Hilton

Old English, meaning 'hill settlement'.

Hiram

Hebrew, meaning 'exalted brother'.

Hiro

Spanish, meaning 'sacred name'.

Hiroshi

Japanese, meaning 'generous'.

Hobart

English, meaning 'bright and shining intellect'. Also the name of the capital of Tasmania.

Hodge

English, meaning 'son of Roger'.

Hogan

Gaelic, meaning 'youth'. Wrestling superstar Terry Bollea is better known as Hulk Hogan.

Holden

English, meaning 'deep valley'.

Hollis

Old English, meaning 'holly tree'.

Homer

Greek, meaning 'pledge'. Name of the Greek poet – and of the TV character Homer Simpson.

Honorius

Latin, meaning 'honourable'. Honorius was a Roman emperor in the fifth century BC.

Horace

Latin, common name of the Roman poet Quintus Horatius Flaccus.

Houston

Old English, meaning 'Hugh's town'. Also a city in the state of Texas, USA.

Howard

Old English, meaning 'noble watchman'. Howard Hughes was a businessman, film-maker and aviator and extremely wealthy. Howard Donald is a founding member of enduringly successful boy band Take That.

Howell

Welsh, meaning 'eminent and remarkable'. Also the name of a town in Lincolnshire.

Hoyt

Norse, meaning 'spirit' or 'soul'. Also believed to be an Old English name, meaning someone who lives on a hill.

Hristo

From Christo, meaning 'follower of Christ'. Hristo Stoichkov is acknowledged to be one of the best footballers of his generation, and the best Bulgarian footballer ever.

Hubbell
(alt. Hubble)

English, meaning 'brave hearted'.

Hubert

German, meaning 'bright and shining intellect'.

Hudson

Old English, meaning 'adventurous' or 'son of Hugh'. Also one of the largest rivers in the USA.

Hugh
(alt. Hubert, Hugo, Huw)

Old German, meaning 'soul, mind and intellect'. Famous Hughs include actors Hugh Grant, Hugh Laurie and Hugh Jackman. Huw Stephens is a Welsh TV and radio presenter.

Humbert

Old German, meaning 'famous giant'. Be warned: it's the name and surname of the paedophile protagonist of Vladimir Nabokov's novel *Lolita*.

Humphrey

Old German, meaning 'peaceful warrior'. Actor Humphrey Bogart is best known for his role in the film *Casablanca*.

Hunter

English. Popular name in the USA for boys, yet to take off in the UK.

Hurley

Gaelic, meaning 'sea tide'.

Huxley

Old English, meaning 'Hugh's meadow'.

Hyrum
(alt. Hiram, Hyram)

Hebrew, meaning 'exalted brother'. Hyrum Smith was one of the founders of the Church of Jesus Christ of Latter Day Saints; also known as the Mormons.

I

Boys' names

Iago
Spanish, meaning 'he who supplants'. Name of the villain in Shakespeare's *Othello*.

Ian
(alt. Ion, Iain)
Gaelic, variant of John, meaning 'God is gracious'. Famous Ians include former cricketer Sir Ian Botham, novelists Ian Fleming and Iain Banks and journalist and satirist Ian Hislop.

Ianto
Welsh, meaning 'gift of God'. Ianto Jones is a featured character in sci-fi drama series *Torchwood*.

Ibaad
Arabic, meaning 'a believer in God'.

Ibrahim
Arabic, meaning 'father of many'. Also the Arabic name for the prophet and father of Islam, Abraham.

Ichabod
Hebrew, meaning 'glory is good'. The protagonist in Washington Irving's short story 'The Legend of Sleepy Hollow' is called Ichabod Crane.

Ichiro
Japanese, meaning 'firstborn son'. A current Japanese superstar baseball player is Ichiro Suzuki.

Idan
Hebrew, meaning 'place in time'.

Idris
Welsh, meaning 'fiery leader'. Actor Idris Elba is known for his roles in *The Wire*, *Luther* and *Mandela: Long Walk to Freedom*.

Ieuan
(alt. Ioan)
Welsh variant of John, meaning 'God is gracious'.

Ignacio

Latin, meaning 'ardent' or 'burning'. More commonly found in South America, particularly Uruguay and Argentina.

Ignatz

German, meaning 'fiery'.

Igor

Russian or Norse origin, meaning 'warrior'.

Ikaika

Hawaiian, meaning 'strong'.

Iku

Japanese, meaning 'nourishing'.

Ilan
(alt. Elan)

Hebrew, meaning 'tree'. Composer Ilan Eshkeri is known for his scores of several films, including Layer Cake and Kick-Ass.

Ilias

Greek variant of Hebrew Elijah, meaning 'the Lord is my God'.

Imanol

Basque-language variant of Immanuel, meaning 'God is with us'.

Indiana

Latin, meaning 'from India'. Also the film character Indiana Jones and the American state.

Indigo

English, describing a deep blue colour derived from a plant. Used as a boys' and girls' name.

Indio

Spanish, meaning 'indigenous people'.

Ingo

Danish, meaning 'meadow'. Also the name of a tropical plant.

Inigo

Spanish, meaning 'fiery'. Famous Inigos include the 16th-century architect Inigo Jones and a character in the film The Princess Bride.

Ian

Welsh, meaning 'gift of God'. Ioan Gruffudd is a Welsh actor.

Ioannis

Greek, meaning 'the Lord is gracious'.

Iovianno

Native American, meaning 'yellow hawk'. More common as a spelling alternative for Giovanni.

Ira

Hebrew, meaning 'full grown and watchful'. In the Hindu faith, Ira-putra is Hanuman the monkey god. Ira Gershwin was a famous 20th-century American lyricist.

Irvin
(alt. Irving, Irwin)

Gaelic, meaning 'green and fresh water'. Composer Irving Berlin is known for songs such as 'White Christmas' and 'Alexander's Ragtime Band'.

Isaac
(alt. Isaak; abbrev. Ike)

Hebrew, meaning 'laughter'. Isaac was the son of Abraham and Sarah in the Bible and the Qur'an. Famous Ikes include singer Ike Turner and former US president Dwight D. Eisenhower (known as Ike).

Isadore
(alt. Isidore, Isidro)

Greek, meaning 'gift of Isis'. Popular name in both ancient Greece and ancient Egypt.

Isai
(alt. Isaiah, Isaias, Izaiah)

Arabic, meaning 'protection and security'.

Iser

Yiddish, meaning 'God wrestler'. Most common in Germany.

Ishedus

Native American, meaning 'on top'.

Ishmael
(alt. Ismael)

Hebrew, meaning 'God listens'. Ishmael was the son of the prophet Abraham and his wife Hagar.

Israel

Hebrew, meaning 'God perseveres'. Also the name of the country.

Istvan

Hungarian variant of Stephen, meaning 'crowned'. Very common in Eastern Europe.

Itai

Hebrew, meaning 'the Lord is with me'. One of the most common names in Israel.

Ivan

Hebrew, meaning 'God is gracious'. Russian Grand Prince Ivan the Terrible conquered so much land to create the vast country of Russia.

Ivanhoe

Russian, meaning 'God is gracious'. Also name of the novel by Walter Scott.

Ivey

English, variant of Ivy usually reserved for boys.

Ivo

French, from the word 'yves', meaning 'yew tree'. Dr Ivo Robotnik is the villain in Sonic the Hedgehog video games.

Ivor

Scandinavian, meaning 'yew'. Welsh-born composer and songwriter Ivor Novello was an influential performer in the first half of the 20th century.

Ivory

Latin, meaning 'white as elephant tusks'. More commonly used as a girls' name.

Izar

Basque, meaning 'star'. The izar is also a piece of Ihram clothing worn during the Islamic Hajj pilgrimage.

Boys' names

Jabari
Swahili, meaning 'valiant'.

Jabez
Hebrew, meaning 'borne in pain'.
Jabez is a well-respected ancestor of
Judah in the Bible.

Jabulani
(alt. Jabulanie, Jabulany, Jabulaney)
Swahili, meaning 'happy one'. The
Jabulani is also a name for a type
of Adidas football used in most
professional Association games.

Jace
(alt. Jaece, Jase, Jayce)
Hebrew, meaning 'healer'.
Sometimes used as a shortened
version of Jason.

Jacek
Polish, meaning 'hyacinth'. Derived
from the Greek name Hyakinthos,
which comes from an ancient myth
about a beautiful boy.

Jacinto
Spanish or Portuguese, meaning
'hyacinth'.

Jack
(alt. Jackie, Jacky)
From the Hebrew John, meaning
'God is gracious'. The UK's most
popular boys' name for 14 years
until fairly recently.

Jackson
(alt. Jaxon, Jaxson)
English, meaning 'son of Jack'.
Jackson Pollock was an abstract
expressionist artist, known for his
large-scale paintings.

Jacob
(alt. Jacobo, Jaco, Jago; abbrev.
Jake)
Hebrew, meaning 'he who
supplants'. Ancestor of the tribes of
Israel in the Bible.

Jacques
(alt. Jaquez)

French form of James, meaning 'he who supplants'. Famous Jacques include Jacques Cousteau, the marine explorer, writer and film-maker, and Jacques Villeneuve, the racing driver.

Jaden
(alt. Jadyn, Jaeden, Jaiden, Jaidyn, Jayden, Jaydin)

Hebrew, meaning 'Jehovah has heard'. Actor Will Smith's eldest child is called Jaden Smith, and has an acting career of his own.

Jaeger
(alt. Jager, Jaecer, Jaegar)

German, meaning 'mighty hunter'. Also the name of a British designer clothing line.

Jafar

Arabic, meaning 'stream'. The name of the villain in Disney's *Aladdin*.

Jagger

Old English, meaning 'one who cuts'. Sir Mick Jagger is the lead singer of the Rolling Stones.

Jaheem
(alt. Jaheim)

Hebrew, meaning 'raised up'. R&B singer Jaheim Hoagland goes by the stage name Jaheim.

Jahir

Hindi, meaning 'jewel'.

Jair
(alt. Jairo)

Hebrew, meaning 'God enlightens'.

Jalen
(alt. Jalon, Jaylon, Jaylan)

American, meaning 'healer' or 'tranquil'. The original spelling was probably Galen, in Greek.

Jali

Gujarati, meaning 'latticed screen'. Popular form of architectural detailing throughout India.

Jamar
(alt. Jamarcus, Jamari, Jamarion, Jamir)

Modern variant of Jamaal, meaning 'handsome'. More common in the USA than in Britain.

Jamel
(alt. Jamal, Jamaal, Jamil)

Arabic, meaning 'handsome'. Actor Jamel Debbouze is a French and Moroccan film star.

James
(alt. Jaime; abbrev. Jamie, Jamey, Jim, Jimmy)

English, meaning 'he who supplants'. An enduringly popular name. Famous actors with this name include James Coburn, James Franco, James Corden, Jamie Bell and Jamie Foxx.

Jameson
(alt. Jamison)

English, meaning 'son of James'.

Jamin
(alt. Yamin)
Hebrew, meaning 'son of the right hand'.

Jan
(alt. Janko, János)
Slavic, from John, meaning 'the Lord is gracious'. Jan is also a term of endearment in Arabic, meaning 'dear'. Used for boys and also girls.

Janesh
Hindi, meaning 'leader of people'.

Janus
Latin, meaning 'gateway'. The two-faced Roman god of doors, beginnings and endings.

Japheth
(alt. Japhet)
Hebrew, meaning 'comely'. One of the sons of Noah in the Bible.

Jared
(alt. Jarem, Jaren, Jaret, Jarod, Jarrod)
Hebrew, meaning 'descending'. Actor Jared Leto is known for his roles in *Fight Club*, *American Psycho* and *Dallas Buyers Club*.

Jarlath
Gaelic, from St Iarlaithe mac Loga.

Jarom
Greek, meaning 'to raise and exalt'. One of the prophets in the Book of Mormon.

Jarrell
Variant of Gerald, meaning 'spear ruler'.

Jarrett
Old English, meaning 'spear-brave'. Sometimes used as an alternative spelling to Garrett.

Jarvis
Old German, meaning 'with honour'. Jarvis Cocker is the singer with the band Pulp.

Jason
Greek, meaning 'healer'. Famous Jasons include actor Jason Statham, and the ancient Greek myth of Jason and the Argonauts.

Jasper
Greek, meaning 'treasure holder' or 'speckled stone'. The stone jasper has been used for thousands of years for carved ornaments and jewellery. Jasper Conran is a modern fashion designer.

Javen
(alt. Javan)
Arabic, meaning 'youth'. Javan was one of Noah's grandsons in the Bible.

Javier
Spanish, meaning 'bright'. Actor Javier Bardem is known for his roles in *No Country for Old Men* and the James Bond movie *Skyfall*.

Jay

Latin, meaning 'jaybird'. Jays are a group of bird species in the crow family.

Jeevan

Sanskrit, meaning 'life'. Often used with a prefix such as 'har', to form other names (such as Harjeevan).

Jefferson

English, meaning 'son of Jeffrey'.

Jeffrey

(abbrev. Jeff)

Old German, meaning 'peace'. Famous Jeffreys include author Jeffrey Archer, and actors Jeff Bridges and Jeff Daniels.

Jensen

(alt. Jenson)

Scandinavian, meaning 'son of Jan'. Has increased in popularity in the UK in recent years, probably linked to the rise of Jenson Button, Formula One racing driver.

Jeremiah

(alt. Jeremia, Jeremias, Jeremiya)

Hebrew, meaning 'the Lord exalts'. One of the main prophets in the Bible.

Jeremy

(alt. Jem)

Hebrew, meaning 'the Lord exalts'. Famous Jeremys include actors Jeremy Irons and Jeremy Renner, and presenter Jeremy Clarkson.

Jeriah

Hebrew, meaning 'Jehovah has seen'.

Jericho

Arabic, meaning 'city of the moon'. An ancient and religious city in the Palestinian West Bank.

Jermaine

Latin, meaning 'brotherly'. Jermaine Jackson was one of the original members of the Jackson 5.

Jerome

Greek, meaning 'sacred name'. Famous Jeromes include actor Jerome Flynn, and St Jerome, who was a medieval priest and theologian.

Jerry

English, from Gerald, meaning 'spear ruler'. Famous Jerrys include presenter Jerry Springer, comedian Jerry Seinfeld and the film *Jerry Maguire*.

Jesse

Hebrew, meaning 'the Lord exists'. Jesse James was a Wild West outlaw and train robber in the 1870s.

Jesus

Hebrew, meaning 'the Lord is Salvation' and the Son of God.

Jet

(alt. Jelt)

English, meaning 'black gemstone'. Jet is a minor gemstone, formed of fossilised wood.

Jethro

Hebrew, meaning 'eminent'. Famous Jethros include Jethro Tull, the agricultural pioineer, who gave his name to a 1970s rock band, and the father-in-law of Moses in the Bible.

Jim
(alt. Jimmy)

From James, meaning 'he who supplants'. Jim is one of the leading characters in Mark Twain's classic novel *Huckleberry Finn*.

Jiri
(alt. Jiro)

Czech, meaning 'farmer'. More commonly used in Czech-speaking communities as an alternative to George.

Joachim
(alt. Joaquin)

Hebrew, meaning 'established by God'. Also the name of the Virgin Mary's father in the Bible. Actor Joaquin Phoenix is known for his roles in *Gladiator*, *Walk the Line* and *Her*.

Joah
(alt. João)

Hebrew, meaning 'God is gracious'.

Joe
(alt. Joey, Jomar)

From Joseph, meaning 'Jehovah increases'. Usually used as a nickname for Joseph, Joel or Josiah, as well as a name in its own right.

Football players

Aaron (Lennon)
Alan (Shearer)
Ashley (Cole)
Daniel (Sturridge)
Darren (Fletcher)
David (Beckham)
Frank (Lampard)
Gareth (Bale)
Gary (Lineker)
Jack (Wilshere)
Joe (Cole)
Rio (Ferdinand)
Scott (Parker)
Steven (Gerrard)
Wayne (Rooney)

Joel

Hebrew, meaning 'Jehovah is the Lord'.

John
(alt. Johan, Johannes, Johnny)

Hebrew, meaning 'God is gracious'. John the Baptist and the apostle John are major characters in the New Testament of the Bible.

Jolyon

English, meaning 'young'. One of the more prominent characters in the 'Tintin' comic series is Jolyon Wagg.

Jonah
(alt. Jonas)

Hebrew, meaning 'dove'. In the Bible, Jonah was swallowed by a whale.

Jonathan
(alt. Johnathan, Johnathon, Jonathon; abbrev. Jon, Jonny, Jonty)

Hebrew, meaning 'God is gracious'. Famous Jonathans include comedian and TV presenter Jonathan Ross, author Jonathan Swift and actor Jonathan Pryce.

Jordan
(alt. Jory, Judd)

Hebrew, meaning 'down-flowing'. Can be used as a girls' name or a boys' name.

Jorge

Spanish or Portuguese version of George, meaning 'farmer'. Actor Jorge Garcia is known for his role as Hurley in the television series *Lost*.

José

Spanish variant of Joseph, meaning 'God increases'. José Mourinho is a football manager known as 'the special one'.

Joseph
(alt. Josef, Joss)

Hebrew, meaning 'Jehovah increases'. Famous Josephs include two Biblical Josephs: the wearer of the many-coloured coat and the father of Jesus Christ; and the actor Joseph Fiennes.

Joshua
(abbrev. Josh)

Hebrew, meaning 'God is salvation'. Joshua was the leader of the Israelites after Moses' death in the Bible.

Josiah

Hebrew, meaning 'God helps'. One of the kings of Judah in the Bible.

Josué

Spanish variant of Joshua, meaning 'God is salvation'.

Jovan

Latin, meaning 'the supreme God'. More commonly used in Serbia and Macedonia.

Joweese

Native American, meaning 'chirping bird'. Originally used more commonly for girls, it has now become a boys' name.

Joyce

Latin, meaning 'joy'. More commonly used as a girls' name but can be used for boys.

Juan

Spanish variant of John, meaning 'God is gracious'. It is also becoming a popular name for girls in China, with the meaning of 'chapter or scroll' in Mandarin.

Jubal

Hebrew, meaning 'ram's horn'. Also the name of the 'father of music' in the Bible.

Jude
(alt. Judson)

Hebrew, meaning 'praise' or 'thanks'. Famous Judes include St Jude, the patron saint of lost causes, actor Jude Law and Thomas Hardy's novel *Jude the Obscure*.

Julian
(alt. Julio, Julien; abbrev. Juels, Jules, Jools)

Greek, meaning 'belonging to Julius'. The original calendar in the Roman empire was called the Julian calendar. Famous Julians include author Jules Verne, DJ Judge Jules and pianist/presenter Jools Holland.

Julius

Latin, meaning 'youthful'. Julius Caesar was dictator of Rome and the first Roman emperor, ruling in the first century BC.

Junior

Latin, meaning 'the younger one'. Can also be used as a suffix to names to denote a name that has been passed down from father to son (such as Steve Jones Sr and Steve Jones Jr).

Junius

Latin, meaning 'young'. The pseudonym of an anonymous and prolific political writer in the 18th century.

Jupiter

Latin, meaning 'the supreme God'. Jupiter was king of the Roman gods and the god of thunder. Jupiter is also the largest planet in the solar system.

Juraj

Hebrew, meaning 'God is my judge'. More popular in Eastern Europe.

Jurgen

German form of George, meaning 'farmer'. Jurgen Klinsmann was a professional football player in the 1980s and '90s.

Justice

English, from the word 'justice', meaning a set of moral values, ethics and law.

Justin
(alt. Justus)

Latin, meaning 'just and upright'. Famous Justins include singers Justin Timberlake and Justin Bieber, and children's TV presenter Justin Fletcher.

Juwan

Hebrew, meaning 'the Lord is gracious'.

Boys' names

Kabelo
Swahili, meaning 'gift'. Popular name in Botswana.

Kade
Scottish, meaning 'from the wetlands'. More commonly used as a spelling alternative to Cade.

Kadeem
Arabic, meaning 'one who serves'. Actor Kadeem Hardison is known for his role in Tv series *A Different World*.

Kaden
(alt. Kadin, Kaeden, Kaedin, Kaiden)
Arabic, meaning 'companion'. Also the name of a town in Germany.

Kadir
Arabic, meaning 'capable and competent'.

Kafka
Czech, meaning 'bird-like'. Often associated with the author Franz Kafka.

Kahekili
Hawaiian, meaning 'the thunder'. Also the name of several kings of Maui.

Kahlil
(alt. Kalil)
Arabic, meaning 'friend'. The Lebanese author Kahlil Gibran is known for his work *The Prophet*.

Kai
Greek, meaning 'keeper of the keys'. Kai has meanings in several languages, including 'dog' in Cornish, 'ocean water' in Hawaiian and 'food' in Maori.

Kaito
Japanese, a combination of the words 'sea, ocean' and 'soar, fly'.

Kalani
Hawaiian, meaning 'sky'.

Kale
German, meaning 'free man'. Also the name of a leafy green vegetable.

Kaleb
(alt. Caleb)

Hebrew, meaning 'dog' or 'aggressive'. Kaleb was also the most prominent King of Aksum, the capital of Abyssinia, in the sixth century.

Kalen

Gaelic, meaning 'uncertain'.

Kaleo

Hawaiian, meaning 'the voice'. Kaleo Kanahele is a silver medal-winning American paralympian in volleyball.

Kamari

Sanskrit, meaning 'the enemy of desire'. Also the name of a popular tourist destination in Greece.

Kamden

English, meaning 'winding valley'. Also an alternative spelling for Camden.

Kamil
(alt. Kaamil)

Arabic, meaning 'perfection'. Also a Polish and Slovak name meaning 'religious service attender'.

Kane

Gaelic, meaning 'little battler'.

Kani

Hawaiian, meaning 'sound'.

Kanye

A town in Botswana. Made popular by rapper Kanye West.

Kareem
(alt. Karim)

Arabic, meaning 'generous'.

Karl
(alt. Karson)

Old German, meaning 'free man'.

Kasey

Irish, meaning 'alert'.

Kaspar

Persian, meaning 'treasurer'. Also an alternative spelling for Casper.

Kavon

Gaelic, meaning 'handsome'. More commonly used in the USA.

Kayden

Arabic, meaning 'companion'. Also an alternative spelling for Caden.

Kazimierz

Polish, meaning 'declares peace'. Also the name of a town in Poland.

Kazuki

Japanese, meaning 'radiant hope'. Kazuki Takahashi is a well-known Japanese artist and video game creator.

Kazuo

Japanese, meaning 'harmonious man'. Depending on the characters/ spellings used, Kazuo can also mean 'first son' or 'first in leadership'.

Keagan
(alt. Keegan, Kegan)

Gaelic, meaning 'small flame'.

Keane
Gaelic, meaning 'fighter'.

Keanu
Hawaiian, meaning 'breeze'. Actor Keanu Reeves is known for his roles in *Bill & Ted's Excellent Adventure*, *Speed* and *The Matrix* trilogy.

Keary
Gaelic, meaning 'black-haired'. Also used as a girls' name.

Keaton
English, meaning 'place of hawks'. Buster Keaton was a famous American actor and director of silent films.

Keefe
(alt. Keef, Keeffe, Kief, Kiefe)
Gaelic, meaning 'cherished, gentle and kind'.

Keeler
Middle English, meaning 'cool'. Also a term used for a small, shallow tub for bathing.

Keenan
(alt. Kenan)
Gaelic, meaning 'little ancient one'.

Keiji
Japanese, meaning 'govern with discretion'. Also a term sometimes used for police officers.

Keir
Gaelic, meaning 'dark-haired' or 'dark-skinned'. James Keir Hardie was a Scottish socialist and labour leader in the 19th and 20th centuries.

Keith
Gaelic, meaning 'woodland'. Famous Keiths include Rolling Stones band member Keith Richards and chef Keith Floyd.

Kekoa
Hawaiian, meaning 'brave one' or 'soldier'.

Kelby
Old English, meaning 'farmhouse near the stream'.

Kell
(alt. Kellan, Kellen, Kelley, Kelly, Kiel)
Norse, meaning 'spring'. Usually associated with the ancient and lavishly illustrated *Book of Kells* (as well as the cartoon movie).

Kelsey
Old English, meaning 'victorious ship'. Actor Kelsey Grammer is known for his roles in *Cheers* and *Frasier*.

Kelton
Old English, meaning 'town of the keels'. Singer Roy Orbison (of 'Oh, Pretty Woman' fame) had the middle name Kelton.

Kelvin
Old English, meaning 'friend of ships'. A kelvin is a unit of measurement for temperature, using the Kelvin scale.

Kemenes
Hungarian, meaning 'maker of furnaces'. More commonly used in Eastern Europe.

Kendal

Old English, meaning 'the Kent river valley'.

Kendon

Old English, meaning 'brave guard'.

Kendrick

Gaelic, meaning 'royal ruler'. Fairly popular in the USA, where famous Kendricks include hip hop artist Kendrick Lamar and record producer Kendrick Dean.

Kenelm

Old English, meaning 'bold'. St Kenelm was a boy king and martyr, mentioned in *The Canterbury Tales*.

Kenji

Japanese, meaning 'intelligent second son'. Also the name of a period in Japanese history in the 13th century.

Kennedy

Gaelic, meaning 'helmet head'. The Kennedy family are a prominent American-Irish Catholic dynasty, whose members have included President John F. Kennedy.

Kenneth

(abbrev, Ken, Kenny, Kenney)
Gaelic, meaning 'born of fire'. Famous Kenneths include actor Sir Kenneth Branagh and designer brand Kenneth Cole.

Kennison

English, meaning 'son of Kenneth'.

Kent

English, meaning 'rim or border'. From the county of the same name in England.

Kenton

English, meaning 'town of Ken'. Kenton Cool is a British mountaineer and mountain guide. He has climbed Mount Everest 11 times.

Kenya

From the country and mountain in Africa.

Kenzo

Japanese, meaning 'wise'. Kenzo Takada is the Japanese designer who founded the fashion brand Kenzo.

Keola

Hawaiian, meaning 'life'.

Keon

(alt. Kean, Keoni)
Persian, meaning 'King of Kings'. In Hawaiian, the same spelling means 'God is gracious'.

Kepler

German, meaning 'hat maker'.

Kerr

English, meaning 'wetland'. Kerr Smith is an American actor.

Kerry

Irish, from the county of the same name. More commonly a girls' name.

Kerwin
(alt. Kermit)

Gaelic, meaning 'without envy'. Most popular in the USA.

Keshav

Sanskrit, meaning 'beautiful-haired'. One of the names for Vishnu in the Hindu religion.

Kevin

Gaelic, meaning 'handsome beloved'. Famous Kevins include former footballer Kevin Keegan and actors Kevin Kline and Kevin Bacon.

Khalid
(alt. Khaled, Khalif, Khalil)

Arabic, meaning 'immortal'. Actor Khalid Abdalla is known for his roles in *United 93* and *The Kite Runner*.

Kian
(alt. Keyon, Kyan)

Persian, meaning 'king or realm'. In Ireland, the same spelling means 'ancient'.

Kiefer

German, meaning 'barrel maker'. Actor Kiefer Sutherland is best known for his role in the series *24*.

Kieran
(alt. Kiaran, Kieron, Kyron)

Gaelic, meaning 'black'. Famous Kierans include gymnast Kieran Behan and actor Kieran Culkin.

Kijana

Swahili, meaning 'youth'.

Kilby

From the English 'Cilebi', a place in Leicestershire.

Kilian

Irish, meaning 'bright headed'. St Kilian was a bishop in Ireland in the seventh century.

Kimani

Swahili, meaning 'beautiful and sweet'. Kenyan Kimani Maruge held the Guinness World Record for being the oldest person to start primary school, at the ripe old age of 84.

King

English, from the word 'male ruler of state'.

Kingsley

English, meaning 'the king's meadow'. Sir Kingsley Amis was an English novelist.

Kirby

German, meaning 'settlement by a church'. Also the name of a small, pink, bubble-like video game character.

Kirk

Old German, meaning 'church'.

Klaus

German, meaning 'victorious'. Also a shortened form of Nikolaus.

Knightley
(alt. Knightly)

English, meaning 'of the knight's meadows'. An English place name in Staffordshire.

Kobe
(alt. Koda, Kody)
Japanese, meaning 'a Japanese city'.

Kofi
Akan, meaning 'born on Friday'. Kofi Annan was Secretary General of the United Nations from 1997 to 2006.

Kohana
Japanese, meaning 'little flower'. The Kohana cat is a hairless breed of cat.

Kojo
Akan, meaning 'Monday'. Kojo is also a type of computer programming language.

Kolby
Norse, meaning 'settlement'. Often used as a spelling alternative for Colby.

Komal
Hindi, meaning 'soft and tender'.

Korben
(alt. Korbin)
Gaelic, meaning 'a steep hill'. Korben Dallas is the protagonist in the sci-fi film *The Fifth Element*.

Kramer
German, meaning 'shopkeeper'. Usually associated with the character Kramer in the 1990s sitcom *Seinfeld*.

Kris
(alt. Krish, Kristoff)
From Christopher, meaning 'Christ bearer'. Can be a short form of Kristopher, Kristian or (for girls) Kristen.

Kurt
German, meaning 'courageous advice'. Famous Kurts include *Glee* character Kurt, actor Kurt Russell and singer Kurt Cobain.

Kurtis
French, meaning 'courtier'.

Kwame
Akan, meaning 'born on Saturday'. Kwame Nkrumah was the first president of Ghana.

Kyden
English, meaning 'narrow little fire'. Sometimes used as a spelling alternative for Caden.

Kyle
(alt. Kylan, Kyleb, Kyler)
Scottish Gaelic, meaning 'narrow and straight'. Originated from the place name in Scotland.

Kyllion
Irish, meaning 'war'.

Kylo
(alt. Kyloh)
American, from the Latin word for 'sky'. Kylo Ren is a main character in the modern *Star Wars* trilogy.

Kyree
From Cree, a Canadian tribe. More commonly used in the USA.

Kyros
Greek, meaning 'legitimate power'. Kyros of Constantinople was an important figure in the Orthodox Church in the eighth century.

L Boys' names

Laban

Hebrew, meaning 'white'. Laban is the brother of Rebekah in the Bible.

Lachlan

Gaelic, meaning 'from the land of lakes'. A popular name in Australia.

Lacy

Old French, after the place in France. The feminine equivalent is Lacey.

Laertes

English, meaning 'adventurous'. Ophelia's brother in Shakespeare's *Hamlet*.

Lalit

Hindi, meaning 'beautiful'. The Lalit is one of the melodic aspects of Indian classical music.

Lamar
(alt. Lemar)

Old German, meaning 'water'. Singer Lemar is known for his songs 'Dance (With U)' and 'If There's Any Justice'.

Lambert
(alt. Lambros)

Scandinavian, two elements meaning 'land' and 'brilliant'. The name has been in use since Roman times.

Lamont

Old Norse, meaning 'law man'.

Lancelot
(abbrev. Lance)

Variant of Lance, meaning 'land'. The name of one of the Knights of the Round Table. Cyclist Lance Armstrong won the Tour de France seven times before being stripped of his titles for cheating.

Landen
(alt. Lando, Landon, Langdon, Landen)

English, meaning 'long hill'. Also the name of a town in Belgium.

Lane
(alt. Layne)

English, from the common word meaning 'narrow road'.

Lang
(alt. Langston)
Norse, meaning 'long meadow'.

Lannie
(alt. Lanny)
German, meaning 'precious'. Sometimes used as a nickname for Roland or Orlando, as well as a name in its own right.

Larkin
Gaelic, meaning 'rough' or 'fierce'. Poet Philip Larkin was known for his works *The Whitsun Weddings* and *High Windows*.

Laron
French, meaning 'thief'.

Larry
Latin, variant of Laurence, meaning 'man from Laurentum'. Famous Larrys include actor Larry Hagman and presenter Larry King.

Lars
Scandinavian variant of Laurence, meaning 'man from Laurentum'. The founder of Swedish electronics brand Ericsson was called Lars Magnus Ericsson.

Lasse
Finnish, meaning 'girl'. (Still, ironically, a boy's name.) Men with the name Lars are sometimes called Lasse as a nickname in Scandinavia. Finn Lasse Viren was one of the greatest long-distance runners of all time. Lasse Hallström is a Swedish film director.

Laszlo
Hungarian, meaning 'glorious rule'. Derived from the name of King/St Ladislaus I of Hungary.

Lathyn
Latin, meaning 'fighter'. Sometimes also used as a name for girls.

Latif
Arabic, meaning 'gentle'. The female equivalent for girls is Latifa.

Laurel
Latin, meaning 'bay'. One of the founders of Jamaican ska music was Laurel Aitken.

Laurence
(alt. Lawrence; abbrev. Larry)
Latin, meaning 'man from Laurentum'. Actor Sir Laurence Olivier was known for his roles in dozens of Shakespeare productions and Hollywood films.

Laurent
French form of Laurence, meaning 'man from Laurentum'. Laurent-Perrier is a champagne brand.

Lazarus
Hebrew, meaning 'God is my help'. In the Bible, Lazarus was said to have been raised from the dead by Jesus Christ.

Leandro
Spanish, meaning 'lion man'. More commonly used in South America.

Lear

German, meaning 'of the meadow'. Shakespeare's play *King Lear* tells the story of a wealthy king decending into madness.

Lee
(alt. Leigh)

English, meaning 'pasture' or 'meadow'. Famous Lees include comedian Lee Mack, *Harry Potter* character Lee Jordan and assassin Lee Harvey Oswald.

Leib

Yiddish, meaning 'lion'.

Leif
(alt. Liev)

Scandinavian, meaning 'heir'. Actor Liev Schreiber is known for his roles in *X-Men Origins: Wolverine*, the *Scream* trilogy and *Ray Donovan*.

Leith

From the name of a busy port town in Scotland.

Lennox

Gaelic, meaning 'with many elm trees'. Lennox Lewis is a retired world heavyweight boxing champion.

Lenny

Shortened form of Lennox or Leonard, as well as a name in its own right. Lenny Kravitz is a musician and Lenny Godber was a much-loved character in the classic TV series *Porridge*.

Leo
(alt. Leon)

Latin, meaning 'lion'. Also the star sign.

Leonard
(alt. Leonardo)

Old German, meaning 'lion strength'. Famous Leonardos include actor Leonardo DiCaprio and artist and inventor Leonardo da Vinci.

Leopold

German, meaning 'brave people'. Prince Leopold was Queen Victoria and Prince Albert's eighth child, who was known to suffer from the blood disorder haemophilia.

Leroy

French, meaning 'king'. The song 'Bad Bad Leroy Brown' was a hit for R&B singer Jim Croce in 1973.

Leslie
(abbrev. Les)

Scottish Gaelic, from the name of the prominent clan. Also meaning 'holly garden'. Usually spet Lesley when used as a name for girls.

Lester

English, meaning 'from Leicester'. Lester Piggott is one of England's most successful jockeys.

Lewis

English form of French Louis, meaning 'famous warrior'. Famous Lewises include Formula One racing driver Lewis Hamilton, comedian Lewis Black and *Alice in Wonderland* author Lewis Carroll.

Lex

English variant of Alexander, meaning 'defending men'. Lex Luthor is the villain of the *Superman* stories.

Liam

German, meaning 'helmet'. Famous Liams include actor Liam Neeson, singer Liam Gallagher and One Direction member Liam Payne.

Lincoln

English, meaning 'lake colony'.

Linden

European, from the tree of the same name. Less commonly used for girls.

Lindsay

Scottish, meaning 'linden tree'. In recent times used more for girls than for boys.

Linus

Latin, meaning 'lion'. Usually associated with the *Peanuts* cartoon strip character, who is known for carrying a blanket everywhere.

Lionel

English, meaning 'lion'. Famous Lionels include dancer/actor Lionel Blair, singer Lionel Richie and composer Lionel Bart.

Llewellyn

Welsh, meaning 'like a lion'.

Lloyd

Welsh, meaning 'grey-haired and sacred'. Famous Lloyds include actor Roger Lloyd Pack, former prime minister David Lloyd George and composer Andrew Lloyd Webber.

Logan

Gaelic, meaning 'hollow'. Usually associated with sci-fi novel *Logan's Run*. Has risen in popularity following 2017's *Logan* Wolverine film.

London

Pre-Celtic, meaning 'place at the navigable or unfordable river'.

Lonnie

English, meaning 'lion strength'.

Lorcan

Gaelic, meaning 'little fierce one'. Also the name of several kings of Leinster in Ireland.

Louis
(alt. Lou, Louie, Luigi, Luis)

French, meaning 'famous warrior'. The given name of the fifth in line to the throne, Prince Louis Arthur Charles, as well as One Direction's Louis Tomlinson, music manager Louis Walsh and designer brand Louis Vuitton.

Lucas
(alt. Lukas, Luca)

English, meaning 'man from Luciana'. Popular in Brazil – there are several Brazilian footballers with this first name.

Lucian
(alt. Lucio)

Latin, meaning 'light'. Lucian of Samosata was an ancient Greek writer. Lucian Freud was a painter.

Ludwig

German, meaning 'famous warrior'. Ludwig van Beethoven was a hugely influential Classical and Romantic composer.

Luke
(alt. Luc, Luka)

Latin, meaning 'from Lucanus'. Famous Lukes include the Gospel of Luke, *Star Wars* protagonist Luke Skywalker and late actor Luke Perry.

Lupe

Latin, meaning 'wolf'. Rapper Lupe Fiasco is known for his songs 'Superstar' and 'The Show Goes On'.

Luther

German, meaning 'soldier of the people'. Famous Luthers include the German church reformer Martin Luther, US civil rights activist Martin Luther King Jr and singer Luther Vandross.

Lyle

French, meaning 'the island'. Lyle Lovett is an American country singer.

Lyn
(alt. Lyndon)

Spanish, meaning 'pretty'. More commonly used as a name for girls.

Lynton

English, meaning 'town of lime trees'. Also a girls' name.

Boys' names

Mabon
(alt. Maban, Mabery)
Welsh, meaning 'our son'. A character in the King Arthur legend.

Mac
(alt. Mack, Mackie)
Scottish, meaning 'son of'.

Macaulay
Scottish, meaning 'son of the phantom'. Actor Macaulay Culkin shot to fame as a child actor in the *Home Alone* films.

Mace
English, meaning 'heavy staff' or 'club'. Can also be a nickname for Mason.

Mackenzie
Scottish, meaning 'the fair one'. Actor Mackenzie Crook is known for his roles in *The Office*, *Pirates of the Caribbean*, *Game of Thrones* and *The Detectorists*.

Mackland
Scottish, meaning 'land of Mac'.

Macon
French, name of towns in France and Georgia (USA).

Macsen
Scottish, meaning 'son of Mac'.

Madden
(abbrev. Mads)
Irish, meaning 'descendant of the hound'.

Maddox
English, meaning 'good' or 'generous'. Derived from Madoc, a legendary Welsh prince who supposedly discovered America years before Christopher Columbus. Maddox Jolie-Pitt is the eldest son of Angelina and Brad.

Madison
(alt. Madsen)
Irish, meaning 'son of Madden'.

Magnus
(alt. Manus)

Latin, meaning 'great'. Famous Magnuses include Magnus Carlsen the chess grand master and former TV presenter Magnus Magnusson.

Maguire

Gaelic, meaning 'son of the beige one'.

Mahabala

Sanskrit, meaning 'great strength'. Also the name of a Buddhist guardian.

Mahesh

Hindi, meaning 'great ruler'. Also one of the names of Lord Shiva in the Hindu faith.

Mahir

Arabic, meaning 'skilful'.

Mahlon

Hebrew, meaning 'sickness'. Found in the Bible.

Mahmoud

Arabic, meaning 'praiseworthy'. Mahmoud Ahmadinejad was the president of Iran until 2013.

Mahoney

Irish, meaning 'bear'.

Major

English, from the word 'major'.

Makal

Alternative to Michael or Mikael, meaning 'close to God'.

Makani

Hawaiian, meaning 'wind'. Also a popular name in Arabic-speaking communities.

Makis

Hebrew, meaning 'gift from God'.

Mako

Hebrew, meaning 'God is with us'.

Malachi
(alt. Malachy)

Hebrew, meaning 'messenger of God', the name of a Jewish prophet in the Bible. Also an Irish name.

Malcolm

English, meaning 'Columba's servant'. Famous Malcolms include activist Malcolm X, actor Malcolm McDowell and bestselling author and journalist Malcolm Gladwell.

Mali

Arabic, meaning 'full and rich'. Also the name of a West African republic.

Manfred

Old German, meaning 'man of peace'. The band Manfred Mann is known for the song 'Blinded by the Light'.

Manish
(alt. Manesh)

English, meaning 'manly'. Extremely popular name in large parts of India.

Manley

English, meaning 'manly and brave'. Also the name of a Cornish village.

Mannix

Gaelic, meaning 'little monk'. Usually associated with the detective series *Mannix*.

Manoi
(alt. Manos)

Japanese, meaning 'love springing from intellect'. Also the name of a Laotian king.

Manuel

Spanish variation of Hebrew Emanuel, meaning 'God is with us'. Usually associated with the character of Manuel in the sitcom *Fawlty Towers*.

Manzi

Italian, meaning 'steer'. Also the old name for parts of southern China.

Marc
(alt. Marco, Marcos, Marcus, Markel)

French, meaning 'from the god Mars'. Famous Marcs include designer brand Marc Jacobs, singer Marc Bolan and drummer Marc Bell.

Marcel
(alt. Marcelino, Marcello)

French, meaning 'little warrior'. One of the most famous mimes of all time was Frenchman Marcel Marceau.

Marek

Polish variant of Mark, meaning 'from the god Mars'.

Mariano

Latin, meaning 'from the god Mars'. Other theories suggest that Mariano is a tribute to the Virgin Mary.

Mario
(alt. Marius)

Latin, meaning 'manly'. Mario is a popular Nintendo video game character, alongside his brother Luigi. Mario Andretti is a retired Formula One world champion racing driver.

Mark
(alt. Markus)

English, meaning 'from the god Mars'. Famous Marks include the Gospel of Mark, actors Mark Hamill and Mark Wahlberg and author Mark Twain.

Marley
(alt. Marlin)

Old English, meaning 'meadow near the lake'. Sometimes used as a short form of Marlon. Famous Marleys include singer Bob Marley.

Marlo

American, meaning 'bitter'.

Marlon

English, meaning 'like little hawk'. Famous Marlons include actor Marlon Brando, singer Marlon Jackson and comedian Marlon Wayans.

Marshall

Old French, meaning 'caretaker of horses'. Also the name of a group of islands in the Pacific Ocean.

Martin
(abbrev. Marty)

Latin, meaning 'dedicated to Mars'. Famous Martins include actors Martin Freeman and Martin Sheen and director Martin Scorsese.

Marvel

English, from the word 'marvel'. Also the name of the long-running comic book company.

Marvin

Welsh, meaning 'sea friend'. Famous Marvins include singer Marvin Gaye and composer Marvin Hamlish.

Mason

English; a mason is a craftsman in either stonework or brickwork.

Massimo

Italian, meaning 'greatest'. The Massimo family were an ancient Roman family with great influence.

Mathias
(alt. Matthias)

Hebrew, meaning 'gift of the Lord'. Matthias was the apostle chosen to replace Judas in the Bible.

Mathieu

French form of Matthew, meaning 'gift of God'.

Matthew
(alt. Mathew)

Hebrew, meaning 'gift of the Lord'. Famous Matthews include the Gospel of Matthew and actors Matthew McConaughey and Matthew Lewis.

Maurice
(alt. Mauricio)

Latin, meaning 'dark skinned' or 'Moorish'. Children's author Maurice Sendak is best known for his work *Where the Wild Things Are*.

Maverick

American, meaning 'non-conformist leader'. Usually associated with the character Maverick from the *Top Gun* films.

Maximillian
(alt. Maximilian; abbrev. Max, Maxie, Maxim)

Latin, meaning 'greatest'. The name of several Roman emperors. Famous Maxes include actor Max Greenfield, the film *Mad Max: Fury Road*, and cosmetics brand Max Factor.

Maximino

Latin, meaning 'little Max'. More commonly used in Spanish-speaking communities.

Maxwell

Latin, meaning 'Maccus' stream'.

Maynard

Old German, meaning 'brave'. John Maynard Keynes was a highly influential British economist.

Mearl

English, meaning 'my earl'. Was used widely in the 19th century.

Mederic

French, meaning 'doctor'. Most commonly used in Quebec, Canada.

Mekhi

Swahili, meaning 'who is God?' Actor Mekhi Phifer is known for his roles in *ER*, *8 Mile* and *Divergent*.

Melbourne

From the city of the same name in Victoria, Australia.

Melchior

Persian, meaning 'king of the city'. The name of one of the three kings in the biblical story of the birth of Jesus.

Melton

English, meaning 'town of Mel'.

Melville

Scottish, meaning 'town of Mel'.

Melvin

(*alt. Melvyn; abbrev. Mel*)

English, meaning 'smooth brow'. Famous Melvins include DJ Melvin O'Doom, presenter Melvyn Bragg and actor Melvyn Douglas. Famous Mels include director Mel Brooks and comedian Mel Smith.

Memphis

Greek, meaning 'established and beautiful'. Also the name of a city in Tennessee, USA.

Mercer

English; a mercer was a man who traded or dealt in textiles.

Meredith

Welsh, meaning 'great ruler'. Used equally for girls and boys.

Merle

(*alt. Merl, Murl*)

French, meaning 'blackbird'.

Merlin

Welsh, meaning 'sea fortress'. Merlin was a magician and wise man in the King Arthur legend.

Merrick

Welsh, meaning 'Moorish'.

Merrill

Gaelic, meaning 'shining sea'.

Merritt

English, from the word 'merit'. Can be used for both boys and girls.

Merton

Old English, meaning 'town by the lake'. Also the name of a London borough.

Meyer

(*alt. Mayer*)

Hebrew, meaning 'bright farmer'.

Michael

(*abbrev. Mick, Micky, Mickey, Mike, Mikey*)

Hebrew, meaning 'resembles God'. Famous Michaels include one of the archangels, Formula One racing legend Michael Schumacher, singer Michael Jackson and comedian Michael McIntyre.

Michalis

Greek form of Michael, meaning 'resembles God'.

Michel

French form of Michael, meaning 'resembles God'. Deutscher Michel is also the cartoon personification of Germany (in the same way that Uncle Sam represents the USA).

Michelangelo

Italian, meaning 'Michael's angel'. Name of the famous painter whose work can still be seen in the Sistine Chapel in Rome.

Michele

Italian form of Michael, meaning 'resembles God'. Elsewhere, more commonly used as a girls' name.

Michio

Japanese, meaning 'a man with the strength of three thousand men'. Michio Kaku is a leading theoretical physicist.

Miguel

Spanish form of Michael, meaning 'resembles God'.

Miklos

Greek form of Nicholas, meaning 'victorious'. Sometimes used as an alternative to Michael as well.

Milan

From the name of the Italian city. Also the name of the son of singer-songwriter Shakira.

Miles

(alt. Milo, Milos, Myles)

English, from the word 'miles'. Famous Mileses include trumpeter Miles Davies, singer Miles Kane and *Star Trek: Next Generation* character Miles O'Brien.

Milton

English, meaning 'miller's town'.

Miro

Slavic, meaning 'peace'.

Misha

Russian, meaning 'resembles God'. Its English equivalent is often thought to be Mike, and the feminine version is Mischa.

Mitchell

(abbrev. Mitch)

English, meaning 'who is like God'. Mitchell Mark was a pioneer in motion picture technology.

Modesto

Italian, meaning 'modest'. Also the name of a town in California, USA.

Mohandas

Sanskrit, meaning 'servant'.

Monroe

Gaelic, meaning 'mouth of the river Rotha'.

Monserrate

Latin, meaning 'jagged mountain'. A mountain in Colombia.

Montague
(abbrev. Monty)
French, meaning 'pointed hill'.

Montana
Latin, meaning 'mountain'. Also a state in the USA.

Monte
Italian, meaning 'mountain'. Also the name of a popular card game.

Montgomery
(abbrev. Monty)
Variant of Montague, meaning 'pointed hill'. Monty Don is a well known TV personality and gardener.

Moody
English, from the word 'moody'. Mad Eye Moody is a prominent character in J.K. Rowling's *Harry Potter* series.

Mordecai
Hebrew, meaning 'little man'.

Morgan
Welsh, meaning 'great and bright'. Can be used for both boys and girls. Famous Morgans include actor Morgan Freeman, film maker Morgan Spurlock and musician Morgan Nicholls.

Moritz
Latin, meaning 'dark skinned and Moorish'. Also the German equivalent of Maurice.

Moroccan
Arabic, meaning 'from Morocco'. Also the name of one of Mariah Carey's twins.

Morpheus
Greek, meaning 'shape'. The name of the god of dreams in the epic poem *Metamorphoses* by Roman poet Ovid. Also a character in *The Matrix*.

Morris
Welsh, meaning 'dark skinned and Moorish'.

Morrison
English, meaning 'son of Morris'.

Mortimer
French, meaning 'dead sea'.

Morton
Old English, meaning 'moor town'. The name of several English towns.

Moses
(alt. Moshe, Moshon)
Hebrew, meaning 'saviour'. In the Bible, Moses receives the Ten Commandments from God.

Moss
English, meaning 'near a peat bog'.

Muhammad

(alt. Mohamed, Mohamet, Mohammad, Mohammed; abbrev. Mo)

Arabic, meaning 'praiseworthy'. Acknowledged as the prophet and founder of Islam. Sir Mo Farah is Britain's most decorated field and track athlete.

Muir

Gaelic, meaning 'of the moor'.

Mungo

Gaelic, meaning 'most dear'.

Murphy

Irish, meaning 'sea warrior'.

Murray

Gaelic, meaning 'lord and master'. Famous Murrays include legendary Formula One commentator Murray Walker and tennis star Andy Murray.

Mustafa

Arabic, meaning 'chosen'. Also a name for the prophet Muhammad in the Muslim faith.

Mwita

Swahili, meaning 'humorous one'.

Myron

Greek, meaning 'myrrh'. Myron was a popular sculptor in ancient Greece.

Boys' names

Nairn

Scottish, meaning 'alder-tree river'. From the Scottish town of the same name.

Najee

Arabic, meaning 'dear companion'. Also the name of an influential jazz musician.

Nakia

Arabic, meaning 'pure'. Also used as a name for girls.

Nakul

Sanskrit, meaning 'mongoose'. Choreographer Nakul Dev Mahajan has made a name for himself choreographing both Bollywood and Hollywood films.

Nana

(alt. Nanna)

Ghanaiian, meaning Your Royal Highness.

Naphtali

(alt. Naftali)

Hebrew, meaning 'wrestling'. One of Joseph's brothers in the Bible.

Napoleon

Italian, meaning 'man from Naples'. The French general Napoleon Bonaparte became Emperor of France.

Narciso

Latin, from the myth of Narcissus, who drowned after falling in love with his own reflection.

Nash

English, meaning 'at the ash tree'.

Nasir

Arabic, meaning 'helper'.

Nathan

(alt. Nathaniel; abbrev. Nat, Nate)

Hebrew, meaning 'God has given'.

Naval

Sanskrit, meaning 'wonder'.

Naveen

Sanskrit, meaning 'new'. Actor Naveen Andrews is known for his roles in *Lost*, *The English Patient* and *Rollerball*.

Ned

Used as a short form of Edward, meaning 'wealthy guard', but can be used in its own right. A character in *Game of Thrones* and *The Simpsons*.

Prime ministers' names

Alexander (Alec) (Douglas-Home)

Andrew (Bonar Law)

Anthony (Eden, Blair)

Arthur (Wellesley, Balfour, Chamberlain)

Benjamin (Disraeli)

Boris (Johnson)

Clement (Attlee)

David (Lloyd George, Cameron)

Edward (Heath)

Gordon (Brown)

Harold (Macmillan, Wilson – though neither of their first names was Harold)

James (Callaghan – whose first name was Leonard)

John (Stuart, Russell, Major)

Neville (Chamberlain)

Ramsay (MacDonald – whose first name was James)

Spencer (Crompton, Perceval)

Stanley (Baldwin)

William (Cavendish, Pitt (Elder and Younger), Wyndham, Lamb, Gladstone)

Winston (Churchill)

– and Margaret (Thatcher) and Theresa (May) for girls.

Nehemiah
Hebrew, meaning 'comforter'.

Neil
(alt. Neal, Niall)
Irish, meaning 'champion'.

Neilson
Irish, meaning 'son of Neil'. Also the name of a prominent train manufacturer in Scotland.

Nelson
Variant of Neil, meaning 'champion'. Admiral Horatio Nelson commanded the British navy at the Battle of Trafalgar. Nelson Mandela was the first black president of South Africa.

Nemo
Latin, meaning 'nobody'. Made famous by the Disney animation *Finding Nemo*.

Neo
Latin, meaning 'new'. Neo is the protagonist in *The Matrix* trilogy.

Nephi
Greek, meaning 'cloud'. The Books of Nephi are some of the subdivisions of the Book of Mormon.

Nessim
(alt. Nasim)
Arabic, meaning 'breeze'. Sham el-Nessim is also the first day of spring in Egypt.

Nestor
Greek, meaning 'traveller'. Nestor was the king of Pylos in ancient Greek mythology.

Neville
Old French, meaning 'new village'. Famous Nevilles include former prime minister Neville Chamberlain and *Harry Potter* character Neville Longbottom.

Newland
(alt. Newlands, Newland, Neuland)
English, meaning 'from a new land'. Also the name of several towns in the UK.

Newton
English, meaning 'new town'.

Neymar
Portuguese contraction of Latin names Netuno and Mars. Made popular by Brazilian footballer Neymar de Silva Santos.

Nicholas
(alt. Nicolas, Niklas; abbrev. Nick, Nicky, Niko, Nikos, Nico)
Greek, meaning 'victorious'. An enduringly popular name. Famous Nicholases include St Nicholas, actor Nicolas Cage and the alchemist Nicholas Flamel.

Nigel
Gaelic, meaning 'champion'. Famous Nigels include actor Nigel Hawthorne, photographer Nigel Barker and producer/presenter Nigel Lythgoe.

Nikhil
Sanskrit, meaning 'whole' or 'entire'.

Nikita
Greek, meaning 'unconquered', also Russian. Nikita Khrushchev was leader of the Soviet Union from 1953 to 1964. Also used as a girls' name.

Nikolai
(alt. *Nikolay*)
Russian variant of Nicholas, meaning 'victorious'. Several Russian emperors were known as either Nicholas or Nikolai.

Nimrod
Hebrew, meaning 'we will rebel'. Also the title of a piece of music by Elgar and the name of a type of aircraft.

Ninian
Gaelic, associated with the fifth-century saint of the same name.

Nissim
Hebrew, meaning 'wonderful things'.

Noah
Hebrew, meaning 'peaceful'. In the Bible, Noah is said to have built an ark to save two of every animal from a flood that covered the earth.

Noel
French, meaning 'Christmas'. Famous Noels include actor/composer Noel Coward and musician Noel Gallagher.

Nolan
Gaelic, meaning 'champion'.

Norbert
Old German, meaning 'Northern brightness'. Norbert is also the name of Hagrid's pet dragon in J.K. Rowling's *Harry Potter* series.

Norman
Old German, meaning 'Northerner'.

Normand
French, meaning 'from Normandy'.

Norris
Old French, meaning 'Northerner'. Norris McWhirter was the co-author with his brother, Ross, of *The Guiness Book of Records*.

Norton
English, meaning 'Northern town'.

Norval
French, meaning 'Northern town'.

Norwood
English, meaning 'Northern forest'. Also the name of several towns in the UK.

Nova
Latin, meaning 'new'.

Nuno
Latin, meaning 'ninth'.

Nunzio
Italian, meaning 'messenger'. A fairly popular name in Italy.

Boys' names

Oakley
English, meaning 'from the oak meadow'. Also the name of a clothing brand.

Obadiah
Hebrew, meaning 'God's worker'. Used throughout the Bible to indicate a servant of God.

Obama
Swahili, meaning 'crooked'. Made famous by the 44th President of the USA, Barack Obama.

Obed
Hebrew, meaning 'servant of God'. Obed was the grandfather of David in the Bible.

Oberon
(abbrev. Obie)
Old German, meaning 'royal bear'. The Fairy King in Shakespeare's *A Midsummer Night's Dream*.

Obijulu
(alt. Obiajulu)
Swahili, meaning 'one who has been consoled'.

Octave
(alt. Octavian, Octavio)
Latin, meaning 'eight'. An octave is a group of eight notes in a musical scale.

Oda
(alt. Odell, Odie, Odis)
Hebrew, meaning 'praise God'. Oda of Canterbury was archbishop in the 10th century.

Ogden
Old English, meaning 'oak valley'. Ogden Nash was an American humorous poet.

Oisin
(alt. Osian, Ossian)
Celtic, meaning 'fawn'. The name of an ancient Irish poet.

Ola

Norse, meaning 'precious'. Ola Nordmann is the personification of Norway, in the same way Uncle Sam represents the USA.

Olaf
(alt. Olan)

Old Norse, meaning 'ancestor'. The name of the snowman in Disney's *Frozen*.

Oleander

Hawaiian, meaning 'joyous'. Also the name of a highly poisonous flowering shrub.

Oleg
(alt. Olen)

Russian, meaning 'holy'. Oleg the Seer was a Grand Prince of Rus', who ruled large parts of eastern Europe in the tenth century.

Olin

Russian, meaning 'rock'.

Oliver
(abbrev. Ollie)

Latin, meaning 'olive tree'. The UK's most popular boys' name in several recent years.

Olivier

French form of Oliver, meaning 'olive tree'.

Omar
(alt. Omari, Omarion)

Arabic, meaning 'speaker'. Extremely popular name in Sunni communities.

Ondrej

Czech, meaning 'manly'. The English equivalent is Andrew.

Ora

Latin, meaning 'hour'.

Oran
(alt. Oren, Orrin)

Gaelic, meaning 'light and pale'.

Orion

Greek, from the legend of a massive hunter who was sent to spend eternity as a star constellation.

Orlando
(alt. Orlo)

Old German, meaning 'old land'. Famous Orlandos include actor Orlando Bloom, the Shakespearean character Orlando in *As You Like It* and the city of Orlando in Florida, USA.

Orpheus

Greek, meaning 'beautiful voice'. Orpheus was an ancient Greek musician and charmer, who tried to rescue his wife from the underworld.

Orrick

English, meaning 'sword ruler'.

Orson

Latin, meaning 'bear'. Film director Orson Welles was known for his radio play *The War of the Worlds*, and films *Citizen Kane* and *Touch of Evil*.

Orville

Old French, meaning 'gold town'. Orville and Wilbur Wright were the American brothers credited with building the first successful aeroplane.

Osaka

From the Japanese city.

Osborne
(alt. Osbourne)

Norse, meaning 'bear god'.

Oscar

Old English, meaning 'spear of the Gods'. Oscar Wilde was an Irish poet and writer, best known for his ready wit.

Osias

Hebrew, meaning 'salvation'. Osias Beert was an influential still-life painter in the 17th century.

Oswald

German, meaning 'God's power'. Oswald the Lucky Rabbit was Walt Disney's original cartoon creation before Mickey Mouse was born.

Othello

Old German, meaning 'wealth'. From the character in Shakespeare's play Othello.

Otis

German, meaning 'wealth'. Singer Otis Redding was known for his songs '(Sittin' on) The Dock of the Bay', 'Respect' and 'Try A Little Tenderness'.

Otten

German, meaning 'son of Otto'.

Otto
(alt. Otha, Otho)

German, meaning 'wealthy'. Famous Ottos include Anne Frank's father, Otto Frank, and Prussian leader Otto von Bismarck.

Ovid

Latin, meaning 'sheep'. Associated with the Roman poet, author of Metamorphoses.

Owain
(alt. Owen)

Welsh, meaning 'noble-born'. Owain Ddantgwyn was a prince of Wales and a contender to be the real King Arthur.

Oz

Hebrew, meaning 'strength'. As well as the fictional land of Oz in the story The Wizard of Oz, this is also a slang term for Australia.

Boys' names

Pablo

Spanish, meaning 'little'. Spanish painter and sculptor Pablo Picasso was one of the most influential artists of the 20th century.

Paco

Native American, meaning 'eagle'. Also a Spanish alternative for Francisco.

Padma

Sanskrit, meaning 'lotus'. Also used as a name for girls.

Padraig

Irish, meaning 'noble'. The English equivalent is Patrick.

Panos

Greek, meaning 'all holy'.

Paolo
(alt. Paulo)

Italian, meaning 'little'. Paolo Nutini is a singer and Paulo Coelho is a Brazilian author.

Paresh

Sanskrit, meaning 'supreme spirit'.

Paris

From France's capital city. Also the Trojan prince in Homer's *Iliad* and Juliet's suitor in Shakespeare's *Romeo and Juliet*. Originally a boys' name, but now also used as a name for girls.

Pascal

Latin, meaning 'Easter child'.

Patrice

French form of Patrick, meaning 'noble'. Also a name given to girls.

Patrick
(abbrev. Pat, Paddy)

Irish, meaning 'noble'. The patron saint of Ireland. Sir Patrick Stewart is an English actor with a long and distinguished career on both stage and screen.

Patten

English, meaning 'noble'.

Paul

Hebrew, meaning 'small'. Pauls
include the biblical Paul the Apostle,
singers Paul Simon and Paul
McCartney and artist Paul Cézanne.

Pavel

Latin, meaning 'small'. The English
equivalent is Paul.

Pax

Latin, meaning 'peace'. From the
Roman goddess of peace.

Paxton

English, meaning 'town of peace'.

Payne

Latin, meaning 'peasant'.

Payton

Latin, meaning 'peasant's town'.

Pedro

Spanish form of Peter, meaning
'rock'. Several kings of Portugal and
Aragon have been named Pedro.

Penn

English, meaning 'hill'. Famous Penns
include magician Penn Jillette and
American actor Penn Badgley.

Percival
(abbrev. Percy)

French, meaning 'pierce the valley'.
One of the Knights of the Round
Table.

Perez

Hebrew, meaning 'breach'. One of
Judah's sons in the Bible.

Pericles

Greek, meaning 'far-famed'. Pericles
was an influential ancient Greek
general and statesman.

Perrin

Greek, meaning 'rock'.

Perry

English, meaning 'rock'. Perry is an
alcoholic drink made from pears.

Pervis

English, meaning 'purveyor'.

Pesah
(alt. Pesach, Pesasch)

Hebrew, meaning 'spared'. Pesach
is the Hebrew name for the Jewish
festival of Passover.

Peter
(abbrev. Pete)

Greek, meaning 'rock'. St Peter was
one of Jesus's disciples in the Bible.
Famous Peters include Peter Pan,
film director Sir Peter Jackson, and
Spiderman's real persona, Peter
Parker.

Petros

Greek form of Peter, meaning 'rock'.

Peyton

Old English, meaning 'fighting man's
estate'.

Philemon

Greek, meaning 'affectionate'. From the New Testament of the Bible.

Philip
(alt. Phillip; abbrev. Phil, Phill, Pip)

Greek, meaning 'lover of horses'. Famous Philips include Prince Philip, Philip the Apostle in the Bible and author Philip Pullman. Pip is usually associated with the lead character in Charles Dickens' novel *Great Expectations*.

Philo

Greek, meaning 'love'. Philo of Alexandria was an ancient Roman Jewish philosopher.

Phineas
(alt. Pinchas)

Hebrew, meaning 'oracle'. Phineas was an ancient Greek king of Thrace.

Phoenix

Greek, meaning 'dark red'. In ancient Greek mythology, a phoenix is a bird that has the power to regenerate itself from its ashes.

Pierre

French form of Peter, meaning 'rock'. A popular French name.

Piers

Old English form of Peter, meaning 'rock'. Journalist and TV presenter Piers Morgan is known for his work with various tabloid newspapers and *Britain's Got Talent*.

Pierson

Variant of Piers, meaning 'son of Piers'.

Placido

Latin, meaning 'placid'. Tenor opera singer Placido Domingo is known for his vast array of operatic roles and performances with Luciano Pavarotti and José Carreras.

Pradeep

Hindi, meaning 'light'.

Pranav

Sanskrit, meaning 'spiritual leader'. Pranava is another way of saying 'Om' in Sanskrit.

Presley

Old English, meaning 'priest's meadow'. Usually associated with music legend Elvis Presley.

Preston

Old English, meaning 'priest's town'. Also the name of a city in England. Preston Sturges was an Oscar-winning playwright.

Primo

Italian, meaning 'first'. Also used as a slang term for 'good' or 'excellent'.

Primus

Latin, meaning 'first'. Primus is often used in cartoons and comic books as a name for villains or superheroes, including in *Transformers* and Marvel comics.

Prince

English, from the word 'prince'. As well as a title of nobility, this name is often associated with the late singer Prince.

Proctor

(alt. Prockter, Procter)

Latin, meaning 'steward'.

Prospero

Latin, meaning 'prosperous'. Prospero is the protagonist in Shakespeare's play *The Tempest*.

Pryor

English, meaning 'first'.

Psalm

Old English, meaning 'hymn'. The name of Kanye West and Kim Kardashian-West's fourth child.

Ptolemy

Greek, meaning 'aggressive' or 'warlike'. Claudius Ptolemy was an ancient Greek mathematician and astronomer.

Purvis

(alt. Purves, Purviss)

French, meaning 'purveyor'.

Boys' names

Qabil
(alt. Quabil)
Arabic, meaning 'accepter'. Qabil is the Arabic name for Cain, who was one of the sons of Adam and Eve in the Bible.

Qadim
(alt. Qaadim, Qadem, Qadeem, Quadim)
Arabic, meaning 'organiser, convenor'. Often used with the prefix 'al', to form Al-Qadim.

Qadir
(alt. Quadir)
Arabic, meaning 'powerful'.

Qino
(alt. Quino)
Chinese, meaning 'handsome'. Also used in Spanish-speaking communities.

Quaid
Irish, meaning 'fourth'.

Qued
Old English, meaning 'bad or ugly'. Also an old name for the devil.

Quemby
Norse, meaning 'from the woman's estate'.

Quentin
(alt. Quinten, Quintin, Quinton, Quintus)
Latin, meaning 'fifth'. Famous Quentins include illustrator Quentin Blake and film director Quentin Tarantino.

Quillan
Gaelic, meaning 'sword'.

Quillon
Gaelic, meaning 'club'. The quillon is the bar on a sword where the handle meets the blade.

Quincy

Old French, meaning 'estate of the fifth son'. Jazz and soul legend Quincy Jones is known for his long career of music production, songwriting and performing.

Quinlan

Gaelic, meaning 'fit, shapely and strong'.

Quinn

Gaelic, meaning 'counsel'. Usually associated with the character from *Glee*.

Quinton

English, meaning 'queen's community'.

Boys' names

Radames

Slavic, meaning 'famous joy'. A character in the Verdi opera *Aïda*.

Rafael

(alt. Raphael; abbrev. Rafa, Rafe, Rafer, Raffi)

Hebrew, meaning 'God has healed'. One of the archangels in the Bible. Rafael Nadal is a Spanish tennis player who has held the world No. 1 ranking.

Ragnar

Old Norse, meaning 'strong counsellor'. Ragnar Lothbrok is a lead character in Amazon Prime's *Vikings*.

Raheem

(alt. Rahim)

Arabic, meaning 'merciful and kind'.

Rahm

Hebrew, meaning 'mercy'.

Rahul

(alt. Raoul, Raul)

Sanskrit, meaning 'efficient'. Rahul was Buddha's son.

Raiden

(alt. Rainen)

From the Japanese god of thunder. It also refers to the combination of lightning and thunder.

Rainer

Old German, meaning 'warrior from the gods'. Rainer Hersch is a British classical music comedian.

Raj

Sanskrit, meaning 'kingdom'. Also a Polish term for 'heaven'.

Rajesh

(alt. Ramesh)

Sanskrit, meaning 'ruler of kings'. Popular in both India and Nepal.

Raleigh

Old English, meaning 'deer's meadow'. Sir Walter Raleigh was an Elizabethan explorer and politician.

Ralph

Old English, meaning 'wolf'. Famous Ralphs include actor Ralph Fiennes, fashion brand Ralph Lauren and cartoon character Ralph from *The Simpsons*.

Ram

English, from the word for a male sheep.

Ramiro

Spanish, meaning 'judicious'. A popular name for boys in Argentina.

Ramone

Spanish, meaning 'wise supporter' or 'romantic'. The Ramones were an American rock band.

Ramsey
(alt. Ramsay)

Old English, meaning 'wild garlic island'. Ramsay MacDonald was the UK's first-ever Labour prime minister.

Randall
(alt. Randal, Randolph; abbrev. Randy)

Old German, meaning 'wolf shield'. Randy Newman is an American singer-songwriter and film composer. In modern English, randy can also mean amorous.

Raniel

English, meaning 'God is my happiness'. Can also be used as an alternative to Daniel.

Ranjit

Sanskrit, meaning 'influenced by charm'. Several Indian cricketers have been called Ranjit.

Rannoch

Gaelic, meaning 'fern'. Also an area in the Scottish Highlands.

Rashad

Arabic, meaning 'good judgement'.

Rashid
(alt. Rasheed)

Sanskrit, meaning 'rightly guided'. Ar-Rashid, meaning The Guide, is one of God's names in the Islamic tradition.

Rasmus

Greek, meaning 'beloved'. Usually used as a shortened form of Erasmus.

Raven

English, from the word 'raven', referring to the black bird.

Ravi

Hindi, meaning 'sun'. Ravivar is the Hindi word for Sunday.

Rawlins

French alternative of Roland, meaning 'renowned land'.

Raymond
(alt. Rayner; abbrev. Ray)

English, meaning 'adviser'. Illustrator and author Raymond Briggs is known for *The Snowman*. Famous Rays include singer Ray Charles and actors Ray Liotta and Ray Winstone.

Raz
Hebrew, meaning 'secret' or 'mystery'.

Reagan
Irish, meaning 'little king'.

Reginald
(abbrev. Reggie)

Latin, meaning 'regal'. Singer Elton John's birth name was Reginald Kenneth Dwight. Reggie Yates is a British actor and TV and radio presenter.

Regis
Latin, meaning 'of the king'.

Reid
Old English, meaning 'by the reeds'.

Reilly
(alt. Rilee, Rileigh, Riley, Ryle, Rylea, Rylei)

Irish, meaning 'courageous'. A very common first name and surname in Ireland.

Remington
English, meaning 'ridge town'.

Remus
Latin, meaning 'swift'. Famous Remuses include the ancient Roman myth of Romulus and Remus, and the character of Remus Lupin in J.K. Rowling's *Harry Potter* series.

Rémy
French, meaning 'from Rheims'.

Ren
Shortened form of Reginald, meaning 'regal'. According to Confucianism, Ren is also the feeling of satisfaction or pleasure after doing something nice for someone else.

Renato
Latin, meaning 'rebirth'.

René
French, meaning 'rebirth'. Traditionally only a name for boys, René is now often given to girls as well – in place of Renée.

Reno
Latin, meaning 'renewed'. Also a gambling city in Nevada, USA.

Reuben
(alt. Ruben)

Spanish, meaning 'a son'. The son of Jacob and eldest brother of Joseph in the Bible.

Reuel
Hebrew, meaning 'friend of God'.

Rex
Latin, meaning 'king'.

Rey

Spanish, meaning 'king'. In Telugu, Rey also means 'friend'.

Reynold

Latin, meaning 'king's adviser'. As a surname, Reynold can be traced back to pre-Norman times.

Rhodes

German, meaning 'where the roses grow'. Also the name of a Greek island and city.

Rhodri

Welsh, meaning 'ruler of the circle'. Rhodri the Great was a Welsh king in the ninth century.

Rhys

(alt. Reece)

Welsh, meaning 'enthusiasm'. Famous Rhyses include actors Rhys Ifans, Griff Rhys Jones and Jonathan Rhys Meyers.

Ricardo

Spanish form of Richard, meaning 'powerful leader'.

Richard

(abbrev. Rich, Richie, Ritchie, Rick, Ricki, Ricky, Dick, Dicky)

Old German, meaning 'powerful leader'. A popular name through many decades, it has dropped off in usage in recent years. Famous Richards include three kings of England. Famous Rickys include actor, writer and comedian Ricky Gervais and singer-songwriter Ricky Wilson.

Ridley

English, meaning 'cleared wood'. Film director Sir Ridley Scott is known for his films *Alien*, *Thelma & Louise* and *Gladiator*.

Rigby

English, meaning 'valley of the ruler'.

Ringo

English, meaning 'ring'. Usually associated with Beatles drummer Ringo Starr, whose birth name is Richard Starkey.

Rio

Spanish, meaning 'river'. Footballer Rio Ferdinand played for Manchester United and England.

Riordan

Gaelic, meaning 'bard'.

Rishi

Sanskrit, meaning 'scribe'. In ancient India, Rishis were the scribes who kept records of hymns and scientific advancement.

River

English, from the body of water. Actor River Phoenix was known for his roles in *Stand By Me*, *Indiana Jones and the Last Crusade* and *My Own Private Idaho*.

Roald

Scandinavian, meaning 'ruler'. Author Roald Dahl is one of the best-loved children's authors of all time, penning books such as *Charlie and the Chocolate Factory*, *Matilda* and *The Witches*.

Robert
(abbrev. Rob, Robbie, Bob, Bobby, Dobbin)

Old German, meaning 'bright fame'. Famous Roberts include Scottish king Robert the Bruce and actors Robert Pattinson and Robert de Niro. Famous Robs include actor Rob Lowe and comedian Rob Brydon. Famous Robbies include singer Robbie Wiliams, actor Robbie Coltrane and poet Robert 'Robbie' Burns.

Roberto
Italian form of Robert, meaning 'bright fame'.

Robin
English, from the word for the small, flame-breasted bird. Famous Robins include comedian Robin Williams, singer Robin Thicke and outlaw legend Robin Hood.

Robinson
English, meaning 'son of Robin'. Usually associated with the novel and title character *Robinson Crusoe*, by Daniel Defoe.

Rocco
(alt. Rocky)

Italian, meaning 'rest'. Rocco Ritchie is the son of Madonna and film director Guy Ritchie.

Rockwell
English, meaning 'of the rock well'.

Rod
Shortened form of Rhodri, Roderick and Rodney. Famous Rods include singer Rod Stewart and journalist Rod Liddle.

Roderick
(abbrev. Rod, Roddy)

German, meaning 'famous power'. Impressionist Rory Bremner's real name is Roderick Bremner.

Rodney
(abbrev. Rod, Roddy)

Old German, meaning 'island near the clearing'. Also a much-loved character in *Only Fools And Horses*.

Rodrigo
Spanish form of Roderick, meaning 'famous power'.

Roger
Old German, meaning 'spear man'. Famous Rogers include athlete Sir Roger Bannister, The Who singer Roger Daltrey and tennis player Roger Federer.

Roland
(alt. Rowland)

Old German, meaning 'renowned land'. Also puppet character Roland Rat.

Rolf
Old German, meaning 'wolf'.

Rollie
(alt. Rollo)

Old German, meaning 'renowned land'. Often used as a shortened version of Rolf or Roland.

Roman

Latin, meaning 'from Rome'.

Romeo

Latin, meaning 'pilgrim to Rome'. Made famous by Shakespeare's play *Romeo and Juliet*. Romeo is the second son of David and Victoria Beckham.

Ronald
(abbrev. Ron, Ronnie)

Norse, meaning 'mountain of strength'. Hollywood actor Ronald Reagan became the 40th president of the United States.

Ronan

Gaelic, meaning 'little seal'. Singer Ronan Keating is known for his career with boy band Boyzone.

Rory

English, meaning 'red king'. Famous Rorys include comedian Rory Bremner, actor Rory MacGregor and comedian Rory McGrath.

Ross
(alt. Russ)

Scottish, meaning 'cape'. Famous Rosses include actor Ross Kemp and comedian Ross Noble.

Rowan
(alt. Roan, Rohan)

Gaelic, meaning 'little red one'. Also reference to the rowan tree. Sir Rowan Atkinson is the comedian, writer and actor best known for his roles in *Blackadder* and as *Mr Bean*.

Roy

Gaelic, meaning 'red'. Famous Roys include England football manager Roy Hodgson and singer Roy Orbison.

Rudolph
(abbrev. Rudy)

Old German, meaning 'famous wolf'. Usually associated with the Christmas reindeer with a shiny red nose.

Rufus

Latin, meaning 'red-haired'. Famous Rufuses include presenter Rufus Hound, actor Rufus Sewell and singer Rufus Wainwright.

Rupert

Variant of Robert, meaning 'bright fame'.

Ruslan

Russian, meaning 'like a lion'.

Russell

Old French, meaning 'little red one'. Famous Russells include comedian Russell Brand, screenwriter Russell T. Davies and astrologer Russell Grant.

Rusty

English, meaning 'ruddy'. Most commonly used in the USA as a name for boys.

Ryan

Gaelic, meaning 'little king'. Famous Ryans include actors Ryan Gosling and Ryan Reynolds and footballer Ryan Giggs.

Ryder

English, meaning 'horseman'.

Rye

English, from the word 'rye'. Also a type of grain.

Ryker

From Richard, meaning 'powerful leader'.

Rylan

English, meaning 'land where rye is grown'. Presenter Rylan Clark-Neale is known for several reality TV programmes, including *Celebrity Big Brother*.

Ryley

Old English, meaning 'rye clearing'. More commonly used as a spelling alternative to Riley.

Rym

Arabic, meaning 'antelope'.

Ryu

Japanese, meaning 'dragon'. A Ryu can also refer to a discipline, such as a martial art, or school of thought.

Boys' names

Saar
Hebrew, meaning 'tempest'.

Saber
(alt. Sabre)
French, meaning 'sword'.

Sagar
Bengali, meaning 'sea'.

Sage
English, meaning 'wise'. Also a herb.

Sakari
Native American, meaning 'sweet'. Most commonly used in Finnish-speaking communities.

Salil
Sanskrit, meaning 'from the water'.

Salim
(alt. Saleem)
Arabic, meaning 'secure'. The Salim Khan family are a Bollywood dynasty, with dozens of members involved as actors, directors, producers or writers.

Salvador
Spanish, meaning 'saviour'. Artist Salvador Dali was known for his surrealist paintings.

Salvatore
Italian, meaning 'saviour'.

Samir
Arabic, meaning 'pleasant companion'.

Samson
Hebrew, meaning 'son of Sam'. Character with supernatural strength in the Bible.

Samuel
(abbrev. Sam, Sama, Sammie, Sammy)
Hebrew, meaning 'God is heard'. Famous Samuels include a prophet in the Bible and actor Samuel L. Jackson.

Sandeep
(alt. Sundeep)

Hindi, meaning 'lighting the way'. Popular in Hindu and Sikh communities.

Sandro

Italian, a shortened form of Alessandro, meaning 'defending men'.

Sandy

Shortened form of Alexander, meaning 'defender of mankind'. Famous Sandys include TV presenter Sandy Toksvig and pro golfer Sandy Lyle.

Sanjay

Hindi, meaning 'victory'. Famous Sanjays include *The Simpsons* character Sanjay, politician Sanjay Gandhi and Hindu narrative *Mahabharata* character Sanjaya.

Santiago

Spanish, meaning 'St James'. Also the name of the capital city of Chile.

Santino

Spanish, meaning 'little St James'. Santino was also the name of the first chimpanzee recognised to have forward-planning skills, in 2009.

Santo
(alt. Santos)

Latin, meaning 'saint'. Also the name of at least 10 separate football clubs around the world, including in Brazil, Mexico and Cape Town.

Sasha
(alt. Sacha)

Shortened Russian form of Alexander, meaning 'defending men'. DJ Sasha is known for his remixes of popular songs by Madonna and The Chemical Brothers. Sasha Baron Cohen is a successful comedian and actor.

Scott
(alt. Scottie)

English, meaning 'from Scotland'. Scott Mills is a radio DJ and TV presenter.

Seamus

Irish variant of James, meaning 'he who supplants'. Irish poet and playwright Seamus Heaney was awarded the Nobel Prize for literature.

Sean
(alt. Shaun, Shawn)

Variant of John, meaning 'God is gracious'. The name originated in the Middle Ages, when French invaders reached Ireland and the Irish began pronouncing the French name Jean as Sean. Famous Seans include legendary Bond actor Sean Connery.

Sebastian
(alt. Sébastien; abbrev. Seb)

Greek, meaning 'revered'. Famous Sebastians include the crab character in Disney's *The Little Mermaid*, novelist Sebastian Faulks and Sebastian Vettel, the Formula One world champion racing driver.

Sergio
(alt. Serge)

Latin, meaning 'servant'. Popular name for boys in parts of Cameroon, Belgium and Haiti.

Seth

Hebrew, meaning 'appointed'. Famous Seths include the third son of Adam and Eve in the Bible, and actors Seth MacFarlane and Seth Greene.

Severus

Latin, meaning 'severe'. Best known now as the character Severus Snape in J.K. Rowling's *Harry Potter* series.

Seymour

English, from Saint-Maur in northern France. Famous fictional Seymours include Seymour of *The Little Shop of Horrors* and Principal Seymour Skinner in *The Simpsons*.

Shalen

Arabic, meaning 'tribal leader'.

Shane

Variant of Sean, meaning 'God is gracious'. Famous Shanes include presenter Shane Richie, novelist Shane Briant and film director Shane Meadows.

Sharif

Arabic, meaning 'honoured'. Also a name for descendants of one of Muhammad's grandchildren.

Shea

Gaelic, meaning 'admirable'.

Shelby

Norse, meaning 'willow'. Also the name of a type of Mustang car.

Sherlock

English, meaning 'fair haired'. Usually associated with the fictional detective Sherlock Holmes.

Sherman

Old English, meaning 'shear man'. Also a type of World War II tank.

Shmuel

Hebrew, meaning 'his name is God'. The English equivalent is Samuel.

Shola

Arabic, meaning 'energetic'. Can be used for boys and girls. Shola Ameobi is a footballer who has played for Fleetwood Town and for Nigeria.

Sidney
(alt. Sydney; abbrev. Sid)

English, meaning 'wide meadow'.

Sigmund

Old German, meaning 'victorious hand'. Neurologist Sigmund Freud was known for his vast work of psychoanalysis.

Silvanus
(alt. Silvio)

Latin, meaning 'woods'. Silvanus was an ancient Roman deity of woods and fields.

Simba
(abbrev. Sim)

Swahili, meaning 'lion'. Usually associated with the character of Simba in Disney's The Lion King.

Simon
(alt. Simeon)

Hebrew, meaning 'to hear'. Famous Simons include music producer Simon Cowell and actor Simon Pegg.

Sinbad
(alt. Sindbad)

Persian, meaning 'Lord of Sages'. Also a literary merchant adventurer.

Sindri

Norse, meaning 'dwarf', from ancient Norse mythology.

Sipho

Swahili, meaning 'the unknown one'.

Sire

English, from the word 'sire'. Used as a form of address or title for reigning kings.

Sirius

Hebrew, meaning 'brightest star'. Name of Harry Potter's godfather, Sirius Black, in J.K. Rowling's Harry Potter series.

Skipper

English, meaning 'ship captain'.

Skyler
(alt. Skylar)

English, meaning 'scholar'. Can be a boys' or girls' name. Now often associated with female Breaking Bad character Skyler White.

Solomon
(alt. Shlomo)

Hebrew, meaning 'peace'. One of the most important kings in the Bible and Torah.

Sonny

American English, meaning 'son'. Singer Sonny Bono was half of the duo Sonny and Cher.

Soren

Scandinavian, meaning 'brightest star'. Also the name of a town in Germany.

Spencer

English, meaning 'guardian'. Actor Spencer Tracy was a star of Hollywood's golden era.

Spike

English, from the word 'spike'. Famous Spikes include film director Spike Lee and comedian and writer Spike Milligan (though neither was actually given the name Spike).

Stamos

Greek, meaning 'reasonable'.

S

Stanford

English, meaning 'stone ford'. Stanford University in the USA is one of the most well-known Ivy League universities.

Stanley
(abbrev. Stan)

English, meaning 'stony meadow'. Famous Stanleys include children's character Flat Stanley, film director Stanley Kubrick and actor Stanley Tucci.

Stavros

Greek, meaning 'cross'.

Stellan

Latin, meaning 'starred'. More commonly used in Swedish-speaking communities.

Steno

German, meaning 'stone'.

Stephen
(alt. Steven, Stefan, Stefano, Steffan; abbrev. Steve, Stevie)

English, meaning 'crowned'. Famous Stephens include actor Stephen Fry, physicist Stephen Hawking and author Stephen King. Famous Stevens include film director Steven Spielberg, Apple founder Steve Jobs and actor Steve Coogan.

Stewart
(alt. Stuart)

English, meaning 'steward'. The House of Stewart was the longest-surviving royal line in the Scottish monarchy. Famous Stuarts include DJ Stuart Maconie, football manager Stuart Pearce and film director Stuart Townsend.

Stoney

English, meaning 'stone like'. More commonly used as a surname.

Storm

English, from the word 'storm'.

Sven

Norse, meaning 'boy'. In the UK, Sven is usually associated with former England football manager Sven-Goran Eriksson.

Syed
(alt. Sayyid)

Arabic, meaning 'lucky'. Also a way of describing decendants of one of Muhammad's grandchildren.

Sylvester

Latin, meaning 'wooded'. Usually associated with the cartoon cat or actor Sylvester Stallone.

Syon

Sanskrit, meaning 'followed by good'. Also the name of a large historical stately home in England.

Boys' names

Tacitus

Latin, meaning 'silent, calm'. From the ancient Roman historian and senator.

Tad

English, from the word 'tadpole'. Also a shortened form of Thaddeus.

Taine

Gaelic, meaning 'river'.

Taj

Sanskrit, meaning 'crown'. Usually associated with the Indian palace the Taj Mahal.

Takashi

Japanese, meaning 'praiseworthy'.

Takoda

Sioux, meaning 'friend to everyone'. Most commonly used in the USA.

Talbot
(alt. Tal)

English, meaning 'command of the valley'. An aristocratic name.

Tamir

Arabic, meaning 'tall and wealthy'.

Taran
(alt. Taron)

Welsh, meaning 'thunder'. Actor Taron Egerton is best known for *Eddie the Eagle*, *Kingsman* and *Rocketman*.

Taras
(alt. Tarez)

Scottish, meaning 'crag'. Taras was the son of Poseidon in ancient Greek mythology.

Tarek
(alt. Tarik, Tariq)

Arabic, meaning 'to strike'.

Tarian

Welsh, meaning 'shield'. Also the name of a breed of Welsh pony.

Tarquin

Latin, from the Roman clan name. Author Tarquin Hall is known for his works *To the Elephant Graveyard* and *Salaam Brick Lane*.

Tarun

Hindi, meaning 'young'. Bollywood star Tarun Kumar Bhatti is known simply as Tarun.

Tatanka

Lakota, meaning 'buffalo'. Legendary Native American leader Sitting Bull's Western name was Tatanka Lyotake.

Tate

English, meaning 'cheerful'.

Taurean

English, meaning 'bull like'. Also used as a term for people born under the Taurus star sign.

Tavares

English, meaning 'descendant of the hermit'. Also found as a last name in Portuguese-speaking communities.

Tave
(alt. Tavian, Tavis, Tavish)

French, from Gustave, meaning 'royal staff'. In Nordic cultures the name also means 'guarantor'.

Tavor

Hebrew, meaning 'misfortunate'. Also the name given to a type of assault rifle.

Taylor

English, meaning 'tailor'. Actor Taylor Lautner appeared in the *Twilight* films. Now used as often for girls as for boys.

Names of poets

Andrew (Marvell)

Benjamin (Zephaniah)

Geoffrey (Chaucer)

Hugo (Williams)

John (Donne, Keats, Milton, Cooper Clarke)

Percy (Bysshe Shelley)

Robert (Burns)

Ted (Hughes)

Walt (Whitman)

William (Blake, Wordsworth)

Ted
(alt. Teddy)

Shortened form of Edward, meaning 'wealthy guard'. Famous Teds include *Father Ted*, and the *Ted* films.

Tennessee

Native American, meaning 'river town'. Also the name of a state in the USA.

Terence
(alt. Terrill, Terrence; abbrev. Terry)

English, meaning 'tender'. Terence was an ancient Roman playwright of comedies.

Tex

English, meaning 'Texan'. More commonly used in the USA.

Thabo

Swahili, meaning 'filled with happiness'. Thabo Mbeki was the president of South Africa from 1999 to 2008.

Thaddaeus

(abbrev. Thad, Thadd)

Greek, meaning 'courageous heart'.

Thane

(alt. Thayer)

Scottish, meaning 'landholder'.

Thelonious

Latin, meaning 'ruler of the people'. Thelonious Monk was an influential jazz pianist and composer.

Theodore

(abbrev. Theo)

Greek, meaning 'God's gift'. St Theodore was a warrior and martyr of the Eastern Orthodox Church.

Theophile

(alt. Theophilus)

Latin, meaning 'God's love'.

Theron

Greek, meaning 'hunter'.

Thierry

French variant of Terence, meaning 'tender'. Striker Thierry Henry played for Arsenal and France.

Thomas

(abbrev. Thom, Tom, Tomaz, Tommy)

Aramaic, meaning 'twin'. An enduringly popular name. Thomas the Tank Engine is one of the most long-standing popular children's characters of book and screen.

Thomson

(alt. Thomsen)

English, meaning 'son of Thomas'. The spelling Thomsen also means 'twin' in Aramaic.

Thor

Norse, meaning 'thunder'. Thor was an ancient Nordic god of thunder and lightning.

Tiago

From Santiago, meaning 'St James'. Used as a shortened form of Santiago as often as a name in its own right, particularly in Portuguese-speaking communities.

Tibor

Latin, from the river Tiber. In Hungary, the name can also mean 'a short meeting'.

Tieman

(alt. Tiemann)

Gaelic, meaning 'lord'.

Tien

Vietnamese, meaning 'first'.

Timothy

(abbrev. Tim, Timmy)

Greek, meaning 'God's honour'. Famous Timothys include actors Timothy Spall, Timothy Olyphant and Timothy Dalton.

Tito

(alt. Titus)

Latin, meaning 'defender'. Usually associated with Tito Jackson, an original member of the Jackson 5.

Tobias
(alt. Toby)
Hebrew, meaning 'God is good'.

Tod
(alt. Todd)
English, meaning 'fox'. Several fictional characters are called Tod or Todd, including Todd Flanders in *The Simpsons*, Todd Alquist in *Breaking Bad* and Todd Grimshaw in *Coronation Street*.

Tonneau
French, meaning 'barrel'. A tonneau is also a word used for the rear section of a car, particularly old-fashioned cars.

Tony
Shortened form of Anthony, from the old Roman family name. Famous Tonys include footballer Tony Adams, former prime minister Tony Blair and comedian, historian and TV presenter Tony Robinson.

Torin
Gaelic, meaning 'chief'. Actor Torin Thatcher was known for his numerous stage roles and films, including *Great Expectations* and *Mutiny on the Bounty*.

Torquil
Gaelic, meaning 'helmet'. In Scandinavia the name is also derived from Thor, the god of thunder and lightning.

Tory
(alt. Torey)
Norse, meaning 'Thor'.

Toshi
Japanese, meaning 'reflection'. More commonly used in Japanese-speaking communities.

Travis
French, meaning 'crossroads'.

Trevelyan
Cornish, meaning 'of the house of Eden'.

Trevor
Welsh, meaning 'great settlement'. Famous Trevors include inventor Trevor Baylis, DJ Trevor Nelson and politician and presenter Trevor Phillips.

Trey
(alt. Tyree)
French, meaning 'three'. Sometimes used as a nickname for a third-born child or person whose name ends in III, such as Microsoft founder Bill Gates, whose birth name is William Henry Gates III.

Tristan
(alt. Tristram)
Celtic, from the Celtic hero. One of the knights of the Round Table.

Troy
Gaelic, meaning 'descended from the soldier'. Troy was a legendary city in ancient Greece.

Tudor

Variant of Theodore, 'God's gift'.
The Tudors were a family dynasty
who ruled England during the 16th
century, including Henry VIII and
Elizabeth I.

Tyler

English, meaning 'tile maker'. The
name can be traced back to the 14th
century and English rebel Wat Tyler,
leader of the Peasants' Revolt.

Tyrell

French, meaning 'puller'. Usually
associated with the House of Tyrell
from *Game of Thrones*.

Tyrone

Gaelic, meaning 'Owen's county'.
Also the name of a county in
Northern Ireland.

Tyson

English, meaning 'son of Tyrone'.
Became popular after the rise of
Mike Tyson, the boxer known for his
aggressive fighting style.

Boys' names

Uberto
(alt. Umberto)
Italian, variant of Hubert, meaning 'bright or shining intellect'. Several kings of Italy were called Umberto.

Udath
(alt. Udathel)
Sanskrit, meaning 'noble'.

Udo
German, meaning 'power of the wolf'.

Ugo
Italian form of Hugo, meaning 'soul, mind and intellect'. Also the name of a town in Japan.

Ulf
German, meaning 'wolf'. Also the name of a Danish Viking chief.

Ulrich
German, meaning 'noble ruler'.

Ultan
Irish, meaning 'from Ulster'. St Ultan was an Irish monk in the seventh century.

Ulysses
Greek, meaning 'wrathful'. Made famous by the mythological voyager of ancient Greece.

Unwyn
(alt. Unwin, Unwine)
English, meaning 'unfriendly'.

Old name, new fashion

Bertrand	Norris
Dexter	Pierce
Felix	Reginald
Hector	Ulysses
Jefferson	Winston

Upton

English, meaning 'high town'.

Urho

Finnish, meaning 'brave'.

Uri

(alt. Uriah, Urias)

Hebrew, meaning 'my light'. Magician Uri Geller is known for his illusions of psychokinesis and telepathy.

Uriel

Hebrew, meaning 'angel of light'. One of the archangels in the Bible.

Usher

English. Made famous by the American R&B star.

Uttam

Sanskrit, meaning 'best'. Actor Uttam Kumar is known as one of the great Bollywood actors of the 20th century.

Uzi

(alt. Uzzi, Uzziah)

Hebrew, meaning 'God is my strength'. Also the name of an Israeli type of submachine gun.

Boys' names

Vaclav

Czech, meaning 'receives glory'. The English form is Wenceslaus.

Vadim

Russian, meaning 'scandal maker'. Vadim the Bold was a legendary warrior in Eastern Europe during the ninth century.

Valdemar

German, meaning 'renowned leader'. Valdemar was a king of Sweden during the 13th century.

Valente

Latin, meaning 'valiant'. More commonly used as a surname, particularly in Italy and Portugal.

Valentine

(alt. Valentin, Valentino; abbrev. Val)
English. St Valentine was a Roman saint associated with the tradition of courtly love, and whose day is celebrated on 14 February. The Spanish variant is Valentin and the Italian is Valentino.

Valerio

Italian, meaning 'to be strong'. Originally a surname in Italy, Valerio is now also being given as a first name to boys.

Valia

Sanskrit, meaning 'king of the monkeys'. Also used as a girls' name.

Van

Dutch, meaning 'son of'. Also a shortened form of Ivan, as with singer Van Morrison.

Vance

English, meaning 'marshland'.

Vangelis

Greek, meaning 'good news'. Vangelis is a modern Greek composer of various music, and is known for his work on films such as *Chariots of Fire*, *Blade Runner* and *Alexander*.

Varro

Latin, meaning 'strong'. There are several ancient Roman generals and poets known as Varro, most of whom were related to each other.

Varun

Hindi, meaning 'water god'. Shortened form of Varuna, who is the Hindu god of all water.

Vasilis

Greek, meaning 'kingly'.

Vaughan
(alt. Vaughn)

Welsh, meaning 'little'.

Vernell

French, meaning 'green and flourishing'. More commonly used in the USA.

Verner

Scandinavian form of the German Werner, meaning 'army defender'.

Vernon
(alt. Vernie)

French, meaning 'alder grove'.

Versilius

Latin, meaning 'flier'. Also the name of a fashionable part of Tuscany, Italy.

Vester

Latin, meaning 'wooded'. Also the name of a manufacturer of guitars.

Vibol

Cambodian, meaning 'man of plenty'.

Victor
(alt. Viktor)

Latin, meaning 'champion'. Author Victor Hugo is known for his novels *Les Miserables* and *The Hunchback of Notre-Dame*.

Vidal
(alt. Vidar)

Spanish, meaning 'life giving'. Hairdresser Vidal Sassoon owned a chain of salons and a range of styling products.

Vijay

Hindi, meaning 'conquering'. Bollywood star Joseph Vijay Chandrasekhar is known simply as Vijay.

Vikram

Hindi, meaning 'sun'. Bollywood star Vikram Kennedy Vinod Raj is known simply as Vikram.

Ville

French, meaning 'town'. The word is used to describe towns or cities throughout France and the UK, usually as a suffix – such as Carville in Yorkshire.

Vincent
(abbrev. Vin, Vince, Vinnie)

English, meaning 'victorious'. Famous Vincents include actor Vince Vaughn, artist Vincent van Gogh and footballer-turned-actor Vinnie Jones.

Virgil

Latin, meaning 'staff bearer'. Ancient Roman poet of the same name.

Vito

Spanish, meaning 'life'. Usually associated with the character Vito Corleone from *The Godfather*.

Vittorio

Italian, meaning 'victory'. The English equivalent is Victor.

Vitus

Latin, meaning 'life'. St Vitus's day was traditionally celebrated with dancing, which led to naming a neurological condition that looks like uncontrolled dancing as 'St Vitus Dance'.

Vivek

Sanskrit, meaning 'wisdom'. Bollywood star Vivekananthan is known simply as Vivek.

Vivian

Latin, meaning 'lively'. Commonly given to both boys and girls.

Vladimir
(abbrev. Vlad)

Slavic, meaning 'prince'. Famous Vladimirs include Russian President Vladimir Putin and legendary warrior Vlad the Impaler – who was also known as Dracula.

Volker

German, meaning 'defender of the people'.

Von

Norse, meaning 'hope'. In Germany, 'von' also means 'of' or 'from', and is used in names to denote origin, such as Ulrich von Liechtenstein.

Boys' names

Wade

English, meaning 'to move forward' or 'to go'. Wade Robson is a prolific choreographer of contemporary dance.

Waldemar

German, meaning 'famous ruler'. A common name for German princes during the Middle Ages.

Walden

English, meaning 'valley of the Britons'. Title of Henry Thoreau's famous book reflecting on simple living off the land.

Waldo

Old German, meaning 'rule'. Famous in the USA for the line of 'Where's Waldo?' books, known as 'Where's Wally?' in the UK.

Walker

German, meaning 'a fuller of cloth'. Most common in late 1800s and early 1900s in America.

Wallace

English, meaning 'foreigner' or 'stranger'. The man of the man-and-dog duo known to children everywhere as Wallace and Gromit.

Walter

(abbrev. Walt, Wally)
German, meaning 'ruler of the army'.

Ward

English, meaning 'guardian'.

Wardell

Old English, meaning 'watchman's hill'.

Warner

German, meaning 'army guard'. Best known for the movie studio Warner Brothers Entertainment, which has released blockbusters such as *Batman* and *Superman*.

Warren

German, meaning 'guard' or 'the game park'. Warren Buffett, an American businessman and philanthropist, is known as one of the richest people in the world.

Warwick

English, meaning 'farm near the weir'. The name of a historic town in England with a castle and a university.

Washington

English, meaning 'clever' or 'clever man's settlement'. The surname of the first president of the USA.

Wasim

Arabic, meaning 'attractive' or 'full of grace'.

Wassily

Greek, meaning 'royal' or 'kingly'. Wassily Kandinsky was an influential Russian painter of abstract art.

Watson

English, meaning 'son' or 'son of Walter'. The right-hand man of the famous fictional detective Sherlock Holmes.

Waverley

(alt. Waverly)

English, meaning 'meadow of aspens'. A common name for towns and cities in the USA.

Waylon

English, meaning 'land by the road'. American Waylon Jennings has been a popular country singer for decades.

Wayne

English, meaning 'a cartwright'. Famous Waynes include footballer Wayne Rooney, comedian Wayne Brady and rapper Lil Wayne.

Webster

English, meaning 'weaver'.

Weldon

English, meaning 'from the hill of well' or 'hill with a well'.

Wendell

(alt. Wendel)

German, meaning 'a wend'. American novelist and poet Wendell Berry has penned dozens of works throughout his career.

Werner

German, meaning 'army guard'.

Werther

German, meaning 'a soldier in the army'.

Weston

English, meaning 'from the west town'.

Wheeler

English, meaning 'wheel maker'.

Whitley

English, meaning 'white wood'.

Whitman

Old English, meaning 'white man'.

Whitney

Old English, meaning 'white island'. Can be used as a boys' or girls' name.

Wilber
(alt. Wilbur)

Old German, meaning 'bright will'. As one of the Wright brothers, Wilbur helped to invent the first powered aeroplanes.

Wildon

English, meaning 'wooded hill'.

Wiley

Old English, meaning 'beguiling' or 'enchanting'. The stage name of English rapper and songwriter Richard Kylea Cowie.

Wilford

Old English, meaning 'the ford by the willows'.

Wilfred
(alt. Wilfredo, Wilfrid; abbrev. Wilf)

English, meaning 'to will peace'.

Wilhelm

German, meaning 'strong-willed warrior'.

Wilkes
(alt. Wilkie)

Old English, meaning 'strong-willed protector' or 'strong and resolute protector'.

Willem

Dutch, meaning 'strong-willed warrior'.

William
(abbrev. Wil, Will, Willie, Willy, Bill, Billy)

Old German, meaning 'strong-willed warrior'. Famous Williams include Prince William, playwright William Shakespeare and rapper Will.i.am.

Willis

English, meaning 'server of William'.

Willoughby

Old Norse and Old English, meaning 'from the farm by the trees'.

Wilmer

English (Teutonic), meaning 'famously resolute'. Wilmer Eduardo Valderrama is an American actor. Wilmer Allison was a tennis champion in the 1930s.

Wilmot

English, meaning 'resolute mind'.

Wilson

English, meaning 'son of William'. Wilson Pickett was an American R&B, soul and rock 'n' roll singer-songwriter.

Wilton

Old Norse and English, meaning 'from the farm by the brook' or 'from the farm by the streams'. A town in Wiltshire with a history dating back to the eighth century.

Windell

German, meaning 'wanderer' or 'seeker'. Windell Middlebrooks is an American actor.

Windsor

Old English, meaning 'river bank' or 'landing place'.

Winfield

English, meaning 'from the field of Wina'.

Winslow

Old English, meaning 'victory on the hill'.

Winter

Old English, meaning 'to be born in the winter'.

Winthrop

Old English, meaning 'village of friends'.

Winton

Old English, meaning 'a friend's farm'.

Wirrin

Aboriginal, meaning 'a tea tree'.

Wistan

Old English, meaning 'battle stone' or 'mark of the battle'. St Wistan was martyred in AD 840 and has his feast day on 1 June.

Wittan

Old English, meaning 'farm in the woods' or 'farm by the woods'. The Witan were a group of advisers to the king that operated from the seventh to 11th centuries.

Wolf
(alt. Wolfe)
English, meaning 'strong as a wolf'.

Wolfgang

Teutonic, meaning 'the path of wolves'. Wolfgang Amadeus Mozart was one of the most important composers of the classical period.

Wolfrom

Teutonic, meaning 'raven wolf'.

Wolter

Dutch, a form of Walter, meaning 'ruler of the army'. Wolter Kroes is a Dutch singer.

Woodburn

Old English, meaning 'a stream in the woods'.

Woodrow
(abbrev. Woody)
English, meaning 'from the row of houses by the wood'. Woodrow Wilson was the 28th president of the USA. Woody is also the well-known cowboy in *Toy Story*.

Woodward

English, meaning 'guardian of the forest'.

Worcester

Old English, meaning 'from a Roman site'.

Worth

American, meaning 'worth much' or 'wealthy place' or 'wealth and riches'.

Wren

Old English, meaning 'tiny bird'. Often associated with the species of small birds found throughout the world.

Wright

Old English, meaning 'to be a craftsman' or 'from a carpenter'.

Wyatt

Teutonic, meaning 'from wood' or 'from the wide water'. Famous Wyatts include wild-west sheriff Wyatt Earp and comedian Wyatt Cenac.

Wyclef

(alt. Wycleff, Wycliff, Wycliffe)

English, meaning 'inhabitant of the white cliff'. Wyclef Jeanelle Jean is an American-Haitian rapper best known for his role in The Fugees.

Wynn

(alt. Wyn)

Welsh, meaning 'very blessed' or 'the fair blessed one'. Also used in old English to mean 'friend'.

Popular song names

Alfie ('Alfie' – Lily Allen)

Carmen ('Carmen' – Lana Del Ray)

Diana ('Diana' – One Direction)

George ('Oh George' – Foo Fighters)

Maddie ('Alone With You (Maddie's Song)' – Ne Yo)

Mary ('Blind Mary' – Gnarls Barkley)

Simone ('Simone' – Goldfrapp)

Stephen ('Hey Stephen' – Taylor Swift)

Wyatt ('Lullaby for Wyatt' – Sheryl Crow)

Boys' names

Xadrian
American, a combination of X and Adrian, meaning 'from Hadria'.

Xander
Greek, meaning 'defender of the people'. A short form of Alexander.

Xannon
American, meaning 'descendant of an ancient family'.

Xanthus
Greek, meaning 'golden-haired'. One of the horses belonging to Achilles.

Xavier
(alt. Xzaviar)
Spanish, meaning 'the new house'. A name originating from the Catholic saint, Francis Xavier.

Xenon
Greek, meaning 'the guest'. Also one of the noble gases.

Xerxes
Persian, meaning 'ruler of the people' or 'respected king'. A king who attempted to invade the Greek mainland, but failed.

Xeven
Slavic, meaning 'lively'.

Xylander
Greek, meaning 'man of the forest'.

Boys' names

Yaal

Hebrew, meaning 'ascending' or 'one to ascend'.

Yadid

Hebrew, meaning 'the beloved one'.

Yadon

Hebrew, meaning 'against judgment'. Name of one of the many Pokemon characters.

Yahir

Spanish, meaning 'handsome one'. A Mexican singer.

Yaholo

Native American, meaning 'yells'.

Yair

Hebrew, meaning 'the enlightening one' or 'illuminating'.

Yakiya

Hebrew, meaning 'pure' or 'bright'.

Yanis
(alt. Yannis)

Greek, a form of John, meaning 'gift of God'.

Yarden

Hebrew, meaning 'to flow downward'. The Hebrew name Jordan comes from Yarden.

Ye

Chinese, meaning 'bright one' or 'light'.

Yehuda
(alt. Yehudi)

Hebrew, meaning 'to praise and exalt'. Often translated to mean Judah. Judah was a son of Jacob in the Bible.

Yered

Hebrew, a form of Jared, meaning 'descending'.

Yerik
Russian, meaning 'God-appointed one'.

Yerodin
Swahili, meaning 'studious'.

Yervant
Armenian, meaning 'king of people'.

Yitzak
(alt. Yitzaak)
Hebrew, meaning 'laughter' or 'one who laughs'.

Ynyr
Welsh, meaning 'to honour'.

Yobachi
Swahili, meaning 'one who prays to God' or 'prayed to God'.

Yogi
Sanskrit, meaning 'master of oneself'. Popularised by the American cartoon character, Yogi Bear.

Yoloti
Aztec, meaning 'heart'.

Yona
Native American, meaning 'bear'; Hebrew, meaning 'dove'. A name used to refer to ancient people who spoke Greek.

York
Celtic, meaning 'yew tree' or 'from the farm of the yew tree'. Used as a surname by people originating from the city of York.

Yosef
Hebrew form of Joseph, meaning 'Jehovah increases'.

Yuri
Aboriginal, meaning 'to hear'; Japanese, meaning 'one to listen'; Russian, a form of George, meaning 'farmer'. Name of a South Korean pop singer.

Yuuta
Japanese, meaning 'excellent'.

Yves
French, meaning 'miniature archer' or 'small archer'. Yves Saint Laurent was a famous French fashion designer.

Z Boys' names

Zachariah
(alt. Zachary, Zecheriah; abbrev. Zac, Zach)
Hebrew, meaning 'remembered by the Lord' or 'God has remembered'.

Zad
Persian, meaning 'my son'.

Zada
(alt. Zadan, Zadin, Zadun)
Dutch, meaning 'a man who sowed seeds'.

Zadok
Hebrew, meaning 'righteous one'. The priest who anointed Solomon, made famous in Handel's anthem.

Zador
Hungarian, meaning 'violent demeanour'.

Long names
Alexander
Bartholomew
Christopher
Demetrius
Giovanni
Montgomery
Obadiah
Roberto
Salvatore
Zachariah

Zafar
Arabic, meaning 'triumphant'. Zafar Younis is a character from the BBC drama *Spooks*.

Zaid
Swahili, meaning 'increase the growth' or 'growth'.

Zaide
Yiddish, meaning 'the elder ones'. An unfinished opera by Mozart.

Zain
(alt. Zane)
Arabic, meaning 'the handsome son'.

Zaire
Swahili, meaning 'river'. Formerly the name of a country in Africa, now known as Democratic Republic of the Congo.

Zander
Greek, meaning 'defender of my people'.

Zarek
Persian, meaning 'God protect our king'. A Marvel comic book character created by Stan Lee and Gene Colan.

Zoltan
(alt. Zoltin)
Hungarian, meaning 'life'. Zoltan Karpathy is a character from the musical *My Fair Lady*.

Zuma
Arabic, meaning 'peace'.

Part three

Girls' names A–Z

Baby names vary widely in spelling and pronunciation. To simplify
things, this book usually lists each name only once: under the most
common initial and spelling. If a name has an alternative spelling
with a different initial, it may be listed under that letter also.

Girls' names

Abigail
(alt. Abagail, Abbiegayle, Abbigail, Abigale, Abigayle; abbrev. Abbey, Abbi, Abi, Abie)

Hebrew, meaning 'my father's joy'. Found in the Bible. Abbey Clancy is a model and TV presenter. Abi Morgan is a screenwriter of films, including *The Iron Lady* and *Shame*.

Abilene
(alt. Abilee)

Latin and Spanish for 'hazelnut'; Greek meaning 'plain' or 'meadow', it is the name of an ancient area of Syria.

Abina
(alt. Abena)

Akan, meaning 'born on Tuesday'.

Abra
Sanskrit, meaning 'clouds'. Female variation of Abraham.

Abril
Spanish for the month of April.

Acacia
Greek, meaning 'point' or 'thorn'. Also a type of flowering tree and shrub.

Ada
(alt. Adair)

Hebrew, meaning 'adornment'. The mathematician Ada Lovelace is generally considered to be the world's first computer programmer, in the 19th century.

Adalee
Derived from German, meaning 'noble'. Sometimes used as a contraction of Ada and Lee.

Adalia
Hebrew, meaning 'God is my refuge'. Also the name of a type of ladybird.

Addison
(alt. Addisyn, Addyson; abbrev. Addie)

English, meaning 'son of Adam'. Used equally for girls and boys.

Adelaide
(alt. Adelaida; abbrev. Addie)
German, meaning 'noble'. Popular after the rule of William IV and Queen Adelaide of England in the 19th century. Also an Australian city and name of Australian actor Adelaide Kane.

Adele
(alt. Adela, Adelia, Adell, Adella, Adelle; abbrev. Addie)
German, meaning 'noble'. Award-winning singer-songwriter Adele Laurie Blue Adkins is better known as simply 'Adele'.

Adeline
(alt. Adalyn, Adalynn, Adelina, Adelyn)
Variant of Adelaide, meaning 'noble'.

Adeola
(alt. Adeolah, Adeolla)
Nigerian, meaning 'weaver of a crown of honour'.

Aderyn
Welsh, meaning 'bird'. Also the name of several places in Wales.

Adesina
Swahili, meaning 'she paves the way'. Often given to a firstborn daughter in Nigerian communities.

Adia
Variant of Ada, meaning 'adornment'. Usually associated with the song 'Adia'.

Adina
(alt. Adena)
Hebrew, meaning 'high hopes' or 'precious'. Found in the Bible.

Adira
Hebrew, meaning 'noble' or 'powerful'.

Adrienne
(alt. Adrian, Adriana, Adriane, Adrianna, Adrianne)
Feminine form of Adrian, from the Latin, meaning 'from Hadria'.

Aegle
Greek, meaning 'brightness' or 'splendour'. Also the name of several characters in ancient Greek mythology.

Aerin
Name of a character in J.R.R. Tolkien's *Lord of the Rings* trilogy.

Aerith
American, from a character in the computer game *Final Fantasy VII*.

Aero
(alt. Aeron)
Greek, meaning 'flight'.

Aerolynn
Combination of the Greek Aero, meaning 'flight', and the English Lynn, meaning 'waterfall'.

Afia
(alt. Aafia, Aff, Affi)
Arabic, meaning 'a child born on Friday'.

Africa
Celtic, meaning 'pleasant'. Also the name of the continent.

Afsaneh
Persian, meaning 'a fairy tale'.

Afsha
Persian, meaning 'one who sprinkles light'.

Afton
Originally the name of a river in Ayrshire, Scotland, or a town on the Isle of Wight.

Agatha
(abbrev. Aggie)
Greek and Latin, meaning 'good'. St Agatha was a third-century Christian saint, patron saint of fire, earthquakes and bells, among other things. Crime writer Agatha Christie is the world's best-selling novelist.

Aglaia
(alt. Aglaya, Aglaja)
Greek, meaning 'brilliance'. In Greek mythology, one of the Three Graces. Also the name of a kind of mahogany tree, an opera, an 18th-century British ship and a saint.

Agnes
Greek, meaning 'virginal' or 'pure'. St Agnes of Rome is the patron saint of chastity and girls, among other things.

Agrippina
Latin, meaning 'born feet first'. The name of several influential women of ancient Rome.

Aida
Arabic, meaning 'reward' or 'present'. Also the name of an opera by Giuseppe Verdi.

Aidanne
(alt. Aden, Aidan, Aidanne, Aiden, Aidenne)
Feminine form of Aidan, from the Gaelic, meaning 'fire'.

Ailbhe
Irish, meaning 'noble' or 'bright'. Has also been used as a boys' name.

Aileen
(alt. Aelinn, Aleen, Aline, Alline, Eileen)
Gaelic variant of Helen, meaning 'light'. Aileen Cust was the first female veterinarian in Great Britain.

Ailith
(alt. Ailish)
Old English, meaning 'seasoned warrior'. Rare since the Middle Ages.

Ailsa
Scottish, meaning 'pledge from God'. Also the name of a Scottish island, Ailsa Craig.

Aimee
(alt. Aimie, Amie)
French form of Amy, meaning 'beloved'. Famous Aimees include actor Aimee Garcia and singer Aimee Mann.

Aina

Scandinavian, meaning 'forever'.

Aine

(alt. Aino)

Celtic, meaning 'happiness'. Aine was a Celtic goddess of summer and prosperity.

Ainsley

(alt. Ansley)

Old English, meaning 'meadow' or 'clearing'. Also variant of an old Scottish last name used as a first name. Both a girls' and a boys' name. Ainsley Hayes was a leading character in TV hit *The West Wing*.

Aisha

(alt. Aeysha, Aysha)

Arabic, meaning 'woman'; Swahili, meaning 'life'. Aisha was one of the prophet Muhammad's wives.

Aishwarya

Variant of the Arabic Aisha, meaning 'woman'. Actor Aishwarya Rai Bachchan is one of the most recognisable Bollywood stars.

Aislinn

(alt. Aislin, Aisling, Aislyn, Alene, Allene)

Irish Gaelic, meaning 'dream'.

Aiyanna

(alt. Aiyana)

Native American, meaning 'forever flowering'.

Aja

Hindi, meaning 'goat'. Also Scandinavian.

Aka

(alt. Akah, Akkah)

Maori, meaning 'loving one' or 'affectionate'.

Akela

(alt. Akilah)

Hawaiian, meaning 'noble'. Also the wolf pack leader Akela in Rudyard Kipling's *The Jungle Book*.

Akilina

Greek or Russian, meaning 'eagle'.

Akiva

Hebrew, meaning 'protect and shelter'.

Alaina

(alt. Alane, Alani, Alayna, Aleena)

Feminine form of Alan, from the Gaelic for 'rock'. Also used as a spelling alternative to Eleanor.

Alana

(alt. Alanna, Alannah)

Gaelic, meaning 'beauty'; Hawaiian, meaning 'beautiful offering'; Old German, meaning 'precious'.

Alanis

(alt. Alarice)

Variant of Alaina, meaning 'rock'. Canadian-American Alanis Morissette is a multi-award-winning singer.

Alba

Latin, meaning 'white'. Also the Gaelic word for Scotland. Name of the central character in the novel *The Time Traveller's Wife*.

Alberta

(alt. Albertha, Albertine)

Feminine of Albert, from the Old German for 'noble, bright, famous'. Also the name of a province in Canada.

Albina

Latin, meaning 'white' or 'fair'. Also the name of an Etruscan goddess of the dawn.

Alda

German, meaning 'old' or 'prosperous'. St Alda was an Italian mystic in the 11th century, who took care of the sick.

Aldis

English, meaning 'battle-seasoned'. Used most commonly for boys but also for girls.

Aleah

Arabic, meaning 'high'; also Persian, meaning 'one of God's beings'. Often used as a spelling alternative for Aliyah.

Alesha

(alt. Alisha, Alysha)

Variant of Alice, meaning 'nobility'. Alesha Dixon is a British singer, dancer, model and TV presenter.

Aleta

(alt. Aletha)

Greek, meaning 'footloose'. Usually associated with the character of Queen Aleta Ellis in the comic strip *The Legend of Prince Valiant*.

Alethea

(alt. Aletheia)

Greek, meaning 'truth'. The first use of this name was in the 17th century.

Alexandra

(alt. Alejandra, Alejhandra, Aleksandra, Alessandra, Alexandria; abbrev. Alex, Alexa, Alexi, Alexia, Alexina)

Feminine form of Alexander, meaning 'defender of mankind'. Also one of the names of the ancient Greek goddess Hera.

Alexis

(alt. Alexus, Alexys)

Greek, meaning 'helper'. Alexis was also an ancient Greek comic poet and an ancient Greek sculptor.

Aleydis

Variant of Alice, meaning 'noble' or 'nobility'. Also an alternative name for St Alice of Scharbeek, patron saint of the blind and paralysed.

Alfreda

(alt. Alfre)

Feminine form of Alfred, from Old English, meaning 'elf' or 'magical counsel'. Alfreda Benge is a lyricist and illustrator and Alfreda Hodgson is a singer.

Ali
(alt. Allie, Ally)

Shortened version of Alexandra, Aliyah, Alison or Alice, as well as a name in its own right.

Alibeth

Variant of Elizabeth, meaning 'consecrated to God'. More commonly used in the Middle Ages.

Alice
(alt. Alicia, Alize, Alyce, Alys, Alyse)

English, meaning 'noble' or 'nobility'. Usually associated with *Alice in Wonderland* by Lewis Carroll. Famous Alicias include singer Alicia Keys and actor Alicia Silverstone. Also the birth name of actor Jodie Foster.

Alida
(alt. Aleida)

Latin, meaning 'small winged one'. More commonly used in Dutch-speaking communities.

Alienor
(alt. Aliana)

Variant of Eleanor, from the Greek for 'light'. Also a spelling variation used by Queen Eleanor of Aquitaine in the 12th century.

Aliki
(alt. Alika)

Variant of Alice, meaning 'noble' or 'nobility'. Actor Aliki Vougiouklaki was considered to be one of Greece's greatest actors of the 20th century.

Alima

Arabic, meaning 'cultured'.

Alina
(alt. Alena)

Variation of Helen, meaning 'light'. More commonly used in Brazil, France, Italy, and Spain.

Alison
(alt. Allison, Allisyn, Allyson, Alyson)

Variant of Alice, meaning 'noble' or 'nobility'. Originally the name was Alis in the Middle Ages, with the suffix 'on', which means 'little'.

Alivia

Variant of Olivia, meaning 'olive tree'. More commonly used in the USA.

Aliya
(alt. Aaliyah, Aleah, Alia, Aliah, Aliyah)

Arabic, meaning 'exalted' or 'sublime'.

Alla

Variant of Ella or Alexandra.

Allegra

Italian, meaning 'joyous'. Allegra Byron was the lovechild of the poet Lord Byron. Allegra Versace is the heiress to the Versace fashion empire.

Allura

French, from the word for entice, meaning 'the power of attraction'.

Allyn

Feminine form of Alan, meaning 'rock'.

Alma

Three possible origins: from Latin meaning 'giving nurture', or Italian meaning 'soul' or Arabic meaning 'learned'.

Almeda

(alt. Almeta)

Latin, meaning 'ambitious'. Also the name of a district in Barcelona, Spain.

Almera

(alt. Almira)

Feminine of Elmer, from the Arabic for 'aristocratic' and the Old English for 'noble'.

Alohi

Variant of the Hawaiian greeting Aloha, meaning 'love and affection'. More commonly used in the USA.

Alona

(alt. Alora)

Hebrew, meaning 'oak tree'.

Alpha

The first letter of the Greek alphabet, usually given to a first-born daughter.

Alta

Latin, meaning 'elevated'. Also the name of many towns throughout Europe and the USA.

Altagracia

Spanish, meaning 'grace'. Alta Gracia is also the name of a city in Argentina.

Althaea

(alt. Altea, Altha, Althea)

Greek, meaning 'healing power'. Althaea was a prominent character in Greek mythology.

Alva

Spanish, meaning 'blonde' or 'fair skinned'. In Norway and Sweden it is considered the feminine form of Alf, which means 'elf'.

Alvena

(alt. Alvina)

Old English, meaning 'elf friend'. In Old German, it is considered the feminine form of Adelwin, which means 'noble friend'.

Alvia

(alt. Alyvia)

Variant of Olivia, meaning 'olive tree'; also variant of Elvira, from the ancient Spanish city.

Alyssa

(alt. Alisa, Alissa, Allyssa, Alysa)

Greek, meaning 'rational'. Usually associated with the flower alyssum.

Amabel

Variant of Annabel, meaning 'grace and beauty'.

Amadea

Feminine form of Amadeus, meaning 'love God'. More commonly used in German-speaking communities.

Amal

Arabic, meaning 'hope and aspiration'.

Amalia

Hebrew, meaning 'labour of love'; German, meaning 'work'.

Amana

Hebrew, meaning 'loyal and true'. Also the name of a type of tulip.

Amanda

(alt. Amandine)

Latin, meaning 'much loved'. Famous Amandas include presenter and actor Amanda Holden, and actors Amanda Bynes and Amanda Seyfried.

Amara

(alt. Amani)

Greek, meaning 'lovely forever'. Actor Amara Miller is known for her role in the film *The Descendants*.

Amarantha

Contraction of Amanda and Samantha, meaning 'much loved listener'. Also associated with the amaranth plant.

Amari

(alt. Amaris, Amasa, Amata, Amaya)

Hebrew, meaning 'pledged by God'. Also the name of a province in Greece.

Amaryllis

(alt. Ameris)

Greek, meaning 'fresh'. Usually associated with the flowering plant.

Amber

French, from the word for the semi-precious stone of the same name. Famous Ambers include actors Amber Heard and Amber Benson.

Amberly

Contraction of Amber and Leigh, meaning 'stone' and 'meadow'.

Amboree

(alt. Amber, Ambree)

American, meaning 'precocious'. More commonly used in the USA.

Amelia

(alt. Aemilia, Amalie, Amelie)

Greek, meaning 'industrious'. Famous Amelias include flying legend Amelia Earhart, and two 18th-century British princesses.

America

From the country of the same name. Actor America Ferrera is known for her roles in *Ugly Betty* and *How to Train Your Dragon*.

Amethyst

Greek, from the word for the precious stone of the same name.

Amina

(alt. Aamina)

Arabic, meaning 'honest and trustworthy'. Also the name of an influential Nigerian princess in the 17th century. Aamina Sheik is a Pakistani–American actor and model.

Amira
(alt. Amiya, Amiyah)
Arabic, meaning 'a high-born girl';
Hebrew, meaning 'rich princess'.

Amity
Latin, meaning 'friendship and
harmony'. Also a name of a faction
in the novel *Divergent*.

Amory
Variant of the Spanish name Amor,
meaning 'love'. Also used as a boys'
(more commonly) and girls' name
in America during the late 1800s to
early 1900s, probably then derived
from the French Ameury.

Amy
*(alt. Aimee, Amee, Ami, Amie,
Ammie, Amya)*
Latin, meaning 'beloved'. Famous
Amys include actor Amy Adams,
Winter Olympic skeleton gold
medallist Amy Williams and singer
Amy Winehouse.

Anafa
Hebrew, meaning 'heron'.

Anaïs
Persian, meaning 'love'.

Ananda
Hindi, meaning 'bliss'. Also the name
of one of the Buddha's disciples.

Anastasia
(alt. Athanasia)
Greek, meaning 'resurrection'.
The Grand Duchess Anastasia of
Russia, was killed in the Bolshevik
Revolution of 1917.

Anat
Jewish, meaning 'water spring'.
Name of a Semitic goddess.

Anatolia
Greek, meaning 'east sunrise'. The
name of a large area within Turkey.
Also a Christian saint.

Andrea
(alt. Andreia, Andria, Andrina)
Feminine form of Andrew, from the
Greek term for 'a man's woman'.
Famous Andreas include singer
Andrea Corr and writers Andrea Levy
and Andrea Dworkin.

Andromeda
Greek, meaning 'leader of men'.
From the heroine of an ancient
Greek legend.

Anemone
Greek, meaning 'breath'. Also the
name of a type of flowering plant.

Angela
*(alt. Angel, Angeles, Angelia, Angelle;
abbrev. Angie)*
Greek, meaning 'messenger from
God' or 'angel'. Famous Angelas
include actor Angela Lansbury and
German Chancellor Angela Merkel.

Angelica
*(alt. Angelina, Angeline, Angelique,
Angelise, Angelita, Anjelica, Anjelina)*
Latin, meaning 'angelic'. Famous
Angelicas include actor Anjelica
Huston and *Rugrats* cartoon
character Angelica Pickle.

Angelina
(alt. Anjelina)

Derived from Angela, meaning 'messenger from God' or 'angel'. Famous Angelinas include actor Angelina Jolie and book and TV mouse Angelina Ballerina.

Anise
(alt. Anisa, Anissa)

French, from the liquorice-flavoured plant of the same name. Feminine form of Anis, a boys' name common in Tunisia and Morocco.

Anita
(alt. Anitra)

Variant of Ann, meaning 'grace'. Famous Anitas include actor Anita Dobson, *Body Shop* founder Anita Roddick and singer Anita Baker.

Anna
(alt. Ana, Anne)

Derived from Hannah, which is Hebrew, meaning 'grace'. Taken from the name of Anna the prophetess in the Bible. Anna Maxwell Martin is a BAFTA award-winning English actor.

Annabel
(alt. Anabel, Anabelle, Annabell, Annabella, Annabelle)

Contraction of Anna and Belle, meaning 'grace' and 'beauty'.

Annalise
(alt. Annalee, Annaliese, Annalisa, Anneli, Annelie, Annelies, Annelise)

Combination of Anna and Lise, meaning 'grace' and 'pledged to God'. More commonly used in the USA and parts of Scandinavia.

Anne
(alt. Ann, Annie)

Derived from Hannah, meaning 'grace'. Famous Annes include actor Anne Hathaway and two wives of Henry VIII, Anne Boleyn and Anne of Cleeves.

Annemarie
(alt. Annamae, Annamarie, Annelle, Annmarie, Anne-Marie)

Combination of Anne and Mary, meaning 'grace' and 'star of the sea'. Actor Anne-Marie Duff is known for her roles in *Shameless* and *The Virgin Queen*.

Annette
(alt. Annetta)

Derived from Hannah, which is Hebrew, meaning 'grace'. Famous Annettes include actors Annette Bening, Annette Crosby and Annette Funicello.

Annis

Greek, meaning 'finished or completed'. May also be a variant of Agnes. In English mythology the Black Annis is a blue-faced witch who eats children.

Annora

Latin, meaning 'honour'. More commonly used in Eastern European communities.

Anoushka
(alt. Anousha, Anushka)

Variant of Anne, meaning 'grace'. Most popular in Russia, Greece and India.

Anthea
(alt. Anthi)

Greek, meaning 'flower-like'. Famous Antheas include presenters Anthea Turner and Anthea Redfern, and director Anthea Benton.

Antigone

In ancient Greek mythology, Antigone was the daughter of Oedipus.

Antoinette
(alt. Antonetta, Antonette, Antonietta)

Both a variation of Ann and the feminine form of Anthony, meaning 'invaluable grace'. Usually associated with 18th-century French queen consort Marie Antoinette. Often shortened to Toni.

Antonia
(alt. Antonella, Antonina)

Latin, meaning 'invaluable'. Also the name of dozens of influential ancient Roman women.

Anwen

Welsh, meaning 'very fair'. Usually associated with the character of Anwen Williams in the TV series *Torchwood*.

Anya
(alt. Aanya, Aniya, Aniyah, Aniylah, Anja)

Russian, meaning 'favour' or 'grace'; Sanskrit, meaning 'the inexhaustible'. Anya Hindmarch is known for designing fashion accessories.

Aoife

Gaelic, meaning 'beautiful joy'. Usually associated with the goddess Esuvia.

Apollonia

Feminine form of Apollo, the Greek god of the sun. St Apollonia was a virgin martyr in the third century and is the patron saint of dentistry.

Apple

From the name of the fruit. Famous Apples include the technology company Apple Inc, and Gwyneth Paltrow's daughter.

April
(alt. Avril)

Latin, meaning 'opening up'. Also the name of the month, which has associations with the goddess Venus.

Aquilina
(alt. Aqua, Aquila)

Spanish, meaning 'like an eagle'. St Aquilina was a child martyr in the third century.

Ara

Arabic, meaning 'brings rain'. Also the name of a star constellation. Used as both a girls' and a boys' name.

Arabella

Latin, meaning 'answered prayer'. Also the name of an opera by Richard Strauss.

Araceli
(alt. Aracely)

Spanish, meaning 'altar of Heaven'.

Araminta
(abbrev. Minnie, Minty)
Hebrew, meaning 'lofty'.

Araylia
(alt. Araelea)
Latin, meaning 'golden'. Associated with aralia, a genus of trees and shrubs.

Arcadia
(alt. Acadia)
Greek, meaning 'paradise'. Also the name of a daughter of the ancient Roman Emperor Arcadius. Acadia was a French colony in what is now Canada.

Ardelle
(alt. Ardell, Ardella)
Latin, meaning 'burning with enthusiasm'. Ardelle Kloss was an early leading American ice skater.

Arden
(alt. Ardis, Ardith)
Latin, meaning 'burning with enthusiasm'.

Arella
(alt. Areli, Arely)
Hebrew, meaning 'angel'. More commonly used in the USA.

Aretha
Greek, meaning 'woman of virtue'. Aretha Franklin was an awrd-winning soul singer.

Aria
(alt. Ariah)
Hebrew, meaning 'lioness', and Italian, meaning 'melody'.

Ariadne
Greek and Latin, meaning 'the very holy one'. In ancient Greek mythology, Ariadne was the daughter of King Minos.

Ariana
(alt. Aaryanna, Ariane, Arianna, Arianne, Arienne)
Derived from the Welsh word for 'silver'. Also the name of a large geographical area in ancient Greek times, covering most of modern-day Afghanistan. Ariana Grande is a popular singer and actor.

Ariel
(alt. Ariela, Ariella, Arielle)
Hebrew, meaning 'lioness of God'. Character in Disney's *The Little Mermaid*.

Arlene
(alt. Arleen, Arlie, Arline, Arly)
Gaelic, meaning 'pledge'. Arlene Phillips is known for her appearances on *Strictly Come Dancing* and *So You Think You Can Dance*, as well as her work as a choreographer.

Armida
Latin, meaning 'little armed one'. Taken from the character of Armida in the epic poem *La Gerusalemme liberata*.

Artemisia
(alt. Artemis; abbrev. Artie, Arti)

Greek and Spanish, meaning 'perfect'. Also the name of a legendary female naval commander in Persia during the fifth century.

Arwen
Welsh, meaning 'fair' or 'fine'. Also an Elven character in J.R.R. Tolkien's *Lord of the Rings* trilogy.

Arya
Fictional brave tomboy character from George R.R. Martin's *A Song of Ice and Fire* series of novels and TV series *Game of Thrones*.

Ashanti
From the geographical area in Ghana, Africa. Singer Ashanti Shequoiya Douglas is better known as just 'Ashanti'.

Ashby
English, meaning 'ash tree farm'.

Ashley
(alt. Ashely, Ashlee, Ashleigh, Ashli, Ashlie, Ashly)

English, meaning 'ash tree meadow'. Also a boys' name. Famous female Ashleys include actors Ashley Jensen and Ashley Judd, and singer Ashley Roberts.

Ashlynn
(alt. Ashlyn)

Irish Gaelic, meaning 'dream'. Also a spelling variation for Aislinn.

Ashton
(alt. Ashtyn)

Old English, meaning 'ash tree town'. Used as a girls' and boys' name, but most commonly for boys.

Asia
From the name of the continent. Also a name for an Oceanid in ancient Greek mythology.

Asma
(alt. Aasmah, Asmara)

Arabic, meaning 'high-standing'. Aasmah Mir is a BBC TV presenter and radio journalist. Asmara is the capital city of Eritrea.

Aspen
(alt. Aspynn)

From the name of the tree. Also the name of a city in the US state of Colorado.

Assumpta
(alt. Asumpta, Assunta)

Irish, meaning 'assumption'; Italian, meaning 'raised up'. Assumpta Serna is a Spanish actor. Several Irish actors have this given name.

Asta
(alt. Asteria, Astor, Astoria)

Greek or Latin, meaning 'star-like'. Also the name of a type of moth.

Astrid
Old Norse, meaning 'beautiful like a God'. Swedish uthor Astrid Lundgren is known for her children's novels such as *Pippi Longstocking*.

Atara

Hebrew, meaning 'diadem' or 'crown'. Also the name of a type of butterfly.

Athena
(alt. Athenais)

Greek, meaning 'wise'. From the ancient Greek goddess of wisdom, mathematics and arts and crafts.

Aubrey
(alt. Aubree, Aubriana, Aubrie)

French, meaning 'elf ruler'. Originally a name for boys, it is now far more common for girls.

Audrey
(alt. Audra, Audrie, Audry, Autry, Audrina)

English, meaning 'noble strength'. St Etheldreda was known as St Audrey, and was an English princess in the seventh century. Famous Audreys include actors Audrey Hepburn and Audrey Tautou.

Augusta
(alt. August, Augustine)

Feminine form of the Ancient Roman name Augustus, which is Latin, meaning 'venerated'.

Aura
(alt. Aurea)

Greek or Latin, meaning either 'soft breeze' or 'gold'.

Aurelia
(alt. Aurelie)

Latin, meaning 'gold'. The name of various Ancient Roman women, including Julius Caesar's mother.

Aurora
(alt. Aurore)

Latin, meaning 'dawn'. In ancient Roman mythology, Aurora was the goddess of sunrise.

Austine
(alt. Austen, Austin)

Feminine form of Austin, which is Latin, meaning 'venerated'.

Autumn

Latin, from the name of the harvest season. Canadian-born Autumn Phillips is granddaughter-in-law to Queen Elizabeth II.

Ava
(alt. Avah, Avia, Avie)

Latin, meaning 'like a bird'. Ava Gardner was an iconic American actor during the 1950s to 1970s.

Avalon
(alt. Avalyn, Aveline)

Celtic, meaning 'island of apples'. The name comes from a mythological island in the legend of King Arthur.

Axelle

Greek, meaning 'father of peace'. More commonly used in French- and Flemish-speaking communities.

Aya
(alt. Ayah)
Hebrew, meaning 'bird'.

Ayanna
(alt. Ayana)
Swahili, meaning 'beautiful flower'.

Azalea
(alt. Azalia)
Latin, meaning 'dry earth'. Also the name of a type of flowering shrub. Often associated with Australian singer Iggy Azalea.

Aziza
Hebrew, meaning 'mighty', or Arabic, meaning 'precious'.

Azure
(alt. Azaria)
French, meaning 'sky-blue'.

Girls' names

Babette

French version of Barbara, from the Greek word meaning 'foreign'. Babette Cole is an author of children's books.

Badia
(alt. Badiyn, Badea)

Arabic, meaning 'elegant'.

Bailey
(alt. Baeli, Bailee)

English, meaning 'law enforcer'. Used as a girls' and boys' name, but more commonly for boys in recent years.

Bambi

Shortened version of the Italian Bambina, meaning 'child'. Usually associated with the cartoon Disney character.

Barbara
(alt. Barbra; abbrev. Barb, Barbie)

Greek, meaning 'foreign'. Famous Barbaras include actor Barbara Windsor, singer Barbra Streisand and Barbara McClintock, who won a Nobel Prize for genetics.

Basma

Arabic, meaning 'smile'.

Bathsheba

Hebrew, meaning 'daughter of the oath'. Usually associated with the story of Bathsheba and King David in the Bible. Also a character in the novel *Far From the Madding Crowd*.

Bay
(alt. Baya, Bae)

From the bay tree, or the indentation in a coastline (e.g. Byron Bay). More commonly used for boys.

Beata

Latin, meaning 'blessed'. Can be used as a shortened form of Beatrice or as a name in its own right.

Beatrice

(alt. Beatrix, Beatriz, Bellatrix, Betrys)

Latin, meaning 'blessed' or 'voyager'. A recent rapid riser in the Top Names list. Famous Beatrices include children's book author Beatrix Potter and Princess Beatrice, granddaughter of Queen Elizabeth II.

Becky

(alt. Becca, Beccie, Beccy, Beckie)

Shortened form of Rebecca, meaning 'joined', used as a name in its own right.

Belinda

(alt. Belen, Belina)

Contraction of Belle and Linda, meaning 'beautiful'. Famous Belindas include singer Belinda Carlisle and actor Belinda Stewart-Wilson.

Bella

(alt. Belle)

Latin, meaning 'beautiful'. Usually associated with the character of Isabella (Bella) Swan from the *Twilight* series or Belle from Disney's film *Beauty and the Beast*.

Belva

Latin, meaning 'beautiful view'. The inspiration for one of the characters in the musical *Chicago* was real-life murderer Belva Gaertner.

Movie inspirations

Bella (*Twilight*)

Elsa (*Frozen*)

Fiona (*Shrek*)

Holly (*Breakfast at Tiffany's*)

Lara (*Tomb Raider*)

Maria (*The Sound of Music*)

Marla (*Fight Club*)

Mary (*Mary Poppins*)

Nina (*Black Swan*)

Pandora (*Avatar*)

Rey (*Star Wars*)

Trinity (*The Matrix*)

Bénédicta

(abbrev. Bennie, Benny)

Feminine form of Benedict, which is Latin, meaning 'blessed'. Benedicta Henrietta of the Palatinate is a common ancestor of many present-day monarchs.

Benita

(alt. Bernita)

Spanish, meaning 'blessed'.

Berit

(alt. Beret)

Scandinavian, meaning 'splendid' or 'gorgeous'.

Bernadette
(alt. Bernadine; abbrev. Bernie)
French, meaning 'courageous'. St Bernadette was known for her visions of the Virgin Mary.

Bernice
(alt. Berenice, Berniece, Burnice)
Greek, meaning 'she who brings victory'. The name of Herod's daughter in the Bible.

Bertha
(alt. Berta, Berthe, Bertie)
German, meaning 'bright'. There are four saints called Bertha, all from the early Middle Ages.

Beryl
Greek, meaning 'pale green gemstone'. Beryl Reid was a classic British actor and Beryl Cook was a 20th-century English artist.

Bess
(alt. Bessie)
Shortened form of Elizabeth, meaning 'consecrated to God'. Queen Elizabeth I has the nickname Good Queen Bess. Bessie Smith was a blues singer.

Beth
Hebrew, meaning 'house'. Also shortened form of Elizabeth, meaning 'consecrated to God'.

Bethany
(alt. Bethan)
Hebrew, referring to a geographical location found in the Bible. The name has seen a return to popularity in recent years.

Bethel
Hebrew, meaning 'house of God'. Also the name of a city in the Bible.

Bettina
Spanish or German version of Elizabeth, meaning 'consecrated to God'.

Betty
(alt. Betsy, Bette, Bettie, Bettye)
Shortened version of Elizabeth, meaning 'consecrated to God', also used in its own right. Famous Bettys include cartoon character Betty Boop and actor Betty White.

Beulah
Hebrew, meaning 'married'. Also the name for a place that exists between Earth and Heaven.

Beverly
(alt. Beverlee, Beverley)
English, meaning 'beaver stream'. Beverley Knight is a British soul singer, actor and TV personality.

Bevin
Celtic, meaning 'fair lady'.

Beyoncé

Modern American, from the singer. Beyoncé's name was created by her parents as a tribute to her mother's maiden name, which was Beyince. However, some sources say the name is Swahili, meaning 'beyond others'.

Bianca
(alt. Blanca)

Italian, meaning 'white'. Famous Biancas include activist Bianca Jagger, model Bianca Gascoigne, the character of Bianca from Shakespeare's *Othello* and the long-running *EastEnders* character of that name.

Bibiana

Greek, meaning 'alive'. St Bibiana was a Roman virgin and martyr during the fourth century.

Bijou

French, meaning 'jewel'.

Billie
(alt. Bill, Billy, Billye)

Shortened version of Wilhelmina, meaning 'determined' as well as a name in its own right. Billie Holiday was an iconic jazz singer. Billie Piper is a singer turned actor.

Bina

Hebrew, meaning 'knowledge'.

Birdie
(alt. Birdy)

English and Swedish, meaning 'little bird'.

Birgit
(alt. Birgitta)

German, meaning 'power and strength'. Used as a variation of Bridget.

Blaer

Icelandic, meaning 'light breeze'.

Blair

Scottish Gaelic, meaning 'flat, plain area'. Blair Waldorf is the main character in *Gossip Girl*, the novel series, TV series and film.

Blaise

French, meaning 'lisp' or 'stutter'. Also common as a boys' name.

Blake
(alt. Blakely, Blakelyn)

Old English, meaning 'dark, black'. More commonly used as a boys' name. Actor Blake Lively is best known for her role in the TV series *Gossip Girl*.

Blanche
(alt. Blanch)

French, meaning 'white or pale'. Extremely common in the Middle Ages, Blanche saw an increase in popularity before World War II, but hasn't been widely used since then.

Blodwen

Welsh, meaning 'white flower'.

Blossom

English, meaning 'flower-like'.

Blythe
(alt. Blithe, Bly)

English, meaning 'happy and carefree'. Actor Blythe Danner is known for her roles in *Will & Grace*, *Meet the Parents*, and for being the mother of Gwyneth Paltrow.

Bobbi
(alt. Bobbie, Bobby)

Shortened version of Roberta, meaning 'bright fame', as well as a name in its own right. Usually associated with the cosmetics brand Bobbi Brown.

Bonamy
(alt. Bomani, Bonamia, Bonamea)

Derived from French, meaning 'close friend'.

Bonita

Spanish, meaning 'pretty'.

Bonnie
(alt. Bonny)

Scottish, meaning 'fair of face'. Actor Bonnie Langford was a child star who grew up to appear in West End musicals and *Dr Who*.

Brandy
(alt. Brandee, Brandi, Brandie)

From the name of the liquor created by distilling wine. Singer Brandy is known for her various pop songs as well as her role in *Moesha*.

Branwen

Welsh, meaning 'a white crow'.

Brea
(alt. Bree, Bria)

Shortened form of Brianna, meaning 'strong', but used in its own right. Also the name of a god in ancient Irish mythology.

Brenda

Old Norse, meaning 'sword'. Can also be used as a feminine form of Brendan.

Brianna
(alt. Breana, Breanna, Breanne)

Irish Gaelic, meaning 'strong'. More commonly used in the USA.

Bridget
(alt. Bridgett, Bridgette, Brigette, Brigid, Brigitta, Brigitte)

Irish Gaelic, meaning 'strength and power'. Famous Bridgets include actor Bridget Fonda, Brigitte Bardot, Brigitte Nielsen and the protagonist in the novel *Bridget Jones's Diary* by Helen Fielding.

Brier
(alt. Briar)

French, meaning 'heather'.

Brit
(alt. Britt, Britta)

Celtic, meaning 'spotted' or 'freckled'. Usually a shortened form of Brittany, though it can be used in its own right. Actors Britt Ekland and Britt Robertson are both Brittanys.

Britannia

Latin, meaning 'Britain'. Britannia is the female personification of Great Britain.

Brittany

(alt. Britany, Britney, Britni, Brittani, Brittanie, Brittney, Brittni, Brittny)

Latin, meaning 'from England', though the name also refers to a region of France. Famous Brittanys include actor Brittany Murphy and singer Britney Spears.

Brontë

Greek, meaning 'the sound of thunder'.

Bronwen

(alt. Bronwyn)

Welsh, meaning 'fair breast'. In Wales it is more common to give the spelling Bronwen to girls and Bronwyn to boys.

Brooke

(alt. Brook)

English, meaning 'small stream'. Brooke Shields is an American actor and model and Brooke Vincent is a British TV actor.

Brooklyn

(alt. Brooklynn)

From the name of a New York borough. More commonly used as a boys' name.

Brunhilda

(alt. Brunhilde, Brynhildr)

German, meaning 'armour-wearing fighting maid'. Brynhildr, from which Brunhilda and Brunhilde orginated, was an important character in Old German mythology.

Bryn

(alt. Brynn)

Welsh, meaning 'mount' or 'hill'. Used more commonly as a boys' name.

Bryony

(alt. Briony)

English, from the name of bryonia, a European vine. Bryony Hannah is an Olivier-nominated British actor and star of *Call the Midwife*.

Buffy

A shortened form of Elizabeth, meaning 'consecrated to God'. Usually associated with the protagonist of the sci-fi series *Buffy the Vampire Slayer*.

C

Girls' names

Cadence
Feminine form of Caden, from Latin, meaning 'with rhythm'

Cadew
Derived from French, meaning 'gift'; English, meaning 'coarse woollen fabric'.

Cai
Vietnamese, meaning 'feminine'.

Caitlin
(alt. Cadyn, Caitlann, Caitlyn, Caitlynn, Katelin, Katelyn, Katelynn, Katlin, Katlyn)
Greek, meaning 'pure'. Caitlin Moran is a British broadcaster, newspaper columnist and author.

Calandra
Greek, meaning 'lark'. The calandra lark is a small bird found in Mediterranean countries. Calandra is also the name of an asteroid belt.

Calantha
(alt. Calanthe)
Greek, meaning 'lovely flower'. Also refers to dozens of flowering shrubs.

Caledonia
Latin, meaning 'from Scotland'. Also an old name for Scotland.

Calia
American, meaning 'renowned beauty'. Also refers to several species of shrubs and trees.

Calista
(alt. Callista, Callisto, Kallista)
Greek, meaning 'most beautiful'. Actor Calista Flockhart is known for her roles in Ally McBeal and Brothers and Sisters.

Calla
Greek, meaning 'beautiful'. Also refers to a type of white-flowered plant.

Callie
(alt. Caleigh, Cali, Calleigh, Cally)
Greek, meaning 'beauty'. Can also be a derivative of Carol, Caroline or Carolyn, as in screen-writer Callie Khouri, who is known for *Thelma & Louise* and *Nashville*.

Calliope
Greek, meaning 'beautiful voice'. From the muse of epic poetry in ancient Greek mythology.

Camas
Native American, from the root and bulb of the same name.

Cambria
Welsh, from the alternative name for Wales.

Camden
(alt. Camdin, Camdyn)
English, meaning 'winding valley'. More popular as a boys' name.

Cameo
Italian, meaning 'skin'. A cameo in the acting world usually refers to a small part played by a big star.

Cameron
(alt. Camryn, Kameron, Kamron)
Scottish Gaelic, meaning 'bent nose'. More often used as a boys' name but also occasionally for girls, as with actor Cameron Diaz.

Camilla
(alt. Camille, Camelia, Camellia, Camila, Camillia)
Latin, meaning 'spiritual serving girl'. Camilla, Duchess of Cornwall, is married to Prince Charles. The French form, Camille, is often also used for boys.

Candace
(alt. Candice, Candis, Kandice; abbrev. Candy, Candi, Kandy, Kandi)
Latin, meaning 'brilliant white'. In the African ancient kingdom of Kush, Candace was the title given to queens and queen mothers.

Candida
Latin, meaning 'white', associated with purity and salvation. Unfortunately, also the name of a fungal infection.

Candra
Latin, meaning 'glowing'. The Candra family dynasty ruled eastern Bengal in the 10th century. Also the name of an immmortal villainess in Marvel comics.

Canei
Greek, meaning 'pure'. Also refers to a type of shrub.

Caoimhe
Celtic, meaning 'gentle' or 'precious'. Can be pronounced as 'kyva' or 'keeva', depending on where in Ireland it is used.

Caprice

Italian, meaning 'ruled by whim'. Caprice Bourret is a model best known simply as 'Caprice'.

Cara

Latin, meaning 'darling'. Cara Delevingne is a top model.

Caren
(alt. Carin, Caron, Caryn)

Greek, meaning 'pure'. Comedian Whoopi Goldberg's real name is Caryn Elaine Johnson.

Carey
(alt. Cari, Carie, Carrey, Carri, Carrie, Cary)

Gaelic, meaning 'love'. Carey Mulligan is an English actor. Can also be used for boys.

Carina
(alt. Corina)

Italian, meaning 'dearest little one'. Also the name of a star constellation.

Carissa
(alt. Carisa)

Greek, meaning 'grace'. Also the name of a type of shrub.

Carla
(alt. Charla)

Feminine of the Old Norse Carl, meaning 'free man'. Singer Carla Bruni Sarkozy is married to the former president of France Nicolas Sarkozy.

Carlin
(alt. Carleen, Carlene)

Gaelic, meaning 'little champion'.

Carlotta
(alt. Carlota)

Italian form of Charlotte, meaning 'little and feminine'. Also the name of a character in The Phantom of the Opera.

Carly
(alt. Carlee, Carley, Carli, Carlie, Karlie, Karly)

Feminine form of Charles, from the German meaning 'free man'. Famous Carlys include singers Carly Simon and Carly Rae Jepson, and model Karlie Kloss.

Carmel
(alt. Carmela, Carmelita, Carmella)

Hebrew, meaning 'God's vineyard'. Mount Carmel is a place mentioned in the Bible.

Carmen
(alt. Carma, Carmina)

Latin, meaning 'song'. Usually associated with the opera Carmen by Georges Bizet.

Carol
(alt. Carole, Carrol, Carroll, Caryl)

Shortened form of Caroline, from the German meaning 'man', but commonly used in its own right. Famous Carols include singer Carole King, former Poet Laureate Carol Ann Duffy and TV personality Carol Vorderman.

Caroline
(alt. Carolann, Carolina, Carolyn, Carolynn)

German, meaning 'man'. Famous Carolines include TV presenter, Caroline Flack and the late writer, actor and comedian Caroline Aherne.

Carrington
English, meaning 'Charles's town'.

Carys
(alt. Cerys)

Welsh, meaning 'love'. Singer and radio presenter Cerys Matthews was a founder member of the band Catatonia.

Casey
(alt. Kacey, Kaci, Kacie, Kacy, Kasey, Kasie, Kassie)

Irish Gaelic, meaning 'watchful'. Used especially in the USA and for both girls and boys.

Cassandra
(alt. Casandra, Cassandre, Kassandra)

Greek, meaning 'one who prophesies doom' or 'entangler of men'. Usually associated with the seer in ancient Greek mythology and sister of Helen of Troy. Cassandra Clare is the pen name of bestselling author Judith Rumelt.

Cassia
(alt. Casia, Casie, Cassie)

Greek, meaning 'cinnamon'. Cassia Leo is an American author.

Cassidy
Irish, meaning 'clever' or 'curly-haired'. Cassidy Wolf is a former American teen beauty queen.

Cassiopeia
(alt. Cassiopia, Cassiopea)

Greek, from the constellation and the ancient Greek myth about a vain queen.

Catalina
(alt. Catarina, Caterina)

Spanish version of Catherine, meaning 'pure'.

Catherine
(alt. Catharine, Cathrine, Cathryn, Katharine, Katherine, Kathryn)

Greek, meaning 'pure'. Famous Catherines include Catherine, Duchess of Cambridge, actor Catherine Zeta Jones, and two wives of King Henry VIII.

Cathleen
(alt. Kathleen)

A spelling variation for Kathleen, the Irish version of Catherine, meaning 'pure'. Actor Cathleen Nesbitt was known for her roles in dozens of West End and Broadway productions.

Cathy
(alt. Caitie, Cathey, Cathi, Cathie, Caty, Cato, Caitia, Kathie, Kathy)

Shortened form of Catherine, meaning 'pure'. Can be used in its own right. Author Cathy Cassidy is known for her young adult fiction.

Catrina
(alt. Caitrina, Catriona)
Greek, meaning 'pure'.

Cayley
(alt. Cayla, Caylee, Caylen)
American, meaning 'pure'.

Cecilia
(alt. Cecile, Cecelia, Cecily, Cicely, Cicily; abbrev. Celia)
Latin, meaning 'blind one'. Associated with the song 'Cecilia' by Simon and Garfunkel.

Celena
Greek, meaning 'goddess of the moon'. A spelling alternative to the Spanish name Selena.

Celeste
(alt. Celestina, Celestine)
Latin, meaning 'heavenly'. American Celeste Holm was an Oscar-winning actor in films and on Broadway.

Celia
Latin, meaning 'heaven'. British actor Celia Imrie has starred in numerous films and television series.

Celine
(alt. Celia, Celina)
French version of Celeste, meaning 'heavenly'. Canadian Celine Dion is one of the most enduringly successful singers in pop music history.

Cerise
French, meaning 'cherry'. The colour cerise is a deep, pinky red.

Chanah
(alt. Chana)
Hebrew, meaning 'grace'. Usually used as a spelling alternative to Hannah.

Chandler
(alt. Chandell)
English, meaning 'candle maker'. Most commonly used as a boys' name.

Chandra
(alt. Chanda, Chandry)
Sanskrit, meaning 'like the moon'. Chandra is a god of the moon in Hinduism.

Chanel
(alt. Chanelle)
French, meaning 'pipe'. Usually associated with the designer and fashion brand Coco Chanel.

Chantal
(alt. Chantel, Chantelle, Chantilly)
French, meaning 'stony spot'. Chantelle Houghton was the first non-celebrity to win Celebrity Big Brother and is now a TV personality and columnist.

Chardonnay
French, from the wine variety of the same name.

Charis
(alt. Charissa, Charisse)
Greek, meaning 'grace'. Charis is one of the Graces in ancient Greek mythology.

Charity

Latin, meaning 'brotherly love'. Of the classic trio of names, Faith, Hope and Charity, this has been the least used.

Charlene
(alt. Charleen, Charline)

German, meaning 'man'. Famous Charlenes include singer Charlene Spiteri, actor Charlene McKenna and Kylie Minogue's character in Aussie soap Neighbours.

Charlotte
(alt. Charnette, Charolette, Charlize; abbrev. Charlie, Charly)

French, meaning 'little and feminine'. Famous Charlottes include author Charlotte Brontë, singer Charlotte Church and, fourth in line to the throne, Princess Charlotte.

Charmaine

Latin, meaning 'clan'. The name possibly comes from Charmian, who was a favourite servant of Cleopatra.

Charnelle
(alt. Charnell, Charnel, Charnele)

American, meaning 'sparkles'. The spelling Charnel refers to a building that houses human remains, often located near a church.

Chastity

Latin, meaning 'purity'.

Chava
(alt. Chaya)

Hebrew, meaning 'beloved'.

Chelsea
(alt. Chelsee, Chelsey, Chelsi, Chelsie, Chelsy)

English, meaning 'port or landing place'. Chelsea Clinton is the only child US political royalty Bill and Hillary Clinton.

Cher

French, meaning 'beloved'. Cher is an American singer and actor.

Cherie
(alt. Cheri, Cherise)

French, meaning 'dear'. Cherie Blair is a barrister and wife of former British prime minister Tony Blair.

Cherish
(alt. Cherith)

English, meaning 'to treasure'.

Chermona

Hebrew, meaning 'sacred mountain'. Sometimes used as a feminine form of Sherman.

Cherry
(alt. Cherri)

English, meaning 'cherry fruit'.

Cheryl
(alt. Cheryle)

English, meaning 'little and womanly'. Singer Cheryl found fame with girl group Girls Aloud and has been a judge on The X Factor.

Chesney

English, meaning 'place to camp'. Used as both a girls' and a boys' name.

Cheyenne
(alt. Cheyanne)
Native American, from the tribe of the same name from the state of Wyoming in the USA.

Chiara
(alt. Ceara, Chiarina)
Italian, meaning 'light'.

China
From the Asian country of the same name.

Chiquita
Spanish, meaning 'little one'.

Chloe
(alt. Cloe)
Greek, meaning 'pale green shoot'. Sometimes spelled with an accent on the 'e'. Famous Chloes include the fashion house Chloé, actors Chloë Moretz and Chloë Sevigny.

Chloris
Greek, meaning 'pale'. Chloris was a nymph in ancient Greek mythology.

Christabel
Latin and French, meaning 'fair Christian'. The title of a poem by Samuel Taylor Coleridge.

Christina
(alt. Christine, Christiana, Cristina; abbrev. Chris, Chrissy, Christa, Christie, Christy, Crissy, Cristy)
Greek, meaning 'anointed Christian'. Feminine form of Christian, and a tribute to Jesus Christ. Christina Aguilera is a world famous pop singer.

Chuma
Aramaic, meaning 'warmth'.

Ciara
Irish, meaning 'dark beauty'. Ciara Princess Harris, known simply as Ciara, is an American singer, dancer, actor and model.

Cierra
(alt. Ciera)
Irish, meaning 'black'. Usually used as a spelling alternative to Sierra.

Cinderella
French, meaning 'little ash-girl'. Most often associated with the fairy tale.

Cinnamon
Greek, from the exotic spice of the same name.

Citlali
(alt. Citlalli)
Nahuatl, meaning 'star'. An ancient Aztec name.

Citrine
Latin, from the gemstone of the same name.

Claire
(alt. Clare, Clara, Claira)
Latin, meaning 'bright'. A very popular name, especially in 1960s and '70s Britain. Famous Claires include actors Claire Danes and Claire Foy, and sports presenter Clare Balding.

Clarabelle
(alt. Clarabella, Claribel)

Contraction of Clara and Isobel, meaning 'bright' and 'consecrated to God'. Clarabelle is a Disney cow character and Clarabella is the title of a Beatles song.

Clarissa
(alt. Clarice, Clarisse)

Variation of Claire, meaning 'bright'. One of the longest novels in English is the 18th-century Clarissa, or, The History of a Young Lady, by Samuel Richardson.

Clarity

Latin, meaning 'lucid'.

Claudette

Latin, meaning 'lame'. The first female prime minister of Haiti was Claudette Werleigh. Claudette Colvin was a pioneer of the American civil rights movement.

Claudia
(alt. Claudie, Claudine)

Latin, meaning 'lame'. TV presenter and film critic Claudia Winkleman co-presents Strictly Come Dancing; Claudia Schiffer is a supermodel.

Clematis

Greek, meaning 'vine'. Also the name of a type of flowering plant.

Clementine
(alt. Clemency, Clementina, Clemmie)

Latin, meaning 'mild and merciful'. Also the name of the sweet orange fruit.

Cleopatra
(alt. Cleo, Clio, Cliona)

Greek, meaning 'her father's renown'. Cleopatra was the last acting Pharaoh of ancient Egypt.

Clodagh

Irish, meaning 'river'.

Clotilda
(alt. Clothilda, Clothilde, Clotilde)

German, meaning 'renowned battle'. St Clotilde was known for her works of charity in the fifth century.

Clover

English, from the flower of the same name.

Coco

Spanish, meaning 'help'. Usually associated with the fashion designer Coco Chanel.

Cody

English, meaning 'pillow'. Used more commonly for boys.

Colleen
(alt. Coleen)

Irish Gaelic, meaning 'girl'. TV presenter Colleen Nolan was the youngest of the singing sisters The Nolans.

Collette
(alt. Colette)

Greek and French, meaning 'people of victory'. Author Sidonie-Gabrielle Colette is known for her novel Gigi.

Connie
(alt. Konnie)

Latin, meaning 'steadfast'. Also used as a shortened version of Constance. Kanak Asha Huq, known as Konnie, is a former *Blue Peter* presenter.

Constance
(alt. Constanza)

Latin, meaning 'steadfast'. Oscar Wilde's wife was Constance Lloyd.

Consuelo
(alt. Consuela)

Spanish, meaning 'comfort'. The name originated from a Spanish name for the Virgin Mary, Our Lady of Consolation.

Cora
Greek, meaning 'maiden'.

Coral
(alt. Coralie, Coraline, Corelia, Corene)

Latin, from the marine life of the same name.

Corazon
Spanish, meaning 'heart'. Also a slang term in Spanish meaning 'darling'.

Cordelia
(alt. Cordia, Cordie)

Latin, meaning 'heart'. Also the name of a tragic character in Shakespeare's play *King Lear*.

Corey
(alt. Cori, Corrie, Cory)

Irish Gaelic, meaning 'the hollow'. Used more commonly, for boys.

Corinne
(alt. Corin, Corinna, Corrine)

French version of Cora, from the Greek meaning 'maiden'. Famous Corinnes include singer-songwriter Corinne Bailey Rae and fashion photographer Corinne Day.

Corliss
English, meaning 'cheery'.

Cornelia
Latin, meaning 'like a horn'. Also the name of several important women in the ancient Roman empire.

Cosette
French, meaning 'people of victory'. Also the heroine in *Les Misérables*.

Cosima
(alt. Cosmina)

Feminine form of Cosmo, from the Greek for 'order'. Cosima Lawson is the daughter of celebrity chef Nigella Lawson.

Courtney
(alt. Cortney)

English, meaning 'court-dweller'. Actor Courtney Cox is known for her roles in *Friends* and *Cougar Town*.

Creola
French, meaning 'American-born, English descent'. Usually associated with the Creole people and language.

Crescent
French, meaning 'increasing'. Usually associated with the shape of the same name.

Cressida

From the Trojan heroine in Greek mythology.

Crystal

(alt. Christal, Chrystal, Cristal, Kristal, Kristel)

Greek, meaning 'ice'. Can also be spelled using a K in all forms.

Csilla

Hungarian, meaning 'defences'. More commonly used in Eastern European countries.

Cyd

Shortened form of Sidney, meaning 'wide island'. Dancer and actor Cyd Charisse was known for her roles in Singin' in the Rain, The Band Wagon and Silk Stockings.

Cynara

Greek, meaning 'thistly plant'. Also the name of a type of thistle plant.

Cynthia

(abbrev. Cinda, Cindi, Cyndi, Cindy)

Greek, meaning 'goddess from the mountain'. Also the name of an ancient Greek goddess of the moon. Famous Cindys include actor Cynthia Nixon (who played Miranda in Sex in the City), supermodel Cindy Crawford and Cyndi Lauper the singer, songwriter and actor.

Cyra

Persian, meaning 'sun'. Also the name of a type of ladybird.

Cyrilla

Latin, meaning 'lordly'. Also the name of a type of flowering plant.

Girls' names

Dacey
Irish Gaelic, meaning 'from the south'.

Dada
Swahili, meaning 'curly haired'.

Daelan
English, meaning 'aware'. More commonly used as a boys' name.

Dagmar
German, meaning 'day's glory'. Dagmar was the stage name of one the first major television stars, Virginia Egnor.

Dagny
Nordic, meaning 'new day'.

Dahlia
Scandinavian, from the flowering plant of the same name.

Dai
Welsh, meaning 'darling'; Japanese meaning 'large, great'. Rarely used for girls.

Daisy
(alt. Dasia)
English, meaning 'eye of the day'. Also the common flower. Daisy has seen a rise in popularity in recent years.

Flower names
Acacia	Lily
Daisy	Petunia
Flora	Poppy
Hyacinth	Primrose
Lilac	Rose

Dakota
Native American, meaning 'allies'. There are two American states named after the Dakota people. Actor Dakota Johnson stars in the film version of *50 Shades of Grey*.

Dalia
(alt. Dalila)

Hebrew, meaning 'delicate branch'. Also the name of a goddess of property in ancient Lithuanian mythology.

Dallas

Scottish Gaelic, from the village of the same name. Also the name of a city in Texas, USA.

Damaris

Greek, meaning 'calf'. Found in the Bible.

Damica
(alt. Damika)

French, meaning 'friendly'. Often used as a spelling alternative to Danica.

Damita

Spanish, meaning 'little noblewoman'.

Dana
(alt. Dania, Danna, Dayna)

English, meaning 'from Denmark'; Persian, meaning 'a perfect and valuable pearl'. Actor Dana Delany played one of the *Desperate Housewives*.

Danae

Greek, from the ancient Greek mythological heroine of the same name.

Danica
(alt. Danika)

Latin, meaning 'from Denmark'. Danica Patrick made waves as one of the most successful female racing drivers in history.

Danielle
(alt. Danelle, Daniela, Daniella, Danila, Danyelle; abbrev. Dani, Danii)

Feminine form of Daniel, which is Hebrew for 'God is my judge'. Model Danielle Lloyd is known for her glamour modelling and *Big Brother* career.

Danita

English, meaning 'God will judge'. More commonly used in the USA.

Daphne
(alt. Dafne, Daphna)

Greek, meaning 'laurel tree'. Daphne was a water nymph in ancient Greek mythology.

Dara

Hebrew and Persian, meaning 'wisdom'. Found in the Bible. Used for both girls and boys.

Darby
(alt. Darbi, Darbie)

Irish, meaning 'a park with deer'.

Darcy
(alt. Darcey, Darci, Darcie)

Irish Gaelic, meaning 'dark'. Ballerina Dame Darcey Bussell is one of the reasons behind the recent rise in popularity of the name in the UK.

Daria

Greek, meaning 'rich'. Usually associated with the teenage cartoon character Daria.

Darla

English, meaning 'darling'. Actor Darla Hood was known for her roles as a child star in the 1930s and '40s.

Darlene
(alt. Darleen, Darline)

American, meaning 'darling'. Actor Darlene Gillespie was one of the original Mickey Mouse Club members.

Darva

Slavic, meaning 'honeybee'. Also the name of several locations in Iran.

Daryl
(alt. Darrell, Darryl)

English, originally used as a surname. Famous Daryls include actor Daryl Hannah; Darrell Rivers was the central character in Enid Blyton's classic Malory Towers books.

Dascha
(alt. Dasha)

Russian, meaning 'of the sea'. Actor Dascha Polanco is known for her role in the US television series Orange is the New Black.

Davina

Hebrew, meaning 'loved one'. English TV presenter Davina McCall is the best-known owner of the name.

Dawn
(alt. Dawna)

English, meaning 'to become day'. Dawn French is one of the most successful comedy actors and writers of recent decades.

Daya

Hebrew, meaning 'bird of prey'. Also the term used for a form of teaching in the Sikh religion.

Deanna
(alt. Dayana, Deana, Deanna, Deanne)

English, meaning 'girl from the valley'. Singer and actor Deanna Durbin was a Hollywood star in the 1930s and '40s. Deanna Troi was a central female character in Star Trek.

Deborah
(alt. Debbra, Debora, Debra, Debrah, Dvora; abbrev. Debbi, Debbie, Debby)

Hebrew, meaning 'bee'. Also the name of a prophetess in the Bible. Among the many famous Deborahs are actor Deborah Kerr and entrepreneur Deborah Meaden, star of Dragons' Den.

December

Latin, meaning 'tenth month'.

Decima
(alt. Decia)

Latin, meaning 'tenth'. Also the name of a goddess in ancient Roman mythology.

Dee

Welsh, meaning 'swarthy'.

Deidre
(alt. Deidra, Deirdre)

Irish, meaning 'raging woman'. Deirdre Barlow was one of *Coronation Street*'s longest-running characters.

Deja
(alt. Dejah)

French, meaning 'already'. The commonly used French phrase *déjà vu* means 'already seen'.

Delaney

Irish Gaelic, meaning 'offspring of the challenger'.

Delia

Greek, meaning 'from Delos'. Delia Smith is one of the most enduringly successful stars of cookery TV programmes and books.

Delilah
(alt. Delina)

Hebrew, meaning 'seductive'. Famous Delilahs include the lover of Samson in the Bible, and the song 'Delilah' by Tom Jones.

Della
(alt. Dell)

Shortened form of Adele, meaning 'noble'. Used as a name in its own right. Donald Duck's twin sister is called Della Duck.

Delores
(alt. Deloris, Dolores, Doloris)

Spanish, meaning 'sorrows'. In Spanish, the shortened form of Delores is Lolita or Lola.

Delphine
(alt. Delpha, Delphia, Delphina, Delphinia)

Greek, meaning 'dolphin'. More commonly used in French-speaking communities.

Delta

Greek, meaning 'fourth child'. Also the name of the fourth letter of the Greek alphabet.

Demelza

Cornish, from the hamlet of the same name in Cornwall. Made popular by the *Poldark* character.

Demetria
(alt. Demetrice, Dimitria)

Greek, from the ancient Greek mythological heroine of the same name.

Demi

French, meaning 'half'. American actor Demi Moore is a star of Hollywood films across several decades.

Dena
(alt. Deena)

English, meaning 'from the valley'. Also the name of a mountain range in Iran.

Denise
(alt. Denice, Denisa, Denisse)

French, meaning 'devoted to Bacchus'. Denise is the feminine French form of Dionysius, the ancient Greek god of wine.

Derora

Hebrew, meaning 'stream'. Also the name of a clan in India.

Desdemona

Greek, meaning 'wretchedness'. A character in Shakespeare's play *Othello*.

Desiree
(alt. Desirae, Des'ree)

French, meaning 'much desired'. Singer Des'ree adapted her name from Desiree, her given name.

Desma

Greek, meaning 'blinding oath'. More commonly used as a shortened version of Desdemona.

Destiny
(alt. Destany, Destinee, Destiney, Destini)

French, meaning 'fate'.

Deva

Hindi, meaning 'God-like'. Deva is also a name for several Buddhist, Hindu and New Age spiritual entities or people.

Devinne
(alt. Devin)

Feminine form of Devin, which is Irish Gaelic for 'poet'.

Devon

English, from the southern English county of the same name.

Diamond

English, meaning 'brilliant'.

Diana
(alt. Dian, Diane, Dianna, Dianne)

Roman, meaning 'divine'. Famous Dianas include Princess Diana, singing legend Diana Ross and Diana the Roman goddess of hunting.

Diandra

Greek, meaning 'two males'.

Dilys

Welsh, meaning 'reliable'. Famous Dilyses include actor Dilys Watling and actor and screenwriter Dilys Laye.

Dimona

Hebrew, meaning 'south'. Also the name of a town in the Bible, now situated in modern Israel.

Dinah
(alt. Dina)

Hebrew, meaning 'justified'.

Dionne

Greek, from the mythological heroine of the same name. Famous Dionnes include singers Dionne Warwick and Dionne Bromfield.

Divine

Italian, meaning 'heavenly'.

Dixie

French, meaning 'tenth'. Usually used as a term for the South of the USA.

Dodie

Hebrew, meaning 'well-loved'. Author Dodie Smith is best known for her children's novel *101 Dalmations*.

Dolly

(alt. Dollie)

Shortened form of Dorothy, meaning 'gift of God'. Can be used in its own right. Dolly Parton is the world-famous country and western singer.

Dominique

(alt. Domenica, Dominica, Domonique)

Latin, meaning 'Lord'. Usually associated with the song 'Dominique' by Soeur Sourire, a singing nun.

Donata

(alt. Donatella)

Latin, meaning 'given', also Italian for 'gift'. Donatella Versace is a leading Italian fashion designer and vice president of the Versace empire.

Donna

(alt. Dona, Donnie)

Italian, meaning 'lady'. Singer Donna Summer had a string of hits in the 1970s and '80s.

Dora

Greek, meaning 'gift'. Usually associated with the cartoon character Dora the Explorer.

Dorcas

Greek, meaning 'gazelle'. Also found in the Bible.

Doreen

(alt. Doren, Dorene, Dorine)

Greek, meaning 'gift'. In Irish Gaelic, the suffix 'een' indicates that a child has the same name as a parent.

Doria

Greek, meaning 'of the sea'. Also the name of an influential Genoese family in the 12th century.

Doris

(alt. Dorris)

Greek, from the region of the same name. Actor and singer Doris Day was a big star in the 1940s and '50s, and was also a leading animal rights campaigner.

Dorothy

(alt. Dorathy, Doretha, Dorotha, Dorothea, Dorthy; abbrev. Dolly, Dot, Dottie, Dotty)

Greek, meaning 'gift of God'. Famous Dorothys include the central character in *The Wizard of Oz* and Dorothy Hodgkin, who won a Nobel Prize for chemistry.

Dorrit

(alt. Dorit)

Greek, meaning 'gift of God'. Usually associated with the novel *Little Dorrit* by Charles Dickens.

Dory

(alt. Dori)

French, meaning 'gilded'. Usually associated with the character from the Disney films *Finding Nemo* and *Finding Dory*.

Dove
(alt. Dovie)

English, from the bird of the same name. Often used as a symbol for peace.

Drew

Greek, meaning 'masculine'. Actor Drew Barrymore became a child star when she appeared in *E.T.*.

Drusilla
(alt. Drucilla)

Latin, meaning 'of the Drusus clan'. Found in the Bible.

Dulcie
(alt. Dulce, Dulcia)

Latin, meaning 'sweet'. Actor Dulcie Gray was known for her roles on stage and screen in the mid-20th century.

Dusty
(alt. Dusti)

Old German, meaning 'brave warrior'. Singer Dusty Springfield was a 1960s star.

Names of Poets

Amy (Lowell)
Anne (Sexton)
Carol Ann (Duffy)
Charlotte (Smith)
Emily (Dickinson)
Flew (Adcock)
Gwyneth (Lewis)
Pam (Ayres)
Ruth (Padel)
Sylvia (Plath)
Wendy (Cope)

Girls' names

Eadlin
(alt. Eadlinn, Eadlyn, Eadlen, Edlin)
Anglo-Saxon, meaning 'royalty'. Can also be a nickname for Adeline.

Earla
English, meaning 'leader'. Also a variation of the German name Herlinde, meaning 'shield'.

Eartha
English, meaning 'earth'. Singer Eartha Kitt was best known for her hit 'Santa Baby'.

Easter
From the festival of the same name.

Ebba
English, meaning 'fortress of riches'. One of the Top 10 names for baby girls in Sweden.

Ebony
(alt. Eboni)
Latin, meaning 'deep black wood'.

Echo
Greek, meaning 'reflected sound'. From the mythological nymph of the same name.

Eda
(alt. Edda)
English, meaning 'wealthy and happy'. An ancient goddess of time and wealth.

Edelmira
Spanish, meaning 'admired for nobility'. Feminine form of Edelmiro.

Eden
Hebrew, meaning 'pleasure'. In the Bible, the Garden of Eden was humankind's first home on Earth.

Edina
Scottish, meaning 'from Edinburgh'. Actor Jennifer Saunders's character in *Absolutely Fabulous* was named Edina Monsoon.

Edith
(alt. Edyth; abbrev. Edie)
English, meaning 'prosperity through battle'. Pulitzer Prize-winner Edith Wharton is the author of *The Age of Innocence*. Actor Edie Falco starred in TV hit *The Sopranos*.

Edna
Hebrew, meaning 'enjoyment'. Australian comedian Barry Humphries is best known for his alter ego Dame Edna Everage.

Edrea
English, meaning 'wealthy and powerful'. Edrea Vorsal was a soprano opera singer.

Edris
(alt. Edriss, Edrys)
Anglo-Saxon, meaning 'prosperous ruler'. Sometimes used as a feminine form of Idris.

Edwina
English, meaning 'wealthy friend'. Edwina Currie was a controversial British politician.

Effie
Greek, meaning 'pleasant speech'. Effie Trinket is a key character in the 'Hunger Games' trilogy, known for her outrageous fashion sense.

Eglantine
French, from the shrub of the same name covered in tiny roses.

Eibhlín
Irish Gaelic, meaning 'shining and brilliant'. Eibhlín Dubh Ní Chonaill was an Irish poet and noblewoman.

Eileen
Irish, meaning 'shining and brilliant'. English version of Eibhlín, and often associated with the song 'Come on Eileen' by Dexys Midnight Runners.

Ekaterina
(alt. Ekaterini)
Slavic, meaning 'pure'.

Elaine
(alt. Elaina, Elayne)
French, meaning 'bright, shining light'. Singer and performer Elaine Paige is a star of West End musical theatre and radio presenter.

Elba
Italian, from the island of the same name.

Elberta
English, meaning 'highborn'.

Eldora
Spanish, meaning 'covered with gold'. Eldora is also the name of a small 'ghost' town in Florida, USA, which has remained uninhabited for over 100 years.

Eldoris
(alt. Eldoriss, Eldorys)
Greek, meaning 'woman of the sea'. Usually found as a variation of Doris.

Eleanor
(alt. Elana, Elena, Elanor, Eleanora)
Greek, meaning 'light'. Queen Eleanor of Aquitaine was married to England's King Henry II, and one of the most influential, wealthy and powerful women of medieval times.

Electra
(alt. Elektra)
Greek, meaning 'shining'. Also a character from an ancient Greek myth. In psychology, Electra is the female counterpart of Oedipus.

Elfrida
(alt. Elfrieda)
English, meaning 'elf power'. Elfrida Andrée was a 19th-century composer and conductor, and the first female organist to be recognised in Sweden.

Eliana
(alt. Eliane)
Hebrew, meaning 'Jehovah is God'. Becoming increasingly popular thanks to the growing trend for names for girls ending in -a.

Elise
(alt. Elisa, Elissa)
French, meaning 'my vow to God'. Commonly associated with Beethoven's 'Für Elise', a piano solo.

Elizabeth
(alt. Elisabet, Elisabeth, Elizabella, Elizabelle, Elsbeth, Elspeth, Elisha; abbrev. Beth, Eliza, Libby, Liz, Lizzie, Lizzy)
Hebrew, meaning 'consecrated to God'. Two queens of England have been named this: Elizabeth I ruled from 1558 to 1603, and Elizabeth II has been on the throne since 1952. Enduringly popular, especially with its many shortened forms.

Elke
(alt. Elkie)
German, meaning 'nobility'. Singer Elkie Brooks had several hits in the 1980s.

Ella
German, meaning 'completely'. Now becoming a name in its own right, Ella is traditionally a shortened version of Eleanor, Elizabeth and Ellen.

Elle
French, meaning 'she'. Elle Macpherson was one of the original supermodels in the 1980s, and known as 'The Body'.

Ellema
(alt. Ellemah, Elema, Ellemma, Elemah)
Swahili, meaning 'dairy farmer' or 'milking a cow'.

Ellen
(alt. Elin, Eline, Ellyn)
Greek, meaning 'shining'. Ellen DeGeneres is a popular actor and TV host.

Ellice
(alt. Elyse)
Greek, meaning 'the Lord is God'.

Ellie
(alt. Elie)

Shortened form of Eleanor which can be used in its own right. Singer and Brit Award winner Ellie Goulding is actually an Elena.

Elma
(alt. Elna)

Latin, meaning 'soul'. Elma Napier was the first woman to be elected to a Caribbean parliament, in 1940.

Elmira
(alt. Elmyra)

Arabic, meaning 'aristocratic lady'. Elmyra Duff is a character in the cartoon *Tiny Toons*.

Elodie

French, meaning 'marsh flower'. Élodie Bouchez-Bangalter is a French actor.

Eloise
(alt. Elois, Eloisa, Elouise)

French, meaning 'renowned in battle'. Also a shortened version and English spelling of French name Héloïse.

Elsa
(alt. Else, Elsie)

Hebrew, meaning 'consecrated to God'. Elsa the Snow Queen is one of the lead characters in Disney's *Frozen*.

Elva

Irish, meaning 'noble'. Also the name of a British sports car manufacturer.

Elvina

English, meaning 'noble friend'. Also an ancient place name.

Elvira
(alt. Elvera)

Spanish, from the ancient city of the same name. Commonly associated with the 1980s film *Elvira, Mistress of the Dark*.

Ember
(alt. Embry)

English, meaning 'spark'. Sometimes used as a shortened version of the name September.

Emerald

English, meaning 'green gemstone'.

Emery
(alt. Emory)

German, meaning 'ruler of work'.

Emiko
(alt. Emuko)

Japanese, meaning 'pretty child'. Popular name for girls in Japan.

Emilia

Latin, meaning 'rival, eager'. British actor Emilia Clarke played lead character Daenerys Targaryen in *Game of Thrones*.

Emily
(alt. Emalee, Emelie, Emely, Emilee, Emili, Emilie, Emlyn)

Latin, meaning 'rival, eager'. Emily Dickinson is one of the most well-known poets of the 19th century. A popular name choice in recent years.

Emma

German, meaning 'embraces everything'. The title character of Jane Austen's novel. Former actor Emma Watson starred as Hermione in the *Harry Potter* films.

Emmanuelle

Feminine form of Emanuel, which is Hebrew for 'God is with us'.

Emmeline

(alt. Emmelina; abbrev. Emmy, Emmie, Emi)

German, meaning 'embraces everything' or 'industrious'. Emmeline Pankhurst was the leader of the Suffragettes, political activists who campaigned in the early 20th century for women's right to vote.

Ena

Shortened form of Georgina, meaning 'farmer'. Ena Sharples was one of the original cast of characters on *Coronation Street*.

Enid

(alt. Eneida)

Welsh, meaning 'life spirit'. Enid Blyton was a hugely popular children's author, known for the *Noddy*, *Famous Five* and *Malory Towers* series, among others.

Enola

Native American, meaning 'solitary'.

Enya

Irish Gaelic, meaning 'fire'. Enya is an Irish singer and songwriter.

Eowyn

Fictional character from J.R.R. Tolkien's *Lord of the Rings* trilogy. Eowyn was a noblewoman who disguised herself as a man in order to fight in a major battle.

Eranthe

Greek, meaning 'delicate like the spring'.

Erica

(alt. Ericka, Erika)

Scandinavian, meaning 'ruler forever'. Also a flowering plant similar to heather.

Erin

(alt. Eryn)

Irish Gaelic, meaning 'from the isle to the west'. Formerly a romanticised name for Ireland. Erin Brockovich is an American housewife turned environmental activist, played by Julia Roberts in the film of the same name.

Eris

Greek, from the mythological goddess. Eris is responsible for chaos, strife and discord.

Erlinda

Hebrew, meaning 'spirited'. Erlinda Cortes was a popular actor after World War II.

Erma

German, meaning 'universal'. Erma Franklin, the sister of soul legend Aretha Franklin, was an American gospel singer.

Ermine
French, meaning 'weasel'. The white winter fur of a stoat is known as ermine.

Erna
English, meaning 'sincere'. Erna was a character in Norse mythology.

Ernestine
(alt. Ernestina)
English, meaning 'sincere'. Ernestine Gilbreth Carey was the co-author of *Cheaper by the Dozen*, the novel upon which the popular films of the same name were based.

Esme
French, meaning 'esteemed'. Esme Cullen is a key character in the *Twilight* series.

Esmeralda
Spanish, meaning 'emerald'. Esmeralda is the female protagonist in *The Hunchback of Notre Dame*.

Esperanza
Spanish, meaning 'hope'. Popular name for girls in Spain.

Estelle
(alt. Estela, Estell, Estella)
French, meaning 'star'. British R&B singer Estelle is known by her first name only.

Esther
(alt. Esta, Ester, Etha, Ethna, Ethne)
Persian, meaning 'star'. Esther is a Jewish and Persian queen mentioned in the Bible.

Eternity
Latin, meaning 'forever'.

Ethel
(alt. Ethyl)
English, meaning 'noble'. Ethel Merman was an enormously popular American actor and singer, and a star of musical theatre.

Etinia
(alt. Eteniah, Etene, Eteniya)
Native American, meaning 'prosperous'.

Etta
(alt. Etter, Ettie)
Shortened form of Henrietta, meaning 'ruler of the house'. Etta James was a blues and soul singer-songwriter.

Eudora
Greek, meaning 'generous gift'.

Eugenia
(alt. Eugenie)
Greek, meaning 'well born'. Also a type of flowering plant. Princess Eugenie is a granddaughter of Queen Elizabeth II.

Eulalia
(alt. Eula, Eulah, Eulalie)
Greek, meaning 'sweet-speaking'. St Eulalia was a Spanish virgin who was martyred for her faith.

Eunice
Greek, meaning 'victorious'. Eunice Kennedy Shriver was John F. Kennedy's sister and the founder of the Special Olympics.

Euphemia

Greek, meaning 'favourable speech'. Great Martyr Euphemia was killed for her Christian faith.

Eva

Hebrew, meaning 'life'. Eva Perón, the First Lady of Argentina from 1946 to 1952, was the inspiration for the musical *Evita*.

Evadne

Greek, meaning 'pleasing one'. Found frequently in Greek mythology.

Evangeline

(alt. Evangelina)

Greek, meaning 'good news'. The very first 'musical comedy' was called *Evangeline*, and it premiered in 1874.

Evanthe

Greek, meaning 'good flower'. Occasionally used as an alternative to the names Eve, Eva and Evelyn.

Eve

(alt. Evie)

Hebrew, meaning 'life'. Found in the Bible.

Evelina

(alt. Evelia)

German, meaning 'hazelnut'. Its popularity was at its peak in the late 18th century, after a novel called *Evelina* by Fanny Burney.

Evelyn

(alt. Evalyn, Evelin, Eveline, Evelyne)

German, meaning 'hazelnut'. Used as a name for girls and boys. Dame Evelyn Glennie is a multi-award-winning Scottish virtuoso percussionist who is profoundly deaf.

Everly

(alt. Everleigh, Everley)

English, meaning 'grazing meadow'.

Evette

French, meaning 'yew wood'. Often used as a spelling variation of Yvette.

Evonne

(alt. Evon)

French, meaning 'yew wood'. Evonne Goolagong was a women's tennis legend in the 1970s.

Girls' names

Fabia
(alt. Fabiana, Fabienne, Fabiola, Fabriana)
Latin, meaning 'one who grows beans'.

Fabrizia
Italian, meaning 'works with her hands'.

Fahari
Swahili, meaning 'splendour'. Can also mean 'magnificent'.

Faith
English, meaning 'loyalty'. Faith Hill and Faith Evans are famous singers.

Faiza
Arabic, meaning 'victorious'. The first ever British Muslim superhero to be created by Marvel comics was Faiza Hussain, codenamed Excalibur.

Fallon
Irish Gaelic, meaning 'descended from a ruler'.

Fanny
(alt. Fannie)
Latin, meaning 'from France'. Extremely popular name in the 18th and 19th centuries. The protagonist of Jane Austen's *Mansfield Park* was Fanny Price.

Farica
German, meaning 'peaceful ruler'. A feminine form of Frederick.

Farrah
English, meaning 'fair haired', and Arabic, meaning 'joy'. Farrah Fawcett was one of TV's original *Charlie's Angels*.

Fatima
Arabic, meaning 'baby's nurse'. Popular in Muslim communities.

Faustine
Feminine form of Faustinus, which is Latin, meaning 'fortunate'.

Fawn

French, meaning 'young deer'.

Fay
(alt. Fae, Faye)

French, meaning 'fairy'. Bestselling author Fay Weldon has written more than 30 books.

Fayola
(alt. Fayolah, Fayeena)

Swahili, meaning 'walks with honour'. Can also mean 'lucky'.

Felicia
(alt. Felicity, Felecia, Felice, Felicita, Felisha)

Latin, meaning 'lucky and happy'. Actor Felicia Day starred in *Buffy the Vampire Slayer*.

Fenella
(abbrev. Fen)

Irish Gaelic, meaning 'white shoulder'. Actor Fenella Fielding is known for her husky voice and sensual image.

Fenia

Scandinavian, from the mythological giantess of the same name.

Fennel

Latin, name of a herb. Also a boys' name.

Fern
(alt. Fearne, Ferne, Ferrin)

English, from the plant of the same name.

Fernanda

German, meaning 'peace and courage'. A popular name in Brazil and Mexico.

Ffion
(alt. Fion)

Irish Gaelic, meaning 'fair and pale' or 'foxglove'. Popular in Wales.

Fia

Italian, meaning 'flame'. Also used as a nickname for Fiona.

Fifi

Hebrew, meaning 'Jehovah increases'.

Filomena

Greek, meaning 'loved one'. Sometimes used as an alternative spelling to Philomena.

Finlay
(alt. Finley)

Irish Gaelic, meaning 'fair-haired courageous one'. More commonly used as a name for boys.

Finola
(alt. Fionnula)

Irish Gaelic, meaning 'white shoulder'. British actor Finola Hughes appears regularly on American TV, having featured in several soap operas.

Fiona
(alt. Fiora)

Scottish, meaning 'fair and pale'. The name was actually invented by poet James Macpherson in the 18th century. Famous Fionas include TV presenter Fiona Bruce and *Shrek* character Princess Fiona.

Fiorella

Feminine form of Fiorello, which is Italian for 'little flower'.

Flanna
(alt. Flannery)

Irish Gaelic, meaning 'russet hair' or 'red hair'.

Flavia

Latin, meaning 'yellow hair'. Popular name in both ancient and modern literature, but rarely used in the UK. Flavia Cacace was an Italian professional dancer on *Strictly Come Dancing*.

Fleur

French, meaning 'flower'. Fleur Delacour is a character in the *Harry Potter* series.

Flora

Latin, meaning 'flower'. Flora was one of the fairy godmothers (the red one) in Disney's *Sleeping Beauty*.

Florence
(alt. Florencia, Florene, Florine; abbrev. Florrie, Flossie, Floy, Flo)

Latin, meaning 'in bloom'. Also an Italian city.

Florida

Latin, meaning 'flowery'. Also a state in the USA.

Fraisine
(alt. Fraise)

French, meaning 'strawberry'.

Frances
(alt. Francine, Francis; abbrev. Fran, Frankie, Frannie)

Latin, meaning 'from France'. Famous Franceses include actor Frances McDormand, author Frances Trollope and playwright Frances Hodgson Burnett.

Francesca
(alt. Franchesca, Francisca; abbrev. Fran, Frankie, Frannie)

Latin, meaning 'from France'. Francesca Simon is the author of the 'Horrid Henry' children's book series.

Freda
(alt. Freeda, Freida, Frida, Frieda)

German, meaning 'peaceful'. Frida Kahlo was a Mexican artist known for her self-portraits and heavy eyebrows.

Frederica

German, meaning 'peaceful ruler'. A popular name for European princesses, it has been used nearly 20 times since the 17th century.

Freya

Old Nordic, meaning 'lady'.

Fuchsia

German, from the flower of the same name. Fuchsia Dunlop is a renowned British chef who specialises in Chinese food.

Fumiko

Japanese, meaning 'little friend' or 'beautiful child'.

Girls' names

Gabrielle
(alt. Gabriel, Gabriela, Gabriella; abbrev. Gabby, Gabbi)
Hebrew, meaning 'heroine of God'. Gabriella Wilde is a British actor. Gabby Logan is a high-profile female TV sports presenter.

Gadara
Armenian, meaning 'mountain's peak'. The ancient town of Gadara is situated in northern Jordan.

Gaia
(alt. Gaea)
Greek, meaning 'the earth'. In ancient Greece, Gaia was the Greek Mother Goddess and the most important.

Gail
(alt. Gale, Gayla, Gayle)
Hebrew, meaning 'my father rejoices'. Badminton player Gail Emms represented England at international level for many years.

Gala
French, meaning 'festive merrymaking'. Used more commonly in Spanish-speaking communities.

Galiena
German, meaning 'high one'.

Galina
Russian, meaning 'shining brightly'. Feminine form of Galen.

Garnet
(alt. Garnett)
English, meaning 'red gemstone'.

Gay
(alt. Gaye)
French, meaning 'glad and lighthearted'.

Gaynor
Welsh, meaning 'white and smooth'.

Gemini
Greek, meaning 'twins'. One of the signs of the zodiac.

Gemma

Italian, meaning 'precious stone'. Actor Gemma Arterton was a Bond girl.

Gene

Greek, meaning 'well born'. More commonly used for boys.

Genesis

Greek, meaning 'beginning'.

Geneva
(alt. Genevra)

French, meaning 'juniper tree'. Also the name of the Swiss city.

Genevieve
(abbrev. Genie)

German, meaning 'white wave'. St Genevieve is said to have saved Paris.

Georgette

French, meaning 'farmer'. Georgette Heyer was an author of historical romance novels.

Georgia
(alt. Georgiana, Georgianna, Georgie)

Greek, meaning 'farmer'. Also the name of the European country and a state in the USA.

Georgina
(alt. Georgene, Georgine, Giorgina)

Greek, meaning 'farmer'. The name's popularity was at its peak during the 1980s. Georgina was the spirited character in Enid Blyton's Famous Five books, who insisted on being referred to as George.

Geraldine
(abbrev. Geri, Gerri, Gerry)

German, meaning 'spear ruler'. Spice Girls singer Geri Halliwell's full name is Geraldine.

Gerda

Nordic, meaning 'shelter'. Gerda is the female protagonist in Hans Christian Andersen's Snow Queen.

Germaine

French, meaning 'from Germany'. Germaine Greer is an Australian author and activist.

Gertrude
(abbrev. Gertie)

German, meaning 'strength of a spear'. Gertrude Stein was an influential 19th-century American author. One of the earliest animated cartoon films was called Gertie the Dinosaur, made in 1914.

Ghislaine

French, meaning 'pledge'. Believed to have derived from Giselle.

Gia
(alt. Ghia)

Italian, meaning 'God is gracious'. Often used by itself, or as a shortened form of Gianna.

Gianina
(alt. Giana)

Hebrew, meaning 'God's graciousness'. Sometimes associated with the town of Ioannina in Greece.

Gigi
(alt. Giget)

Shortened form of Georgina, meaning 'farmer'. Also the name of a successful 1958 musical film.

Gilda

English, meaning 'gilded'. The name of Rigoletto's daughter in Verdi's opera *Rigoletto*.

Gilia

Hebrew, meaning 'joy of the Lord'. Also the name of a genus of flowering plants.

Gillian
(abbrev. Gill, Gilly, Gillie)

Latin, meaning 'youthful'. Famous Gillians include actor Gillian Anderson and children's author Gillian Cross.

Gina
(alt. Geena, Gena)

Shortened form of Regina, meaning 'queen', often used in its own right. Bestselling author Gina Ford has published over 20 parenting books.

Ginger

Latin, from the spicy root of the same name. Ginger Rogers was an Oscar-winning American singer, dancer and actor, best known for dancing with Fred Astaire. Her real first name was Virginia.

Ginny

Shortened form of Virginia, meaning 'virgin'. Made popular by the character of Ginny Weasley in the *Harry Potter* series.

Giovanna

Italian, meaning 'God is gracious'. The English equivalent is Joanna or Jane.

Giselle
(alt. Gisela, Gisele, Giselle, Gisselle)

German, meaning 'pledge'. *Giselle* is the name of a romantic ballet. Gisele Bündchen is a Brazilian supermodel and actor.

Gita
(alt. Geeta)

Sanskrit, meaning 'song'. *Bhagavad Gita* is a 700-verse Hindu scripture.

Giulia
(alt. Giuliana)

Italian, meaning 'youthful'. The Italian form of the name Julia.

Gladys
(alt. Gladyce)

Welsh, meaning 'lame'. Singer Gladys Knight is known as the 'Empress of Soul'.

Glenda

Welsh, meaning 'fair and good'. A variation of Glenna and Glynda. Glenda Jackson is a British actor turned politician.

Glenna
(alt. Glennie)

Irish Gaelic, meaning 'glen'. Feminine form of Glenn.

Gloria
(alt. Glory)

Latin, meaning 'glory'. Famous Glorias including singers Gloria Estefan and Gloria Gaynor.

Glynda
(alt. Glinda)

Welsh, meaning 'fair'. The good witch in the *Wizard of Oz*.

Less common three-syllable names

Cassandra	Jessamy
Dolores	Julia
Gloria	Marilyn
Harriet	Miranda
Imogen	Nigella

Glynis

Welsh, meaning 'small glen'. The first Olympic gold medallist of the heptathlon was Australian athlete Glynis Nunn.

Golda
(alt. Goldia, Goldie)

English, meaning 'gold'. Golda Meir was the prime minister of Israel from 1969 to 1974.

Grace
(alt. Graça, Gracie, Gracin, Grayce)

Latin, meaning 'grace'. Film actor Grace Kelly became Princess Grace of Monaco.

Gráinne
(alt. Grania)

Irish Gaelic, meaning 'love'.

Gratia
(alt. Grasia)

Latin, meaning 'blessing'. Gratia was the ancient Greek goddess of charm, beauty and fertility, among other things.

Greer
(alt. Grier)

Latin, meaning 'alert and watchful'.

Gregoria

Latin, meaning 'alert'. Empress Gregoria was a key figure in the Byzantine empire.

Greta
(alt. Gretel)

Greek, meaning 'pearl'. Gretel is the name of the female protagonist in the fairy tale Hansel and Gretel. Greta also refers to a genus of butterfly.

Gretchen

German, meaning 'pearl'. Actor Gretchen Mol is known for her role in TV series *Boardwalk Empire*.

Griselda
(alt. Griselle; abbrev. Selda, Zelda)

German, meaning 'grey fighting maid'.

Grytha

English, meaning 'fiery'. Denmark's Queen Grytha ruled during the fifth century.

Gudrun

Scandinavian, meaning 'battle'. Key recurring figure in Norse and Germanic literature.

Guinevere

Welsh, meaning 'white and smooth'. The queen in Arthurian legend.

Gwen

Shortened form of Gwenda or Gwendolyn, as well as a name in its own right. Gwen Stefani is a singer-songwriter and member of No Doubt.

Gwenda

Welsh, meaning 'fair and good'. As well as a name in its own right, Gwenda can also be a shortened form of Gwendolyn or Gwyneth.

Gwendolyn

(alt. Gwendolen, Gwenel)

Welsh, meaning 'fair bow'. Gwendolyn Brooks was a Pulitzer Prize-winning poet.

Gwyneth

(alt. Gwynneth, Gwynyth; abbrev. Gwyn, Gwynn)

Welsh, meaning 'happiness'. Actor and author Gwyneth Paltrow is mum to Apple and Moses.

Gypsy

English, meaning 'of the Roma tribe'.

Girls' names

Habibah
(alt. Habiba)
Arabic, meaning 'beloved'.

Hadassah
Hebrew, meaning 'myrtle tree'. Usually associated with the character of Esther in the Bible, whose Hebrew name is Hadassah.

Hadley
English, meaning 'heather meadow'. Hadley Freeman is an author and journalist.

Hadria
Latin, meaning 'from Hadria'. Also the name of two ancient cities in Italy.

Hala
Arabic, meaning 'halo'. Also the name of a female weather demon in Serbian and Bulgarian mythology.

Halima
(alt. Halimah, Halina)
Arabic, meaning 'gentle'. The prophet Mohammad's foster mother was called Halimah.

Hallie
(alt. Halle, Halley)
German, meaning 'ruler of the home or estate'. Oscar-winning actor Halle Berry was originally given the name Maria Halle.

Hannah
(alt. Haana, Hana, Hanna)
Hebrew, meaning 'grace'. Famous Hannahs include Hannah Cockroft, the wheelchair athlete and world record holder, and American teen sitcom *Hannah Montana*.

Harika
Turkish, meaning 'superior one'. In India, the name is associated with Parvati, the Hindu goddess of power and creation.

Harley
(alt. Harlene)
English, meaning 'the long field'.

Harlow
English, meaning 'army hill'.

Harmony

Latin, meaning 'harmony'.

Harper

English, meaning 'minstrel'. Harper Lee is the author of classic novel *To Kill a Mockingbird*. Harper Seven is the name of David and Victoria Beckham's fourth child.

Harriet
(alt. Harriett, Harriette; abbrev. Hattie)

German, meaning 'ruler of the home or estate'. Famous Harriets include activist Harriet Tubman, author Harriet Beecher Stowe, and politician Harriet Harman.

Haven

English, meaning 'a place of sanctuary'.

Hayden
(alt. Haydn)

Old English, meaning 'hedged valley'. Also ussed as a boys' name.

Hayley
(alt. Haelee, Haely, Hailee, Hailey, Hailie, Haleigh, Haley, Hali, Halie, Haylee, Hayleigh, Haylie)

English, meaning 'hay meadow'.

Hazel
(alt. Hazle)

English, from the tree of the same name. Famous Hazels include children's author Hazel Hutchins, singer Hazel O'Connor and politician Hazel Blears.

Heather

English, from the flower of the same name. Famous Heathers include actors Heather Graham and Heather Locklear, and model Heather Mills.

Heaven

English, meaning 'everlasting bliss'.

Hedda

German, meaning 'warfare'. Also the name of the protagonist in the play *Hedda Gabler*, by Henrik Ibsen.

Hedwig

German, meaning 'warfare and strife'. The name stems from two different St Hedwigs, but is now most associated with Harry Potter's owl!

Heidi
(alt. Heidy)

German, meaning 'nobility'. One of the top-selling children's books of all time is the Swiss novel *Heidi*, by Johanna Spyri.

Helen
(alt. Halen, Helena, Helene, Hellen)

Greek, meaning 'light'. In ancient Greek mythology Helen of Troy was considered to be the most beautiful woman in the world.

Helga

German, meaning 'holy and sacred'. Extemely popular name in Germany and Norway.

Helia

Greek, meaning 'sun'.

Héloïse

French, meaning 'renowned in war'. Héloïse d'Argenteuil was a nun and writer known for having an affair with the theologian Peter Abelard in the 12th century.

Henrietta
(alt. Henriette)

German, meaning 'ruler of the house'. Usually associated with Henrietta Maria of France, who was queen consort to Charles I.

Hephzibah
(alt. Hefzibah)

Hebrew, meaning 'my delight is in her'. Found in the Bible.

Hera

Greek, meaning 'queen'. Hera is the Queen of the Gods, and the goddess of marriage, women and birth in ancient Greek mythology.

Hermia
(alt. Hermina, Hermine, Herminia)

Greek, meaning 'messenger'. Also the name of a character in Shakespeare's play *A Midsummer Night's Dream*.

Hermione

Greek, meaning 'earthly'. Now inseparable from the main female character in the *Harry Potter* series.

Hero

Greek, meaning 'brave one of the people'.

Hertha

English, meaning 'earth'. Also another name for Nerthus, the goddess of fertility in ancient German mythology.

Hesper
(alt. Hesperia)

Greek, meaning 'evening star'.

Hester
(alt. Hestia)

Greek, meaning 'star'. Also the name of the protagonist in *The Scarlet Letter* by Nathaniel Hawthorne.

Hettie

Shortened form of Hester or Henrietta, also used as a name in its own right.

Hilary
(alt. Hillary)

Greek, meaning 'cheerful and happy'. Also a boys' name. Famous Hilarys include US politician Hillary Rodham Clinton and actor Hilary Swank.

Hilda
(alt. Hildur)

German, meaning 'battle woman'. Famous Hildas include the first female pilot to hold a licence, Hilda Hewlett, and author Hilda Doolittle – known as H.D.

Hildegarde
(alt. Hildegard)

German, meaning 'battle stronghold'.

Hildred

German, meaning 'battle counsellor'. More commonly used as a boys' name.

Hilma

German variant of Wilhelmina, meaning 'helmet'. The feminine form of Hilmar or Hilmer.

Hirkani

Sanskrit, meaning 'like a diamond'.

Hollis

English, meaning 'near the holly bushes'.

Holly
(alt. Holli, Hollie)

English, from the tree of the same name. Famous Hollys include TV presenter Holly Willoughby and actor Holly Hunter.

Honey

English, from the word 'honey'.

Honor
(alt. Honour, Honora, Honoria)

Latin, meaning 'woman of honour'. Actor Honor Blackman played the Bond girl Pussy Galore.

Hope

English, meaning 'desire and expectation'. One of three virtues in most religions: faith, hope and charity. Hope Powell represented England in football for many years before becoming the England Women's coach for more than a decade.

Hortense
(alt. Hortencia, Hortensia)

Latin, meaning 'of the garden'. Also the name of one of Napoleon Bonaparte's stepdaughters, and a character in Charles Dickens's novel *Bleak House*.

Hudson

English, meaning 'adventurous'.

Hulda

German, meaning 'loved one'. Also the name of a prophetess in the Bible.

Hyacinth

Greek, from the flower of the same name. Hyacinth was also a hero in ancient Greek mythology.

Girls' names

Ianthe
(alt. Iantha)
Greek, meaning 'purple flower'. Also the name of a character in ancient Greek mythology.

Ichigo
Japanese, meaning 'strawberry'.

Ida
English, meaning 'prosperous'. Also the name of several characters in both ancient Greek mythology and the Hindu religion.

Idella
(alt. Idell)
English, meaning 'prosperous'. Idella Purnell was an academic and author of children's books, best known in the 1930s and '40s.

Idona
Nordic, meaning 'renewal'.

Ignacia
(alt. Iggy)
Latin, meaning 'ardent' or 'burning'. The feminine form of Ignatius.

Ila
French, meaning 'island'. In Hindu mythology Ila is a character able to change sex at will.

Ilana
Hebrew, meaning 'tree'. Ilana Vered is a classical pianist known for her work with dozens of major international orchestras.

Ilaria
Italian, meaning 'cheerful'. The English equivalent is Hilary.

Ilene
American, meaning 'light'. Ilene Woods was a voice actor known for being the voice of Cinderella in the Disney film.

Iliana
(alt. Ileana)
Greek, meaning 'Trojan'. Actor Ileana D'Cruz is a star in Bollywood films.

Ilona
Hungarian, meaning 'light'. Also the name of the Queen of the Fairies in Magyar mythology.

Ilsa
German, meaning 'pledged to God'. Also the name of Ingrid Bergman's character in the film *Casablanca*.

Ima
German, meaning 'embraces everything'. Ima Hogg was an influential philanthropist in the early 20th century.

Iman
Arabic, meaning 'faith'. The Somali supermodel known simply as Iman is also an entrepreneur and was married to David Bowie.

Imara
Hungarian, meaning 'great ruler'. Also the name of a genus of moths.

Imelda
German, meaning 'all-consuming fight'. Famous Imeldas include actor Imelda Staunton, politician Imelda Marcos and actor Anne Crawford, whose real name was Imelda.

Imogen
(alt. Imogene)
Latin, meaning 'last-born'.

Ina
Latin, meaning 'to make feminine'. Famous Inas include author and presenter Ina Garten and childbirth pioneer Ina May Gaskin.

Inaya
Arabic, meaning 'taking care'. Singer Inaya Day's voice features on many dancefloor house music classics.

India
(alt. Indie)
Hindi, from the country of the same name. India Knight is a British journalist and author.

Indiana
Latin, meaning 'from India'. Also the name of a state in the USA.

Indigo
Greek, meaning 'deep blue dye'. Also one of the seven colours of the rainbow.

Indira
(alt. Inira)
Sanskrit, meaning 'beauty'. Indira Gandhi was the first and, to date, only female prime minister of India.

Inez
(alt. Ines)
Spanish, meaning 'pure'. Also a spelling variation of Agnes.

Inga
(alt. Inge, Ingeborg, Inger)
Scandinavian, meaning 'guarded by Ing'. Also the name of a type of tropical shrub and tree.

Ingrid

Scandinavian, meaning 'beautiful'. Actor Ingrid Bergman was known for her roles in *Casablanca*, *Notorious* and *Gaslight*.

Io
(alt. Eyo)

Greek, from the mythological priestess and heroine of the same name in ancient Greek mythology.

Ioanna

Greek, meaning 'grace'. Usually used as a spelling alternative to Joanna.

Iola
(alt. Iole)

Greek, meaning 'cloud of dawn'. The novel *Iola Leroy*, by Frances Harper, was one of the first novels published by a black female author.

Iolanthe

Greek, meaning 'violet flower'. Usually associated with the opera *Iolanthe* by Gilbert and Sullivan.

Iona

Greek, from the island of the same name. Also the name of a small island off the coast of Scotland.

Ione

Greek, meaning 'violet'. Also the name of a type of orchid.

Iorwen

Welsh, meaning 'fair'.

Iphigenia

Greek, meaning 'sacrifice'. Iphigenia was an ancient Greek victim of slaughter whose name became synonymous with strength and being the mother of strong children.

Ira
(alt. Iva)

Hebrew, meaning 'watchful'. More commonly used as a boys' name.

Irene
(alt. Irelyn, Irena, Irina, Irini)

Greek, meaning 'peace'.

Iris

Greek, meaning 'rainbow'. Also from the flower of the same name.

Irma

German, meaning 'universal'. Often associated with Irma Bunt, a Bond villainess.

Isabel
(alt. Isabela, Isabell, Isabella, Isabelle, Isabeth, Isobel, Izabella, Izabelle)

Spanish, meaning 'pledged to God'. Dozens of royals have been called Isabel or Isabella over the centuries, including Queen Isabella I of Spain, who financed Christopher Columbus' voyage to North America.

Isadora

Latin, meaning 'gift of Isis'. Isadora Duncan was a famed dancer at the turn of the 20th century, whose life was made into the film *Isadora*.

Ishana

Sanskrit, meaning 'desire'. One of the names for Shiva in the Hindu faith.

Isis

From the ancient Egyptian goddess of motherhood, magic and fertility.

Isla

(alt. Isa, Isela, Isley)

Scottish Gaelic, meaning 'river'. Actor Isla Fischer was born in Oman to Scottish parents and raised in Australia.

Isolde

Welsh, meaning 'fair lady'. Usually associated with the opera *Tristan und Isolde* by Richard Wagner.

Istas

Native American, meaning 'snow'. In Latin, 'istas' also refers to the feminine form of 'that person'.

Ivana

Slavic, meaning 'Jehovah is gracious'. Model Ivana Trump is known for her former marriage to the 45th US President Donald Trump.

Ivette

Variation of Yvette, meaning 'yew wood'. This spelling is more commonly used in Spanish-speaking communities.

Ivonne

Variation of Yvonne, meaning 'yew wood'. This spelling is more commonly used in Spanish-speaking communities.

Ivory

Latin, meaning 'white as elephant tusks'.

Ivy

English, from the plant of the same name. Famous Ivys include elderly internet sensation Ivy Bean, the first British female lawyer, Ivy Williams, and children's author Ivy Wallace.

Ixia

Afrikaans, from the flower of the same name.

Girls' names

Jaamini
Hindi, meaning 'evening'.

Jacinda
(alt. Jacinta)

Spanish, meaning 'hyacinth'. Jacinda Ardern is the Prime Minister of New Zealand. Jacinda Barrett is an Australian-American model turned actor.

Jacqueline
(alt. Jacalyn, Jacklyn, Jaclyn, Jacquelin, Jacquelyn, Jacquline, Jaqlyn, Jaquelin, Jaqueline; abbrev. Jack, Jacky, Jackie, Jacque, Jacqui)

French, meaning 'he who supplants'. Famous Jacquelines include children's author Jacqueline Wilson, actor Jacqueline Bisset and cellist Jacqueline du Pré.

Jade
(alt. Jada, Jaida, Jayda, Jayde)

Spanish, meaning 'green stone'. Famous Jades include athletes Jade Jones and Jade Johnson and designer Jade Jagger.

Jaden
(alt. Jadyn, Jaiden, Jaidyn, Jayden)

Hebrew, meaning 'Jehovah has heard'. More commonly used as a boys' name.

Jael
Hebrew, meaning 'mountain goat'. Found in the Bible.

Jaime
(alt. Jaima, Jaimie, Jami, Jamie)

Spanish, meaning 'he who supplants'. Jamie is a common short form of James, more commonly used for boys.

Jamila
Arabic, meaning 'lovely'. Author Jamila Gavin is known for her children's books, most of which have an Indian influence.

Jan
(alt. Jana, Jann, Janna, Janae)

Hebrew, meaning 'the Lord is gracious'; Arabic, meaning 'dear'; Persian meaning 'life'.

Jane
(alt. Jayne, Janie)

Feminine form of the Hebrew John, meaning 'the Lord is gracious'. A popular name in the 1960s and '70s but less common now. Famous Janes include Tarzan's friend Jane and Henry VIII's third wife, Jane Seymour.

Janelle
(alt. Janel, Janell, Jenelle)

American, meaning 'the Lord is gracious'. A popular name in the 1970s and '80s in both America and Australia but less common now.

Janet
(alt. Janette)

Scottish, meaning 'the Lord is gracious'. Singer Janet Jackson is known for being part of the musical Jackson family, as well as a performer in her own right.

Janice
(alt. Janis)

American, meaning 'the Lord is gracious'. Famous Janices include rower Janice Meek, former supermodel Janice Dickinson and the character of Janice Battersby in Coronation Street.

Janine
(alt. Janeen)

English, meaning 'the Lord is gracious'.

Janoah
(alt. Janiya, Janiyah)

Hebrew, meaning 'quiet and calm'. Also used as a spelling alternative for Genoa.

January

Latin, meaning 'the first month'. Actor January Jones is known for her roles in Mad Men, Unknown and X-Men: First Class.

Jarita

Hindi-Sanskrit, meaning 'famous bird'. Usually associated with the bird character in the Hindu Mahabharata.

Jasmine
(alt. Jasmin, Jazim, Jazmine)

Persian, meaning 'jasmine flower'.

Jay

Latin, meaning 'jaybird'. Jays are colourful birds from the crow family.

Jayna

Sanskrit, meaning 'bringer of victory'. More commonly used in Indian communitites.

Jean
(alt. Jeane, Jeanne)

Scottish, meaning 'the Lord is gracious'. Famous Jeans include actors Jean Harlow and Jean Marsh and author Jean Auel.

Jeana
(alt. Jeanna)
Latin, meaning 'queen'.

Jeanette
(alt. Jeannette, Janette; abbrev. Jeannie, Jeanie)
French, meaning 'the Lord is gracious'. Jeanette Winterson is a BAFTA-winning British author and journalist. The shortened form is commonly associated with the sitcom *I Dream of Jeannie*.

Jeanine
(alt. Jeannine)
Latin, meaning 'the Lord is gracious'. Jeanine Tesori is known for her musical theatre arrangements and compositions.

Jemima
Hebrew, meaning 'dove'. Jemima Khan is a writer and campaigner.

Jemma
English variant of Gemma, meaning 'precious stone'. Actor Jemma Redgrave is a fourth-generation member of the Redgrave acting dynasty.

Jena
Arabic, meaning 'little bird'. Actor Jena Malone starred in *Donnie Darko*, *Pride and Prejudice* and *The Hunger Games: Catching Fire*.

Jenna
Shortened form of Jennifer, meaning 'white and smooth'. The name was very popular in the 1980s, especially in the USA.

Jennifer
(alt. Jenifer; abbrev. Jenny, Jennie, Jenni)
Cornish alternative to Guinevere, meaning 'white and smooth'. Famous Jennifers include actors Jennifer Lawrence and Jennifer Aniston and singer Jennifer Hudson.

Jerri
(alt. Jeri, Jerrie, Jerrie, Jerry)
German, meaning 'spear ruler'. Famous Jerries include actor Jerri Manthey, model Jerry Hall and pioneering South Pole physician Dr Jerri Nielsen.

Jerusha
Hebrew, meaning 'married'. Jerusha Hess and husband Jared Hess are filmmakers whose films include *Napoleon Dynamite*.

Jeryl
English, meaning 'spear ruler'. Jeryl Prescott is an American actor.

Jessa
Shortened form of Jessica, meaning 'He sees'. Jessa Gamble is an English-Canadian author and scientific researcher.

Jessamy
(alt. Jessame, Jessamine, Jessamyn)
Persian, meaning 'jasmine flower'. Usually associated with the children's book *Jessamy* by Barbara Sleigh.

Jessica
*(alt. Jesica, Jesika, Jessika; abbrev.
Jess, Jessi, Jessie, Jessye)*
Hebrew, meaning 'He sees'. A
popular name over several decades.
Famous Jessicas include actor Jessica
Alba and athlete Jessica Ennis-Hill.
Famous Jessies include singer Jessie J.

Jesusa
Spanish, meaning 'mother of the
Lord'. Also a shortened form of
Jerusalem.

Jethetha
Hebrew, meaning 'princess'.

Jette
(alt. Jetta, Jettie)
Danish, meaning 'black as coal'. Also
the name of a town in Belgium.

Jewel
(alt. Jewell)
French, meaning 'delight'. Singer-
songwriter, producer and actor Jewel
is professionally known just by her
first name.

Jezebel
(alt. Jezabel, Jezabelle)
Hebrew, meaning 'pure and virginal'.
Conversely, widely used as a term for
'bad women' after the misbehaving
wife of a king in the Bible.

Jill
Latin, meaning 'youthful'. Famous
Jills include actor Jill Clayburgh,
presenter Jill Dando and children's
author Jill Murphy.

Jillian
(abbrev. Jill, Jilly)
Latin, meaning 'youthful'. Often used
as a spelling alternative to Gillian.

Jimena
Spanish, meaning 'heard'. Jimena
Diaz was the ruler of Valencia in the
12th century.

Jo
Shortened form of Joanna, meaning
'the Lord is gracious'. Famous
Jos include supernanny Jo Frost,
presenter Jo Coburn and athlete Jo
Ankier.

Joan
Hebrew, meaning 'the Lord is
gracious'. Famous Joans include
St Joan of Arc, actor Joan Collins and
comedian Joan Rivers.

Joanna
*(alt. Joana, Joanie, Joann, Joanne,
Johanna, Joni)*
Hebrew, meaning 'the Lord is
gracious'. Famous Joannas include
actors Joanna Lumley and Joanna
Page. Author J.K. Rowling's first name
is Joanne.

Jocasta
Italian, meaning 'lighthearted'.
Jocasta was an influential character in
ancient Greek mythology.

Jocelyn
(alt. Jauslyn, Jocelyne, Joscelin, Joslyn)
German, meaning 'cheerful'.

Jody
(alt. Jodee, Jodi, Jodie)

Shortened form of Judith, meaning 'Jewish'. Famous Jodys include actor Jodie Foster and singer Jody Watley.

Joelle
(alt. Joela)

Hebrew, meaning 'Jehovah is the Lord'. Famous Joelles include teen singer Joelle and actor Joelle Carter.

Joie

French, meaning 'joy'.

Jolene
Contraction of Joanna and Darlene, meaning 'gracious darling'. Usually associated with the song 'Jolene' by Dolly Parton.

Jolie
(alt. Joely)

French, meaning 'pretty'.

Jordan
(alt. Jordana, Jordin, Jordyn)

Hebrew, meaning 'down-flowing'. Model and reality television star Katie Price is known by her professional name Jordan. Also used for boys.

Josephine
(alt. Josefina, Josephina; abbrev. Jo, Joss, Josie)

Hebrew, meaning 'Jehovah increases'. Famous Josephines include the first Empress of France, wife of Napoleon, pioneering actor Josephine Baker and mystery author Josephine Bell.

Jovita
(alt. Jovie)

Latin, meaning 'made glad'. St Jovita was a Christian martyr with her brother St Faustinus during the second century.

Joy
Latin, meaning 'joy'. Famous Joys include comedian Joy Behar, actor Joy Lauren and poet Joy Harjo.

Joyce
Latin, meaning 'joyous'. Famous Joyces include author Joyce Carol Oates and actors Joyce Blair and Joyce DeWitt.

Juanita
(alt. Juana)

Spanish, meaning 'the Lord is gracious'.

Jubilee
Hebrew, meaning 'horn of a ram'. Usually associated with the celebration of an anniversary, such as the Queen's Diamond Jubilee.

Judith
(alt. Judit; abbrev. Judi, Judie, Judy)

Hebrew, meaning 'Jewish'. Found in the Bible. Very popular in the 1940s and '50s. Actor Judy Garland was the star of *The Wizard of Oz*.

Jules
French, meaning 'Jove's child'. Sometimes used as a variant of Julie or Julia, but more commonly used as a boys' name.

Julia
(alt. Julie, Juli)

Latin, meaning 'youthful'. Famous Julias include actors Julia Roberts and Julia Sawalha and TV chef Julia Child, while famous Julies include three Golden Globe and BAFTA-winning actors: Julie Andrews, Julie Christie and Julie Walters.

Julianne
(alt. Juliana, Juliann, Julianne)

Latin, meaning 'youthful'. Oscar-nominated British-American actor Julianne Moore has starred in a string of blockbuster films and is also a children's author.

Juliet
(alt. Joliet, Juliette)

Latin, meaning 'youthful'. Usually associated with the heroine of Shakespeare's play *Romeo and Juliet*.

June
(alt. Juna)

Latin, after the month of the same name. Famous Junes include actor June Bland, singer June Carter Cash and presenter June Sarpong.

Juniper

Dutch, from the shrub of the same name, used for distilling the spirit gin.

Juno
(alt. Juneau)

Latin, meaning 'queen of heaven'. Juno was an ancient Roman Queen of the Gods, and the goddess of marriage and Rome.

Justice

English, meaning 'to deliver what is just'.

Justine
(alt. Justina)

Latin, meaning 'fair and righteous'. Famous Justines include singer Justine Frischmann and actors Justine Bateman and Justine Waddell.

Jørgina

Dutch, meaning 'farmer'. More commonly used as a spelling alternative for Georgina.

Girls' names

Kadenza
(alt. Kadence)
Latin, meaning 'with rhythm'. A spelling alternative for Cadenza.

Kadisha
Hebrew, meaning 'religious one'.

Kaitlin
(alt. Kaitlyn)
Greek, meaning 'pure'. Variant of Caitlin that became popular, especially in the USA, after the 1970s. Kaitlin Doubleday is a Hollywood actor.

Kala
(alt. Kaela, Kaiala, Kaila)
Sanskrit, meaning 'black one'. Also known for being the great ape that saved Tarzan as a baby.

Kali
(alt. Kailee, Kailey, Kaleigh, Kaley, Kalie, Kalli, Kally, Kaylee, Kayleigh)
Sanskrit, meaning 'black one'. Also known in Hinduism as the Goddess of Time and Change.

Kalila
Arabic, meaning 'beloved'.

Kalina
Slavic, meaning 'flower'.

Kalliope
(alt. Calliope)
Greek, meaning 'beautiful voice'. From the muse of the same name.

Kama
Sanskrit, meaning 'love'. Known in Hinduism as one of the four goals of life, kama refers to intellectual fulfilment.

Kami
Japanese, meaning 'lord'.

Kamilla
(alt. Kamilah)
Slavic, meaning 'serving girl'. A spelling alternative for Camilla.

Kana

Hawaiian, from the demi-god of the same name. In Hawaiian mythology Kana could take the form of a rope that could stretch from the island of Molokai to Hawaii.

Kanika

Swahili, meaning 'black cloth'. The stage name of Indian actor Divya Venkatasubramaniam.

Kara

Latin, meaning 'dear one'.

Karen

(alt. Karan, Karalyn, Karin, Karina, Karon, Karren; abbrev. Kari, Karrie)

Greek, meaning 'pure'. Very popular during the 1960s and '70s. Famous Karens include comedian Karen Taylor and musician Karen Carpenter. Kari is one of Saturn's moons.

Karimah

Arabic, meaning 'giving'. A spelling variation of Karima.

Karishma

(alt. Karisma)

Sanskrit, meaning 'miracle'. Both Karisma and Karishma are popular names in India.

Karla

German, meaning 'man'. A spelling variation for Carla.

Karly

(alt. Karlee, Karley, Karli)

German, meaning 'free man'. Popular in Scotland especially, from where both Karly Robertson the ice skater and Karly Ashworth from *Big Brother* hail.

Karma

Hindi, meaning 'destiny'. Known as a principle of Buddhism where good deeds lead to a positive influence on a person's future.

Karol

(alt. Karolina, Karolyn)

Slavic, meaning 'little and womanly'. A spelling variation of Carol.

Kasumi

Japanese, meaning 'of the mist'.

Katarina

(alt. Katarine, Katerina, Katharina)

Greek, meaning 'pure'. Katarina was one of the first companions of Doctor Who.

Kate

(alt. Kat, Katie, Kathi, Kathie, Kathy, Kati, Katy)

Shortened form of Katherine, meaning 'pure'. Famous Kates include actors Kate Winslet and Kate Hudson and the Duchess of Cambridge, Kate Middleton.

Katherine

(alt. Katharine, Katheryn, Kathrine, Kathryn; abbrev. Kathie, Kathy)

Greek, meaning 'pure'. A spelling variation for Catherine.

Kathleen
(alt. Kathlyn)

Greek, meaning 'pure'. Very popular in the 1960s and shared by many actors, politicans and scientists from that generation.

Katrina
(alt. Katina)

Greek, meaning 'pure'. More commonly used as a shortened version of Katherine.

Kaveri

Sanskrit, meaning 'sacred river'. Known for the large river that flows across India.

Kay
(alt. Kaye)

Shortened form of Katherine, meaning 'pure'.

Kaya

Sanskrit, meaning 'nature', or Turkish, meaning 'rock'. Kaya also refers to a sweet coconut jam popular in Asia.

Kayla
(alt. Kaylah)

Greek, meaning 'pure'. Kayla Harrison won a gold medal in judo at the 2012 and 2016 Olympics.

Kayley
(alt. Kayley, Kayli)

American, meaning 'pure'. Also known as one of the main characters in *The Magic Sword: Quest for Camelot*.

Kaylin

American, meaning 'pure'. A spelling variation for Caylin.

Keary

Gaelic, meaning 'black-haired'. Also a boys' name.

Keeley
(alt. Keely)

Irish, meaning 'battle maid'. Actor Keeley Hawes is a popular star of British TV drama.s

Keila

Hebrew, meaning 'citadel'.

Keira

Irish Gaelic, meaning 'dark'. A rise in popularity of the name followed the success of actor Keira Knightley.

Keisha
(alt. Keesha)

Arabic, meaning 'woman'. Keisha Castle-Hughes is an Australian actor.

Kelis

American, meaning 'beautiful'. Award-winning singer Kelis is known widely by her first name only.

Kelly
(alt. Keli, Kelley, Kelli, Kellie)

Irish Gaelic, meaning 'battle maid'. Famous Kellys include singer Kelly Clarkson, TV personality Kelly Osbourne and Olympic athlete Kelly Holmes.

Kelsey
(alt. Kelcee, Kelcie, Kelsea, Kelsi, Kelsie)
Old English, meaning 'victorious ship'. More popular in the USA, where it is the name of several cities and is used for both girls and boys.

Kendall
(alt. Kendal)
English, meaning 'the valley of the River Kent'. Also a place in Cumbria.

Kendra
English, meaning 'knowing'. Name of a character in *Buffy The Vampire Slayer*. Kendra Wilkinson is an American TV personality.

Kenna
Irish Gaelic, meaning 'handsome'.

Kennedy
(alt. Kenadee, Kennedi)
Irish Gaelic, meaning 'helmet head'. Also used as a boys' name.

Kenzie
Shortened form of Mackenzie, meaning 'son of the wise ruler'. Mackenzie is also commonly used as a boys' name.

Kerensa
Cornish, meaning 'love'. Also a variation on the name Karen.

Kerrigan
Irish, meaning 'black haired'.

Kerry
(alt. Keri, Kerri, Kerrie)
Irish, from the county of the same name. Used for both girls and boys.

Khadijah
(alt. Khadejah)
Arabic, meaning 'premature baby'. Khadija bint Khuwaylid was the first wife of Muhammad and is known as the 'Mother of Islam'.

Khaleesi
Dothraki, meaning 'queen'. Royal title from *Game of Thrones*.

Kiana
(alt. Kia, Kianna)
American, meaning 'fibre'. Kiana is an American TV personality known for her physical fitness and physical training videos.

Kiara
It is possible that the name could come from two sources – Irish 'ciar' meaning 'dark' or 'dark haired', or the Latin 'chiara', meaning 'light'.

Kiki
Spanish, meaning 'home ruler'. Also an American slang term for a party centred around gossip and laughter.

Kimana
Native American, meaning 'butterfly'.

Kimberly
(alt. Kimberleigh, Kimberley; abbrev. Kim)
Old English, meaning 'royal forest'. Famous Kimberlys include rapper Kimberly 'Lil' Kim' Denise Jones. Famous Kims include TV personality Kim Kardashian, actor Kim Basinger and singer Kim Wilde.

Kingsley
(alt. Kinsley, Kynslee)
English, meaning 'king's meadow'. More commonly used for boys.

Kinsey
English, meaning 'king's victory'.

Kira
Greek, meaning 'lady'.

Kiri
Maori, meaning 'tree bark'. Dame Kiri Te Kanawa is known for her opera singing career spanning nearly 50 years.

Kirsten
(alt. Kirstin; abbrev. Kirstie, Kirsty)
Scandinavian, meaning 'Christian'. Kirsten Dunst is a German-American actor, singer and model. Famous Kirsties include TV presenters Kirsty Young and Kirstie Allsopp and American actor Kirstie Alley.

Kitty
(alt. Kittie)
Shortened form of Katherine, meaning 'pure'. Can be used in its own right.

Kizzy
Hebrew, meaning the plant 'cassia'. Singer Kizzy Crawford sings in both English and Welsh.

Klara
Hungarian, meaning 'bright'. Commonly used in German-speaking communities.

Komal
Hindi, meaning 'soft and tender'. Most commonly used for boys.

Konstantina
Latin, meaning 'steadfast'. Feminine form of Constantine.

Kora
(alt. Kori)
Greek, meaning 'maiden'. A spelling variation for Cora.

Kristen
(alt. Kristan, Kristin, Kristine, Krysten; abbrev. Kris, Krista, Kristie, Kristy)
Greek, meaning 'Christian'. Actor Kristen Stewart is known for her roles in the *Twilight* films.

Kwanza
(alt. Kwanzaa)
Swahili, meaning 'beginning'. Also known for the week-long celebration of African–American culture near Christmas time.

Kyla
(alt. Kya, Kylah, Kyle)
Scottish, meaning 'narrow spit of land'.

Kylie
(alt. Kiley, Kylee)
Irish Gaelic, meaning 'graceful'. The rise in popularity of this name is linked to actor and singer Kylie Minogue.

Kyoko
Japanese, meaning 'girl who sees her own true image'.

Girls' names

Lacey
(alt. Laci, Lacie, Lacy)
French, from a nobleman's surname. Most popular in North America, but Lacey Turner is an English actor and *EastEnders* star.

Ladonna
Italian, meaning 'lady'. Also a spelling alternative to Madonna.

Lady
English, meaning 'bread kneader'. Also an aristocratic title.

Laidh
Scottish meaning 'a ship's course'. Also a spelling alternative to Lady.

Laila
(alt. Laelia, Layla, Leila, Lejla, Lela, Lelah, Lelia)
Arabic, meaning 'night'. Famous Lailas include boxer Laila Ali and the song 'Layla' by Eric Clapton. Has become popular in recent years.

Lainey
(alt. Laine, Laney, Lany)
French, meaning 'bright light'. In Poland, the most common spelling is Lany, whereas in other countries it can be Lainey or Laney.

Lakeisha
(alt. Lakeshia)
American, meaning 'woman'. Its origins seem to be a combination of La and Keisha.

Lakshmi
(alt. Laxmi)
Sanskrit, meaning 'good omen'. Also the Hindu goddess of wealth.

Lana
Greek, meaning 'light'. Famous Lanas include singer Lana Del Rey, actor Lana Turner and the language-communication chimpanzee Lana.

Lani
(alt. Lanie)
Hawaiian, meaning 'heaven and sky'.

Lara
Latin, meaning 'famous'. Famous Laras include actor Lara Flynn Boyle, *Tomb Raider* protagonist Lara Croft, and the ancient Roman nymph of the same name.

Larissa
(alt. Larisa)
Greek, meaning 'lighthearted'. Larissa was a nymph in ancient Greek mythology.

Lark
(alt. Larkin)
English, meaning 'playful songbird'.

Larsen
(alt. Larsen)
Scandinavian, meaning 'son of Lars'.

Latifa
(alt. Latifah)
Arabic, meaning 'gentle and pleasant'. Queen Latifah is the stage name of the singer and pioneer of female hip hop.

Latika
(alt. Lotika)
Hindi, meaning 'a plant'. Usually associated with the character of Latika from *Slumdog Millionaire*.

Latisha
Latin, meaning 'happiness'. More commonly used in the USA.

Latona
(alt. Latonia)
Roman, from the ancient Roman mythological heroine of the same name who had twin sons with the god Zeus.

Latoya
Spanish, meaning 'victorious one'. Singer LaToya Jackson is known for being a member of the musical Jackson family.

Latrice
(alt. Latricia)
Latin, meaning 'noble'. More commonly used in the USA.

Laura
(alt. Lora)
Latin, meaning 'laurel'. Famous Lauras include designer Laura Ashley, author Laura Ingalls Wilder and actor Laura Dern.

Laurel
Latin, meaning 'laurel tree'. A Laurel is also a term used for young women in the Mormon Church.

Lauren
(alt. Lauran, Loren)
Latin, meaning 'laurel'. Famous Laurens include actors Lauren Bacall and Lauren Crace and DJ Lauren Laverne.

Laveda
(alt. Lavada)
Latin, meaning 'cleansed'.

Lavender

Latin, from the flowering plant of the same name.

Laverne
(alt. Lavern, Laverna)

Latin, from the goddess of the same name. Famous Lavernes include the Andrews Sisters member Laverne Andrews, and US sitcom *Laverne & Shirley*.

Lavinia
(alt. Lavina)

Latin, meaning 'woman of Rome'. Lavinia was an ancient Roman character whose hair caught fire during sacrifices to the gods.

Lavita

American, meaning 'charming'. The original 'la vita' means 'life' in Latin.

Lavonne
(alt. Lavon)

French, meaning 'yew wood'. More commonly used in the USA.

Leah
(alt. Lea, Leia)

Hebrew, meaning 'weary'.

Leandra

Greek, meaning 'lion man'. In the novel *Don Quixote* by Miguel de Cervantes, Leandra is a beautiful woman whose many suitors withdraw to the mountains to write about how beautiful she is.

Leanne
(alt. Leann, Leanna, Leeann, Lee Ann)

Contraction of Lee and Ann, meaning 'meadow grace'. Famous Leannes include singers LeAnn Rimes and Lee Ann Womack and actor Leanne Wilson.

Leda

Greek, meaning 'gladness'. Leda was an ancient Greek character seduced by the god Zeus in the form of a white swan, and whose children included Helen of Troy.

Lee
(alt. Leigh)

English, meaning 'pasture' or 'meadow'. Used equally for girls and boys.

Leilani

Hawaiian, meaning 'flower from heaven'. Actor Leilani Jones is known for her roles in *Little Shop of Horrors* and various voice acting roles.

Leith

Scottish Gaelic, meaning 'broad river'.

Lena
(alt. Leena, Lina)

Latin, meaning 'light'. Famous Lenas include actors Lena Dunham, Lena Headey and Lena Ashwell.

Lenna
(alt. Lennie)

German, meaning 'lion's strength'.

Lenore
(alt. Lenora, Leonora, Leonor, Leonore)

Greek, meaning 'light'. Usually associated with the poem *Lenore* by Edgar Allan Poe.

Léonie
(alt. Leona, Leone)

Latin, meaning 'lioness'. Poet Leonie Adams wrote during the mid-20th century.

Leora
(alt. Liora)

Hebrew, meaning 'light'. The masculine form of Leora is Leor.

Lerola

Latin, meaning 'like a blackbird'.

Lesley
(alt. Leslee, Lesli)

Scottish Gaelic, from the name of the prominent clan. Also meaning 'holly garden'. The boys' variation is usually spelt Leslie.

Leta

Latin, meaning 'glad and joyful'. Leta Hollingworth was an influential child psychologist in the 20th century.

Letha

Greek, meaning 'forgetfulness'. Also the name of a type of butterfly.

Letitia
(alt. Leticia, Lettice, Lettie)

Latin, meaning 'joy and gladness'. St Leticia was a Spanish virgin martyr.

Lexia
(alt. Lexi, Lexie)

Greek, meaning 'defender of mankind'. Also the name of a type of butterfly.

Lia

Italian, meaning 'bringer of the gospel'. Actor Lia Williams is known for her roles in both theatre and film.

Liana

French, meaning 'to twine around'. Also the name of a type of vine.

Libby
(alt. Libbie)

Shortened form of Elizabeth, meaning 'consecrated to God'. Famous Libbys include journalist Libby Purves and singer Libby Holman.

Liberty

English, meaning 'freedom'.

Lida

Slavic, meaning 'loved by the people'.

Liese
(alt. Liesel, Liesl)

German, meaning 'pledged to God'. Also used as a shortened form of Elizabeth.

Lila
(alt. Lilah)

Arabic, meaning 'night'. In the Hindu faith, Lila refers to playtime or pastimes.

Lilac

Latin, from the flower of the same name. Also associated with the pale purple colour.

Lilia
(alt. Lilias)

Scottish, meaning 'lily'. More commonly used in Russian and Ukrainian communities.

Lilith

Arabic, meaning 'ghost'. Also the name of a female demon in Hebrew mythology.

Lillian
(alt. Lilian, Liliana, Lilla, Lillianna)

Latin, meaning 'lily'. Famous Lillians include actor Lillian Gish, playwright Lillian Hellman and pioneering nurse Lillian Wald.

Lily
(alt. Lili, Lillie, Lilly)

Latin, from the flower of the same name. Famous Lilys include singer Lily Allen, actor Lily Collins and model Lily Cole.

Linda
(alt. Lynda)

Spanish, meaning 'pretty'. Famous Lindas include presenter Linda Barker, actor Linda Blair and singer Linda Ronstadt.

Linden
(alt. Lindie, Lindy)

From the tree of the same name. Used more commonly for boys.

Lindsay
(alt. Lindsey, Linsey)

English, meaning 'island of linden trees'. Famous Lindsays include actors Lindsay Lohan, Lindsay Sloane and Lindsay Wagner.

Linnea
(alt. Linnae, Linny)

Scandinavian, meaning 'lime or linden tree'.

Lirit

Hebrew, meaning 'musically talented'.

Lisa
(alt. Leesa, Lise, Liza)

Hebrew, meaning 'pledged to God'. Famous Lisas include singer Lisa Bonet, *Friends* actor Lisa Kudrow and *The Simpsons* character Lisa Simpson.

Lissa

Greek, meaning 'bee'. Also used as a shortened form of Melissa.

Lissandra
(alt. Lisandra)

Greek, meaning 'man's defender'.

Liv

Nordic, meaning 'defence'. Actor Liv Tyler appeared in the *Lord of the Rings* trilogy.

Livia

Latin, meaning 'olive'. Livia Drusilla was a prominent ancient Roman woman, wife of the Emperor Augustus.

Liz
(alt. Lizzie, Lizzy)

Shortened form of Elizabeth, meaning 'consecrated to God'. Many Elizabeths go by Liz, including actor Liz Taylor.

Logan

Irish Gaelic, meaning 'small hollow'. More commonly used as a name for boys.

Lois

German, meaning 'renowned in battle'. Usually associated with the character of Lois Lane from the Superman comic series.

Lola

Spanish, meaning 'sorrows'. Also used as a shortened form of Delores.

Lolita
(alt. Lollie)

Spanish, meaning 'sorrows'. Usually associated with the character of Lolita in Vladimir Nabokov's novel *Lolita*.

Lona

Latin, meaning 'lion'. Lona is a moon deity in Hawaiian mythology.

Lora

Latin, meaning 'laurel'. Sometimes used as a spelling alternative to Laura.

Lorelei
(alt. Loralai, Loralie)

German, meaning 'dangerous rock'. Ancient German mythology tells of a maiden who lives on the Lorelei Rock in the river Rhine and lures sailors to their deaths.

Lorenza

Latin, meaning 'from Laurentium'.

Loretta
(alt. Loreto)

Latin, meaning 'laurel'. Mostly used in the USA, where actors with this name include Loretta Devine and Loretta Swit.

Lori
(alt. Laurie, Lorie, Lorri)

Latin, meaning 'laurel'. Actor Lori Petty is known for her roles in *Point Break*, *A League of Their Own* and *Tank Girl*.

Lorna

Scottish, from the town of Lorne. Usually associated with the protagonist in R.D. Blackmore's novel *Lorna Doone*.

Lorraine
(alt. Laraine, Loraine)

French, meaning 'from Lorraine'. TV presenter Lorraine Kelly is best known for breakfast TV and chat show work.

Lottie
(alt. Lotta, Lotte)

French, meaning 'little and womanly'. Usually used as a shortened form of Charlotte.

Lotus

Greek, meaning 'lotus flower'.

Louise
(alt. Louisa, Luisa; abbrev. Lou, Louie)

German, meaning 'renowned in battle'.

Lourdes

French, from the town of the same name. Madonna famously chose this name for her daughter in 1996.

Love

English, from the word 'love'.

Lowri

Welsh, meaning 'crowned with laurels'. Lowri Turner is a TV presenter.

Luanne
(alt. Luann, Luanna)

German, meaning 'renowned in battle'. In Hawaiian, the name also means 'enjoyment'.

Luba

Hebrew, meaning 'dearly loved'.

Lucia
(alt. Luciana)

Italian, meaning 'light'. Feminine form of the ancient Roman name Lucius.

Lucille
(alt. Lucile, Lucilla)

French, meaning 'light'. American Lucille Ball was the star of *I Love Lucy*.

Lucinda

English, meaning 'light'. Lucinda Green (Lucinda Prior-Palmer) was a world champion equestrian who won Badminton six times.

Lucretia
(alt. Lucrece)

Spanish, meaning 'light'. Also an important character in ancient Roman mythology.

Lucy
(alt. Lucie)

Latin, meaning 'light'. St Lucy was a martyr in the fourth century.

Ludmilla

Slavic, meaning 'beloved of the people'.

Luella
(alt. Lue)

English, meaning 'renowned in battle'. Designer Luella Bartley is known for her fashion brands and journalism for various fashion magazines.

Lulu
(alt. Lula)

German, meaning 'renowned in battle'. Singer Lulu became a star in the 1960s and is still successful today.

Luna

Latin, meaning 'moon'. Luna was the personification of the moon in ancient Roman mythology.

Lupita

Spanish, short form of Guadelupe. Actor Lupita Nyong'o is known for her role in *12 Years a Slave*.

Luz

Spanish, meaning 'light'. Also the name of an ancient city in the Bible.

Lydia
(alt. Lidia)

Greek, meaning 'from Lydia'. Famous Lydias include activist Lydia Becker, ballerina Lydia Lopokova and the character of Lydia Bennet in *Pride and Prejudice*.

Lyla

Hebrew, meaning 'night'.

Lynette
(alt. Linette)

Welsh, meaning 'idol'.

Lynn
(alt. Lyn, Lynne)

Spanish, meaning 'pretty'; English, meaning 'waterfall'. Actor Lynn Redgrave is part of the Redgrave acting dynasty.

Lynton

English, meaning 'town of lime trees'. Also the name of a town in Devon. Most commonly used for boys.

Lyra

Latin, meaning 'lyre'. The central character in Philip Pullman's *His Dark Materials* trilogy.

Girls' names

Mab

Irish Gaelic, meaning 'joy'. Queen Mab is a character in Shakespeare's play *Romeo and Juliet*.

Mabel
(alt. Mabelle, Mable)

Latin, meaning 'loveable'. Although the name Mabel is very old and dates from the fifth century, it did not become popular until the 19th century, when the novel *The Heir of Redclyffe* was published.

Macaria

Spanish, meaning 'blessed'.

Machiko

Japanese, meaning 'knowledgeable child'. Machiko Kawana is a Japanese voice artist.

Macy
(alt. Macey, Maci, Macie)

French, meaning 'weapon'. Macy Gray is the stage name of the award winning R&B singer-songwriter and actor Natalie McIntyre.

Mada

English, meaning 'from Magdala'. In Hindu mythology, Mada also refers to an enormous monster who is able to swallow the entire universe.

Madaio

Hawaiian, meaning 'gift from God'.

Madden
(alt. Maddyn)

Irish, meaning 'little dog'.

Madeline
(alt. Madaline, Madalyn, Madeleine, Madelyn, Madelynn, Madilyn; abbrev. Maddy, Maddi, Maddie, Madie)

Greek, meaning 'from Magdala'. Madeleine Albright was the first female Secretary of State in the US. Maddy Prior is one of the best-known English folk singers.

Madge

Greek, meaning 'pearl'. Also a shortened form of several names including Margaret, Madeline and Marjorie. Madge was especially common around 1880–1900, being the name of several actors of that time. More recently, it's the nickname of pop icon Madonna.

Madhuri

Hindi, meaning 'sweet girl'. Madhuri Dixit is one of Bollywood's most well-known and popular actors, appearing in dozens of Hindi films.

Madison

(alt. Maddison, Madisen, Madisyn, Madyson)

English, meaning 'son of the mighty warrior'. The increase in the popularity of Madison can be traced back to the mermaid character of Madison in the film *Splash*, played by Daryl Hannah.

Madonna

Latin, meaning 'my lady'. Usually associated with the pop legend Madonna, or as one of the Virgin Mary's many names.

Maeve

Irish Gaelic, meaning 'intoxicating'. Famous Maeves include Queen Maeve from Irish mythology, author Maeve Binchy and writer Maeve Brennan.

Mafalda

Spanish, meaning 'battle-mighty'. Mafalda is a popular Argentine comic strip.

Magali

Greek, meaning 'pearl'. More commonly used in French- or Portuguese-speaking communities.

Magdalene

(alt. Magdalen, Magdalena)

Greek, meaning 'from Magdala'. Mary Magdalene was one of Jesus's disciples in the Bible.

Magnolia

Latin, from the flowering plant of the same name.

Mahala

(alt. Mahalia)

Hebrew, meaning 'tender affection'.

Maia

(alt. Maja, Maya)

Greek, meaning 'mother'. Also an important character in ancient Greek mythology.

Maida

English, meaning 'maiden'.

Maisie

(alt. Maisey, Maisy, Maizie, Masie, Mazie)

Greek, meaning 'pearl'. Famous Maisies include children's book character Maisey Mouse and Maisie Williams, star of *Game of Thrones*.

Malin

Hebrew and English, meaning 'of Magdala'. Malin is most common in Sweden.

Maliya
(alt. Malia, Maliyah)
Hawaiian, meaning 'beloved'. Malia Obama is the daughter of the 44th President of the USA, Barack Obama.

Malka
Hebrew, meaning 'queen'.

Mallory
(alt. Malorie)
French, meaning 'unhappy'. Author Malorie Blackman is known for her children's literature.

Malvina
Gaelic, meaning 'smooth brow'. The name was invented by poet James Macpherson in the 18th century.

Mamie
(alt. Maimie, Mammie)
Shortened form of Margaret, meaning 'pearl'. Famous Mamies include former US first lady Mamie Eisenhower, wife of President Dwight Eisenhower.

Mandy
(alt. Mandie)
Shortened form of Amanda, meaning 'much loved'. Famous Mandys include actor Mandy Moore and the song *Mandy* by Barry Manilow.

Manisha
Sanskrit, meaning 'desire'. Manisha is the goddess of wisdom in the Hindu faith.

Mansi
Hopi, meaning 'plucked flower'. Also the name of an indigenous group of people in Russia.

Manuela
Spanish, meaning 'the Lord is among us'. More commonly used in German-speaking communities.

Mara
Hebrew, meaning 'bitter'. Famous Maras include actor Mara Wilson and children's author Mara Bergman.

Marcela
(alt. Marceline, Marcella, Marcelle)
Latin, meaning 'war-like'.

Marcia
(alt. Marcy, Marci, Marcie)
Latin, meaning 'war-like'. Famous Marcias include legendary British leader Queen Marcia, actor Marcia Cross and voice actor Marcia Wallace.

Margaret
(alt. Margarete, Margaretta, Margarette, Margret; abbrev. Maggie)
Greek, meaning 'pearl'. Famous Margarets include former prime minister Margaret Thatcher, author Margaret Atwood and actor Margaret Rutherford. Famous Maggies include actors Maggie Gyllenhaal and Maggie Grace, and the song 'Maggie May' by Rod Stewart.

Margery
(alt. Marge, Margie, Margit, Margy, Marjorie)
French, meaning 'pearl'. Author Margery Kempe wrote the first English-language autobiography, *The Book of Margery Kempe*, in the 15th century. Marjorie Bruce was daughter of Robert the Bruce of Scotland.

Margot
(alt. Margo)

French, meaning 'pearl'. Famous Margots include ballerina Margot Fonteyn, actor Margot Robbie and the sister of Anne Frank, Margot Frank.

Marguerite
(alt. Margarita)

French, meaning 'pearl'. Marguerite de Valois was Queen of France during the 16th century.

Maria
(alt. Mariah)

Latin, meaning 'bitter'. Famous Marias include tennis pro Maria Sharapova, performer Maria von Trapp and the character of Maria from the musical *West Side Story*.

Marian
(alt. Mariam, Mariana, Mariann, Marianne, Maryann, Maryanne, Marion)

French, meaning 'bitter grace'. Usually associated with the character of Maid Marian from the legend of Robin Hood. Marianne Faithfull is an English singer-songwriter.

Maribel

Hebrew, meaning 'bitter'. Also used as a contraction of Maria and Isabel.

Marie

French, meaning 'bitter'. Famous Maries include French Queen Marie Antoinette, physicist Marie Curie, and singer Marie Osmond.

Mariel
(alt. Mariela, Mariella)

Dutch, meaning 'bitter'. Also the name of a city in Cuba.

Marietta
(alt. Marieta)

French, meaning 'bitter'. Activist Marietta Stow was an influential campaigner for women's suffrage during the 19th century.

Marigold

English, from the flowering plant of the same name.

Marika

Dutch, meaning 'bitter'. More commonly used in Greek-speaking communities.

Marilyn
(alt. Marilee, Marilene, Marilynn)

English, meaning 'bitter'. Marilyn Monroe starred in films such as *Gentlemen Prefer Blondes*, *The Seven Year Itch* and *Some Like It Hot*.

Marina
(alt. Marine)

Latin, meaning 'from the sea'. Marina is a truly global name, with famous Marinas of many nationalities and backgrounds. Journalist Marine Hyde is… is one of few Brits with the name.

Mariposa

Spanish, meaning 'butterfly'. Also the name of a group of lilies.

Marisa
(alt. Maris, Marissa)

Latin, meaning 'of the sea'.
Famous Marisas include actor Marisa
Tomei and the notorious Yahoo!
business executive Marissa Mayer.

Marisol

Spanish, meaning 'bitter sun'. Also a
contraction of Maria de la Soledad,
which is another title for the Virgin
Mary in Spain.

Marjolaine

French, meaning 'marjoram'.

Marlene
(alt. Marlen, Marlena; abbrev. Marla)

Hebrew, meaning 'bitter'. Actor
Marlene Dietrich was German born
but became an American in 1939
and was a front-line entertainer for
the troops during World War II. The
character of Marla Singer in the film
Fight Club, was played by Helena
Bonham Carter.

Marley
(alt. Marlee)

American, meaning 'bitter'.

Marlo
(alt. Marlowe)

American, meaning 'bitter'. More
commonly used as a boys' name.

Marnie
(alt. Marney)

Scottish, meaning 'from the sea'.
Famous Marnies include the character
of Marnie from *Girls* and the film
Marnie by Alfred Hitchcock. It was
also the birth name of ballerina Dame
Darcey Bussell.

Marseille

French, from the city of the same
name in France.

Marsha

English, meaning 'war-like'. Famous
Marshas include actor Marsha
Thomason, singer Marsha Hunt and
playwright Marsha Norman.

Martha
(alt. Marta)

Aramaic, meaning 'lady'. Found in
the Bible. Martha Lane Fox was a
leading dotcom entrepreneur in the
2000s, later becoming the youngest
female member of the House of
Lords.

Martina

Latin, meaning 'war-like'. Famous
Martinas include tennis pros Martina
Hingis and Martina Navratilova and
Martina, Empress of the Byzantine
empire.

Marvel

French, meaning 'something to
marvel at'. Usually associated with
the comic book brand.

Mary

Hebrew, meaning 'bitter'. Famous Marys include the Virgin Mary, author Mary Shelley and morality campaigner Mary Whitehouse.

Masada

Hebrew, meaning 'foundation'. Also the name of an ancient Jewish fortification in Israel.

Matilda
(alt. Mathilda, Mathilde, Matilde)

German, meaning 'battle-mighty'. Famous Matildas include the lead character from the novel *Matilda* by Roald Dahl, Queen consort of England Matilda of Flanders, and 12th-century Queen Matilda of England.

Mattea

Hebrew, meaning 'gift of God'.

Maude
(alt. Maud)

German, meaning 'battle-mighty'. Usually associated with the character of Maude Flanders from *The Simpsons* or the film *Harold and Maude*.

Maura

Irish, meaning 'bitter'. Also the name of a French saint of the fourth century.

Maureen
(alt. Maurine)

Irish, meaning 'bitter'. Famous Maureens include actors Maureen Lipman, Maureen McCormick and Maureen O'Hara.

Mavis

French, meaning 'thrush'. The name originated in the 19th century after the publication of the novel *The Sorrows of Satan*.

Maxine
(alt. Maxie)

Latin, meaning 'greatest'. Famous Maxines include the Andrews Sisters member Maxine Andrews, and actors Maxine Audley and Maxine Peake.

May
(alt. Mae, Maye)

Hebrew, meaning 'gift of God'. Also the name of the fifth month.

Maya
(alt. Mya, Myah)

Greek, meaning 'mother'. Famous Mayas include author Maya Angelou, comedian Maya Rudolph and the Mayan people of Central America.

Mckenna
(alt. Mackenna)

Irish Gaelic, meaning 'son of the handsome one'.

Mckenzie
(alt. Mackenzie, Mckenzy, Mikenzi)

Irish Gaelic, meaning 'son of the wise ruler'. More commonly used as a boys' name.

Meara

Gaelic, meaning 'filled with happiness'.

Medea
(alt. Meda)

Greek, meaning 'ruling'. Also the name of a prominent figure in ancient Greek mythology.

Meg

Shortened form of Margaret, meaning 'pearl'. Famous Megs include actor Meg Ryan and the character of Meg from Disney's Hercules.

Megan
(alt. Meagan, Meghan, Meghann)

Welsh, meaning 'pearl'. Famous Megans include actors Megan Fox and Megan Mullally and Duchess of Sussex, Meghan Markle.

Mehri

Persian, meaning 'kind'. Also the name of a group of people and a language spoken in southern Arabia.

Meiwei

Chinese, meaning 'forever enchanting'.

Melanie
(alt. Melania, Melany, Melonie; abbrev. Mel)

Greek, meaning 'dark-skinned'. Famous Melanies include singers Melanie Brown and Melanie Chisholm of the Spice Girls. Melania Trump is the current First Lady of the USA.

Melba

Australian, meaning 'from Melbourne'.

Melia
(alt. Meliah)

German, meaning 'industrious'.

Melina

Greek, meaning 'honey'. Actor Melina Kanakaredes has appeared in several US-based crime dramas, including CSI:NY.

Melinda

Latin, meaning 'honey'. Famous Melindas include TV presenter and model Melinda Messenger, philanthropist Melinda Gates and actor Melinda Clarke.

Melisande

French, meaning 'bee'. Melisandre is a character from George R.R. Martin's A Song of Ice and Fire series.

Melissa
(alt. Melisa, Mellissa)

Greek, meaning 'bee'. Famous Melissas include singer Melissa Etheridge and actors Melissa Joan Hart and Melissa George.

Melody
(alt. Melodie)

Greek, meaning 'song'. Aptly, there are a number of Melodys who have gone on to be singers as well as actors. Melody is also a character in Disney's The Little Mermaid.

Melvina

Celtic, meaning 'chieftain'.

Menora
(alt. Menorah)
Hebrew, meaning 'candlestick'.

Mercedes
Spanish, meaning 'mercies'. Usually associated with the luxury car manufacturer Mercedes-Benz.

Mercy
English, meaning 'mercy'.

Meredith
(alt. Meridith)
Welsh, meaning 'great ruler'.

Merle
French, meaning 'blackbird'. Used equally for girls and boys, though not a common name anywhere.

Merritt
English, from the word 'merit'. Can be used for both boys and girls.

Merry
English, meaning 'light-hearted'.

Meryl
(alt. Merrill) ·
Irish Gaelic, meaning 'sea-bright'. Actor Meryl Streep is Hollywood royalty, having starred in a string of hugely successful films.

Meta
German, meaning 'pearl'. Also a Greek term for 'after or beyond'.

Mia
Italian, meaning 'mine'. Famous Mias include actors Mia Wasikowska and Mia Farrow and singer M.I.A.

Michaela
(alt. Makaela, Makaila, Micaela, Mikaila, Mikayla)
Hebrew, meaning 'resembles God'. Famous Michaelas include presenter Michaela Strachan, actor Michaela Conlin, and gymnast McKayla Maroney.

Michelle
(alt. Machelle, Mechelle, Michaele, Michal, Michele, Michen; abbrev. Mickey, Mickie)
French, meaning 'resembles God'. Famous Michelles include actor Michelle Rodriguez and the former First Lady of the USA, Michelle Obama.

Mieko
(alt. Meiko)
Japanese, meaning 'born into wealth'.

Migdalia
Greek, meaning 'from Magdala'.

Mignon
French, meaning 'sweet'.

Mika
(alt. Micah)
Hebrew, meaning 'resembles God'.

Milada
Czech, meaning 'my love'. More commonly used in Slavic and Czech communities.

Milagros

Spanish, meaning 'miracles'. Also a term used for folk charms with healing properties in Mexico.

Milan

Italian, from the city of the same name in Italy.

Mildred

English, meaning 'gentle strength'. Famous Mildreds include the character of Mildred Hubble from the *Worst Witch* series, author Mildred B. Davies and actor Mildred Dunnock.

Milena

Czech, meaning 'love and warmth'.

Miley

American, meaning 'smiley'. Made popular by singer and actor Miley Cyrus.

Millicent
(alt. Milicent; abbrev. Millie, Milly)

German, meaning 'high-born power'. Famous Millicents include suffragist Millicent Fawcett and British spy Milicent Bagot.

Mimi

Italian, meaning 'bitter'. Also the name of the female protagonist in the opera *La bohème*, by Giacomo Puccini.

Mina
(alt. Mena)

German, meaning 'love'; Persian, meaning 'coloured glass'.

Mindy
(alt. Mindi)

Latin, meaning 'honey'. Used as a shortened form of Melinda as well as a name in its own right. Mindy Kaling is an American-Indian actor and comedian.

Minerva

Latin, from the goddess of the same name. Minerva was the goddess of wisdom, the arts and defence, in ancient Roman mythology.

Ming

Chinese, meaning 'bright'. Usually associated with the Ming Dynasty, which ruled China from the 14th to the 17th century.

Minnie
(alt. Minna)

German, meaning 'helmet'. Usually associated with the Disney character Minnie Mouse and actor Minnie Driver.

Mira
(alt. Meera)

Latin, meaning 'admirable'. Also the name of a giant red star.

Mirabel
(alt. Mirabella, Mirabelle)

Latin, meaning 'wonderful'. Also the name of a type of plum.

Miranda
(alt. Meranda; abbrev. Randi, Randy)

Latin, meaning 'admirable'. Famous Mirandas include actors Miranda Richardson and Miranda Hart and model Miranda Kerr.

Mirella
(alt. Mireille, Mirela)

Latin, meaning 'admirable'. Opera singer Mirella Freni is known in Italy as being one of the finest in her art.

Miriam

Hebrew, meaning 'bitter'. Also the name of a prophetess in the Bible. Miriam Margolyes is a popular British BAFTA-winning character actor.

Mirta

Spanish, meaning 'crown of thorns'.

Missy

Shortened form of Melissa, meaning 'bee'. Famous Missys include musician Missy Elliot, singer Missy Higgins, and performer Missy Malone.

Misty
(alt. Misti)

English, meaning 'mist'. Misty Copeland was the first black ballerina to become a principal dancer with a national ballet company.

Mitzi

German, meaning 'bitter'. Actor Mitzi Gaynor appeared in *South Pacific*.

Miu

Japanese, meaning 'beautiful feather'. Also the name of an endangered language spoken in Papua New Guinea.

Moana

Maori, meaning 'ocean'. Made famous by the Disney animation of the same name.

Moira
(alt. Maira)

Irish, meaning 'bitter'. Famous Moiras include actor Moira Brooker, ballet dancer Moira Shearer and news presenter Moira Stuart.

Molly
(alt. Mollie)

American, meaning 'bitter'. Famous Mollys include actors Molly Ringwald and Molly Sims.

Mona

Irish Gaelic, meaning 'aristocratic'. A character from the children's television programme *Mona the Vampire*.

Monica
(alt. Monika, Monique)

Latin, meaning 'adviser'. Famous Monicas include singer Monica, infamous White House intern Monica Lewinsky and tennis pro Monica Seles.

Monroe

Gaelic, meaning 'mouth of the river Rotha'. Usually associated with Marilyn Monroe.

Montserrat
(alt. Monserrate)

Spanish, from the town of the same name. Opera singer Montserrat Caballe is known for her work in the bel canto technique, and for the song 'Barcelona' with Freddie Mercury.

Morag

Scottish, meaning 'star of the sea'. Also the pet name of a monster that supposedly inhabits Loch Morar in Scotland.

Morgan
(alt. Morgann)

Welsh, meaning 'great and bright'. Used for both girls and boys.

Moriah

Hebrew, meaning 'the Lord is my teacher'. Also the name of a mountain mentioned in the Bible.

Morwenna
(alt. Modwenna)

Welsh, meaning 'maiden'. Morwenna Banks is a British comedy actor, writer and producer. She is known to toddlers everywhere as the voice of Mummy Pig in Peppa Pig.

Moselle
(alt. Mozell, Mozella, Mozelle)

Hebrew, meaning 'saviour'. Also the name of a river and a German wine.

Mulan

Chinese, meaning 'wood orchid'. Usually associated with the protagonist from the Disney film Mulan.

Munin

Scandinavian, meaning 'good memory'.

Muriel

Irish Gaelic, meaning 'sea-bright'. Author Muriel Spark was known for her novel The Prime of Miss Jean Brodie.

Myfanwy

Welsh, meaning 'my little lovely one'. The name originally appeared in a song called 'Myfanwy' by Joseph Parry.

Myleene

English, from the Latin Melaine meaning 'dark as night'. Associated with musician and presenter Myleene Klass.

Myra

Latin, meaning 'scented oil'. Famous Myras include pioneering lawyer Myra Bradwell and pianist Myra Hess, and also Moors murderer Myra Hindley.

Myrna
(alt. Mirna)

Irish Gaelic, meaning 'tender and beloved'. Actor Myrna Fahey appeared in Walt Disney's Zorro.

Myrtle

Irish, from the flowering shrub of the same name. Usually associated with the character of Myrtle Wilson from F. Scott Fitzgerald's novel The Great Gatsby.

Girls' names

Nadia
(alt. Nadya)

Russian, meaning 'hope'. Romanian Nadia Elena Comăneci was the first female Olympic gymnast to be awarded a perfect score of 10, and has three gold medals. Nadia Petrova is a tennis pro and Nadia Sawalha is a TV presenter and actor.

Nadine

French, meaning 'hope'. Also the title of a Chuck Berry song. Nadine Gordimer is a South African writer and activist who won the Nobel Prize for literature.

Nahara

Aramaic, meaning 'light'.

Nahla
(alt. Nala, Nalo)

Arabic, meaning 'first drink of water', and Sanskrit meaning 'hollow reed'. Made popular by the character from Disney's *The Lion King*.

Naima

Arabic, meaning 'water nymph'. Naima Belkhiata is a singer with the group Honeyz.

Nakia

Egyptian, meaning 'pure'.

Nalani

Hawaiian, meaning 'serenity of the skies'.

Nan
(alt. Nanna, Nannie)

Hebrew, meaning 'grace'. A character in Louisa May Alcott's *Little Women*.

Nancy
(alt. Nanci, Nancie)

Hebrew, meaning 'grace'. Nancy Reagan was a First Lady of the USA and anti-drug advocate who began her career as a film actor.

Nanette
(alt. Nannette)

French, meaning 'grace'. *No, No Nanette* is a musical comedy from the 1920s. Nanette Lepor is an American fashion designer and Nanette Newman is a British actor.

Naomi
(alt. Naoma, Noemi)

Hebrew, meaning 'pleasant'. Found in the Bible. Naomi Campbell is one of the original five supermodels.

Narcissa
Greek, meaning 'daffodil'. Narcissa Whitman, a missionary, became one of the most famous women of the early American West.

Nastasia
Greek, meaning 'resurrection'. Can also mean 'born on Christmas Day'.

Natalie
(alt. Natalee, Natalia, Natalya, Nathalie)

Latin, meaning 'birth day'. From the Latin name Natalia, meaning 'Christmas Day'. Its popularity increased in the USA after the 1940s due to actor Natalie Wood, who was the daughter of Russian immigrants.

Natasha
(alt. Natasa)

Russian, meaning 'birth day'. A character in Leo Tolstoy's *War and Peace*. Used in the English-speaking world only since the 20th century.

Natividad
Spanish, meaning 'Christmas'.

Neda
English, meaning 'wealthy'. Neda was also an Arcadian nymph who nursed the infant Zeus.

Nedra
English, meaning 'underground'.

Neema
Swahili, meaning 'born of prosperity'.

Neka
Native American, meaning 'goose'.

Nell
(alt. Nelda, Nell, Nella, Nellie, Nelly)

Shortened form of Eleanor, meaning 'light'. May have roots in old German *nelle*, meaning 'crown of the head', perhaps suggesting an obstinate person.

Nemi
Italian, from the lake of the same name.

Neoma
Greek, meaning 'new moon'.

Nereida
Spanish, meaning 'sea nymph'. A mermaid in Greek mythology.

Nerissa
Greek, meaning 'sea nymph'. The name of Portia's waiting woman in Shakespeare's *The Merchant of Venice*.

Nettie
(alt. Neta)

Shortened form of Henrietta, meaning 'ruler of the house'.

Neva

Spanish, meaning 'snowy'.

Nevaeh

American, meaning 'heaven'. The name Nevaeh is the word 'Heaven' spelled backwards. May also be linked with Neva, Spanish for 'snowy'.

Neytiri

Na'vi, meaning 'princess'. From the *Avatar* film series.

Nhung

Vietnamese, meaning 'velvet'.

Niamh
(alt. Neave, Neve)

Gaelic, meaning 'brightness'. In Irish mythology, Niamh was a goddess, the daughter of the god of the sea and a queen of the land of eternal youth.

Nicola
(alt. Nichola, Nichole, Nicole, Nicolette, Nicolle, Nikole; abbrev. Nicky, Nicki, Nikki)

Greek, meaning 'victory of the people'. Nicola is a boys' name in Italy, but became widely used in England and Germany as a girls' name, perhaps due to the -a ending of the name. Nicole Kidman is an Oscar-winning Australian actor. Nicole Farhi is a French fashion designer and sculptor.

Nidia

Spanish, meaning 'graceful'.

Nigella

Irish Gaelic, meaning 'champion'. Nigella Lawson is a TV chef and author, famous for her sensual style of cookery.

Nikita

Greek, meaning 'unconquered'. Popular in Russia. Also the one-word title of a song by Elton John, a film and a US TV series.

Nila

Egyptian, meaning 'Nile'.

Nilda

German, meaning 'battle woman'.

Nimra

Arabic, meaning 'number'. Also a name of Punjabi origin, meaning 'humble'.

Nina

Spanish, meaning 'girl'. One of the three ships used by Christopher Columbus on his first voyage. Nina Conti is a comedian and ventriloquist and Nina Simone was a jazz singing legend and civil rights campaigner.

Nissa

Hebrew, meaning 'sign'.

Nita

Spanish, meaning 'gracious'.

Nixie

German, meaning 'water sprite'.

Noel
(alt. Noelle)

French, meaning 'Christmas'. Noel is used most commonly for boys; Noelle is the feminine variant.

Nola

Irish Gaelic, meaning 'white shoulder'. Also a city and area in Italy.

Nona

Latin, meaning 'ninth'.

Nora
(alt. Norah)

Shortened form of Eleanor, meaning 'light', used in its own right. Nora Roberts is an American author who has written over 200 romance novels, some under pseudonyms.

Noreen
(alt. Norine)

Irish, meaning 'light'. Professor Noreen Murray was a highly regarded molecular geneticist who helped develop a vaccine against hepatitis B.

Norma

Latin, meaning 'pattern'. In Bellini's tragic opera of the same name, Norma is a druidess at the time of the Roman occupation of England. Norma Jeane was the real name of Marilyn Monroe.

Normandie
(alt. Normandy)

French, from the province of the same name.

Novia

Latin, meaning 'new'.

Nuala

Irish Gaelic, meaning 'white shoulder'. A popular name in Ireland.

Nydia

Latin, meaning 'nest'.

Nyimbo

Swahili, meaning 'song'.

Nyoko

Swahili, meaning 'snake'. Made popular by the 'Nyoka the Jungle Girl' comic book series.

Nysa
(alt. Nyssa)

Greek, meaning 'ambition'. A mountainous district in Greek mythology.

Girls' names

Oceana
(alt. Ocean, Océane, Ocie)
Greek, meaning 'ocean'.

Octavia
Latin, meaning 'eighth'. Sister to Caesar and wife to Antony in Shakespeare's *Antony and Cleopatra*.

Oda
(alt. Odie)
Shortened form of Odessa, meaning 'long voyage'. Also Germanic, meaning 'wealth' or 'inheritance'.

Odele
(alt. Odell)
English, meaning 'woad hill'. Woad is a plant used as a natural blue dye.

Odelia
Hebrew, meaning 'I will praise the Lord'. Also an eighth-century French saint.

Odessa
(alt. Odyssey)
Greek, meaning 'long voyage'. A place in the Ukraine, known as the pearl of the Black Sea.

Odette
(alt. Odetta)
French, meaning 'wealthy'. In the famous ballet *Swan Lake*, Odette is the good swan.

Odile
(alt. Odilia)
French, meaning 'prospers in battle'. The evil black swan in the famous ballet *Swan Lake*.

Odina
Feminine form of Odin, from the Nordic god of the same name, meaning 'creative inspiration'.

Oksana

Russian, meaning 'praise to God'. Famous Oksanas include Oksana Baiul, a Ukrainian Olympic figure-skater; Oksana Grigorieva, a Russian pianist; and a character in the hit TV series *Killing Eve*.

Ola
(alt. Olie)

Greek, meaning 'man's defender'.

Olena
(alt. Olene)

Russian, meaning 'light'.

Olga

Russian, meaning 'holy'. The first Russian female ruler, later canonised as the first Russian saint of the Orthodox Church.

Oliana

American, meaning 'the Lord has answered'.

Olivia
(alt. Olive, Olivev, Oliviana, Olivié; abbrev. Ollie)

Latin, meaning 'olive'. Has featured in the Top 10 names for girls in England for several years now, including at number one.

Olwen

Welsh, meaning 'white footprint'. Olwen Hufton is a British historian of early modern Europe, women's history and social history.

Olympia
(alt. Olimpia)

Greek, meaning 'from Mount Olympus'. A sanctuary of ancient Greece, known as the site of the Olympic Games in classical times.

Oma
(alt. Omie)

Arabic, meaning 'leader'. In German, oma often refers to 'grandmother'.

Omyra

Latin, meaning 'scented oil'.

Ondine

French, meaning 'wave of water'. Also the name of a French play.

Oneida
(abbrev. Ona, Onnie)

Native American, meaning 'long awaited'. The Oneida Indians were believed to have emerged as a tribe in the 14th century.

Onyx

Latin, meaning 'veined gem'. A precious stone.

Oona
(alt. Oonagh)

Irish, meaning 'unity'.

Opal

Sanskrit, meaning 'gem'. A gemstone made of this mineral, noted for its rich iridescence.

Ophelia
(alt. Ofelia, Ophélie)

Greek, meaning 'help'. Lead character from Shakespeare's play *Hamlet*.

Oprah

Hebrew, meaning 'young deer'. Most often associated with Oprah Winfrey.

Orabela
(abbrev. Ora)

Latin, meaning 'prayer'.

Oralie
(alt. Oralia)

French, meaning 'golden'. Oralia Dominguez is a Mexican opera singer.

Orane

French, meaning 'rising'.

Orchid

Greek, from the flower of the same name.

Oriana
(alt. Oriane)

Latin, meaning 'dawning'. Oriana was the nickname for Queen Elizabeth I.

Orla
(alt. Orlaith, Orly)

Irish Gaelic, meaning 'golden lady'. Orla Kiely is an Irish fashion designer.

Orlean

French, meaning 'plum'. Orleans is a city in France.

Ornelia

Italian, meaning 'flowering ash tree'.

Orsa
(alt. Osia, Ossie)

Latin, meaning 'bear'.

Otthid

Greek, meaning 'prospers in battle'.

Ottilie
(alt. Ottie)

French, meaning 'prospers in battle'. Ottilie Metzger was a German opera singer well known in the early 1900s.

Ouida

French, meaning 'renowned in battle'. Pseudonym of the English novelist Maria Louise Ramé, known for her extravagant melodramatic romances.

Oyintsa

Native American, meaning 'white duck'.

Ozette

Native American, from the village of the same name.

Girls' names

Pacifica
(alt. Pacifika)

Spanish, meaning 'peaceful'. Pacifica Fernández was once Costa Rica's first lady; she also designed the Costa Rican flag.

Padma

Sanskrit, meaning 'lotus'. A major Buddhist symbol. Padma Lakshmi is an Indian-born American chef, cookbook author, model and TV presenter.

Paige
(alt. Page)

French, meaning 'serving boy'.

Paisley

Scottish, from the town of the same name.

Palma
(alt. Palmira)

Latin, meaning 'palm tree'.

Paloma

Spanish, meaning 'dove'. Paloma Picasso is the youngest daughter of artist Pablo Picasso. Singer Paloma Faith is known for her eccentric style.

Pamela
(alt. Pamala, Pamella, Pamla; abbrev. Pam)

Greek, meaning 'all honey'. Pamela Stephenson is an actor and comedian turned clinical psychologist and author. Pamela (P.L.) Travers is the author of *Mary Poppins*.

Pandora

Greek, meaning 'all gifted'. Also from the Greek myth, Pandora was given a box containing all the evils of the world, not to be opened. Now also commonly associated with the jewellery company.

Pangiota

Greek, meaning 'all is holy'. Comes from a Greek epithet widely used in reference to the Virgin Mary.

Paniz

Persian, meaning 'candy'.

Pansy

French, from the flower of the same name. Pansy Potter is a strong girl character in comic *The Beano* and Pansy Parkinson appears in the *Harry Potter* series.

Paprika

English, meaning 'spice'.

Paradisa
(alt. Paradis)

Greek, meaning 'garden orchard'.

Paris
(alt. Parisa)

Greek, from the mythological hero of the same name. Also from the city. Paris Hilton is the hotel heiress and socialite.

Parker

English, meaning 'park keeper'.

Parthenia

Greek, meaning 'virginal'.

Parthenope

Greek, from the mythological Siren of the same name. Parthenope Nightingale was the elder sister of Florence Nightingale.

Parvati

Sanskrit, meaning 'daughter of the mountain'. The Hindu goddess of love and devotion.

Pascale

French, meaning 'Easter'.

Patience

French, meaning 'the state of being patient'. A Shakespearean name. Patience Wheatcroft was a respected journalist, and is now in the House of Lords.

Patricia
(alt. Patrice; abbrev. Pat, Patsy, Patti, Pattie, Patty)

Latin, meaning 'noble'. Patricia Routledge and Patricia Hodge are English actors. Patricia Neal was an American actor whose birth name was Patsy Louise Neal.

Paula

Latin, meaning 'small'. Paula Radcliffe is a British long-distance runner, and current world record holder for the marathon.

Pauline
(alt. Paulette, Paulina)

Latin, meaning 'small'. The name of a British opera.

Paxton

Latin, meaning 'town of peace'.

Paz

Spanish, meaning 'peace'.

Pazia

Hebrew, meaning 'golden'.

Peace

English, meaning 'peace'.

Peaches

English, from the fruit of the same name. Rarely used. Peaches Geldof was the most famous bearer of the name.

Pearl
(alt. Pearle, Pearlie, Perla)

Latin, meaning 'pale gemstone'. Pearl Buck was an American author.

Peggy
(alt. Peggie)

Greek, meaning 'pearl'. Peggy Parish was the author of the children's story series Amelia Bedelia.

Pelia

Hebrew, meaning 'marvel of God'.

Penelope
(abbrev. Penny, Penni, Pennie)

Greek, meaning 'bobbin worker'. In Homer's *Odyssey*, Penelope is the faithful wife of Odysseus.

Peony

Greek, from the flower of the same name.

Perdita

Latin, meaning 'lost'. Perdita is one of the heroines of William Shakespeare's play *The Winter's Tale*.

Peri
(alt. Perri)

Hebrew, meaning 'outcome'. In Persian mythology, the Peri are spirits who have been denied paradise until they have done penance.

Perry
(alt. Perrie)

French, meaning 'pear tree'. Also an English alcoholic drink made from pears. Perrie Edwards is part of the pop group Little Mix.

Persephone

Greek, meaning 'bringer of destruction'. In Greek mythology, Queen of the Underworld.

Petra
(alt. Petrina)

Greek, meaning 'rock'. City in Jordan dating back to the time of Jesus and the Apostles.

Petula

Latin, meaning 'to seek'. Petula Clark is an English singer, actor and composer.

Petunia

Greek, from the flower of the same name.

Phaedra

Greek, meaning 'bright'.

Philippa
(abbrev. Pippa, Pippie)

Greek, meaning 'lover of horses'. Philippa Foot was a 20th-century philosopher and pioneer in the field of modern ethics.

Philomena
(alt. Philoma)

Greek, meaning 'loved one'. Also a Catholic saint.

Phoebe

Greek, meaning 'shining and brilliant'. In Greek mythology, Phoebe was one of the original Titans and is associated with the moon.

Phoenix

Greek, meaning 'dark red'. In ancient Greek mythology, a phoenix is a bird that has the power to regenerate itself from its ashes.

Phyllida

Greek, meaning 'leafy bough'. Phyllida Lloyd is a British director, best known for her work in theatre and as the director of *Mamma Mia!* and *The Iron Lady*.

Phyllis
(alt. Phillia, Phylis)
Greek, meaning 'leafy bough'.

Pia

Latin, meaning 'pious'.

Piera

Italian, meaning 'rock'.

Pilar

Spanish, meaning 'pillar'. In Latin America, Nuestra Señora del Pilar (Our Lady of the Pillar), the name given to the Blessed Virgin Mary.

Piper

English, meaning 'pipe player'. Piper Laurie, an American actor, was born Rosetta Jacobs. Piper Kerman is the real-life inspiration behond the character Piper Chapman in hit TV series *Orange is the New Black*.

Plum

Latin, from the fruit of the same name.

Polly

Hebrew, meaning 'bitter'. A nickname for 'Mary'. Polly Dunbar is a British author-illustrator.

Pomona

Latin, meaning 'apple'. Pomona was a goddess of fruitful abundance in ancient Roman religion and myth.

Poppy

Latin, from the flower of the same name. Poppy Delevingne is a British socialite and model.

Portia
(alt. Porsha)
Latin, meaning 'from the Portia clan'. The heroine in Shakespeare's *The Merchant of Venice*.

Posy

English, meaning 'small flower'. Posy Hawthorne is a character in *The Hunger Games* series.

Precious

Latin, meaning 'of great worth'.

Priela

Hebrew, meaning 'fruit of God'.

Primavera

Italian, meaning 'springtime'. Also the name of a painting by Botticelli.

Primrose

English, meaning 'first rose'.

Princess

English, meaning 'daughter of the monarch'.

Priscilla
(alt. Prisca, Priscila)

Latin, meaning 'ancient'. Priscilla Wakefield was an 18th-century Quaker educational writer and philanthropist. Priscilla Presley is an actor, businesswoman and was the wife of Elvis Presley.

Priya

Hindi, meaning 'loved one'.

Prudence
(abbrev. Pru, Prue, Prudie)

Latin, meaning 'caution'. Known as the mother of all virtues.

Prunella

Latin, meaning 'small plum'. Prunella Clough was a prominent British artist and Prunella Scales is an actor best known for playing Sybil in *Fawlty Towers*.

Psyche

Greek, meaning 'breath'. In Greek mythology, the wife of Eros. Also the name of an opera.

Girls' names

Qiana
(alt. Qianah, Qiania, Qyana, Qianne)
American, meaning 'gracious'. Qiana Chase is an American model.

Qiturah
Arabic, meaning 'incense'.

Queen
(alt. Queenie)
English, meaning 'queen'.

Quiana
American, meaning 'silky'. Quiana Grant is an American model.

Quincy
(alt. Quincey)
French, meaning 'estate of the fifth son'. Also used as a boys' name.

Quinn
Irish Gaelic, meaning 'counsel'. Quinn Fabray is a character from the American musical comedy-drama series *Glee*.

Quintessa
Latin, meaning 'creative'.

Girls' names

Rachel
(alt. Rachael, Rachelle)
Hebrew, meaning 'ewe'. Rachel is a figure in the Bible. Famous Rachels include actors Rachel Weisz and Rachel Bilson, and the character of Rachel Green from *Friends*.

Radhika
(alt. Raadhika)
Sanskrit, meaning 'prosperous'. Raadhika Sarathkumar is one of Bollywood's most prolific actors and producers.

Rae
(alt. Ray)
Shortened form of Rachel, meaning 'ewe'. Rae Armantrout is known for her poetry and academic writing.

Rafferty
Irish, meaning 'abundance'. More commonly found as a surname.

Rahima
Arabic, meaning 'compassionate'.

Raina
(alt. Rain, Raine, Rainey, Rayne)
Latin, meaning 'queen'.

Raisa
(alt. Raissa)
Yiddish, meaning 'rose'. Extremely popular name in Russia, particularly as Mikhail Gorbachev's wife was called Raisa.

Raleigh
(alt. Rayleigh)
Old English, meaning 'deer's meadow'.

Rama
(alt. Ramey, Ramya)
Hebrew, meaning 'exalted'. Also one of the god Vishnu's avatars in the Hindu faith.

Ramona
(alt. Romona)

Spanish, meaning 'wise guardian'. Also the *Ramona* children's novels and the film *Ramona and Beezus*, by Beverly Cleary.

Ramsey
(alt. Ramsay)

Old English, meaning 'wild garlic island'. Can be used for girls and boys.

Rana
(alt. Rania, Rayna)

Arabic, meaning 'beautiful thing'.

Rani

Sanskrit, meaning 'queen'. Also a character from *Doctor Who*.

Raphaela
(alt. Rafaela, Raffaella)

Spanish, meaning 'God has healed'. Feminine form of Raphael, name of the painter and artist.

Raquel
(alt. Racquel)

Hebrew, meaning 'ewe'. Famous Raquels include actor Racquel Welch and the character in *Only Fools and Horses*.

Rashida

Turkish, meaning 'righteous'. Rashida Jones is an actor.

Raven
(alt. Ravyn)

English, from the black bird of the same name. Raven-Symoné is an actor often known as just Raven.

Razia

Arabic, meaning 'contented'. Razia Sultan was the only female ruler of the Sultanate Delhi and of the Mughal period of Indian history, during the 13th century.

Reagan
(alt. Reagen, Regan)

Irish Gaelic, meaning 'descendant of Riagán'.

Reba

Shortened form of Rebecca, meaning 'joined'. Reba McEntire is an American country singer.

Rebecca
(alt. Rebekah; abbrev. Becca, Becky, Becs, Beka, Bex, Reb)

Hebrew, meaning 'joined'. Rebecca is a figure in the Bible. Also a classic novel by Daphne Du Maurier. An enduringly popular name.

Reese

Welsh, meaning 'fiery and zealous'. Actor Reese Witherspoon starred in *Legally Blonde* and *Walk the Line*.

Regina

Latin, meaning 'queen'. Famous Reginas include actors Regina King and Regina Hall and the character of Regina George in the film *Mean Girls*.

Reiko

Japanese, meaning 'thankful one'.

Reina
(alt. Rey, Reyna, Rheyna)

Spanish, meaning 'queen'.

Rena
(alt. Reena)
Hebrew, meaning 'serene'.

Renata
Latin, meaning 'reborn'. Renata Tebaldi was one of the best-loved post-war opera singers.

Rene
Greek, meaning 'peace'. Actor Rene Russo appeared in *Get Shorty*, *The Thomas Crown Affair* and the *Thor* series.

Renée
(alt. Renae, Renee)
French, meaning 'reborn'. Famous Renées include actors Renée Zellweger and Renee Roberts, and one half of the singing duo Renée and Renato.

Renira
A rare name with no clear agreed origin. Used, but rarely, in a range of countries including England and Scotland, the USA, Germany, Brazil and Hungary.

Renita
Latin, meaning 'resistant'. Most commonly used in the USA.

Reshma
(alt. Resha)
Sanskrit, meaning 'silk'.

Reta
(alt. Retha, Retta)
Shortened form of Margaret, meaning 'pearl'. In Portuguese the name also means 'straight'.

Rhea
Greek, meaning 'earth'. Also the name of the mother of the gods in ancient Greek mythology.

Rheta
Greek, meaning 'eloquent speaker'.

Rhiannon
(alt. Reanna, Reanne, Rhian, Rhianna)
Welsh, meaning 'witch'. Also the name of the mother of Pryderi, King of Dyfed, in Welsh mythology.

Rhoda
Greek, meaning 'rose'. Found in the Bible.

Rhona
Nordic, meaning 'rough island'. Popular in Scotland. Rhona Martin represented Britain in curling at the 2002 Salt Lake City Olympics. Rhona Cameron is a comedian.

Rhonda
(alt. Ronda)
Welsh, meaning 'noisy'.

Ría
(alt. Rie, Riya)
Shortened form of Victoria, meaning 'victor'.

Ricki
(alt. Rieko, Rika, Rikki)
Shortened form of Frederica, meaning 'peaceful ruler'. Actor and presenter Ricki Lake hosted a talk show bearing her name for a decade.

Riley

Irish Gaelic, meaning 'courageous'. Used equally for both boys and girls.

Rilla

German, meaning 'small brook'.

Rima

Arabic, meaning 'antelope'. Rima the Jungle Girl is the fictional heroine of novel *Green Mansions* and was briefly a comic book character also.

Riona

Irish Gaelic, meaning 'like a queen'. Sometimes used as a spelling alternative to Fiona.

Ripley

English, meaning 'shouting man's meadow'.

Risa

Latin, meaning 'laughter'. More commonly used in Japanese- and Spanish-speaking cultures.

Rita

Shortened form of Margaret, meaning 'pearl'. Famous Ritas include actors Rita Hayworth and Rita Moreno and singer Rita Coolidge.

River
(alt. Riviera)

English, from 'river'. Used as both a boys' and a girls' name, sometimes in the plural.

Roberta
(abbrev. Robbie, Robi, Roby, Bobby, Bobbie)

English, meaning 'bright fame'. Singer Roberta Flack is best known for the songs 'The First Time Ever I Saw Your Face' and 'Killing Me Softly with His Song'.

Robin
(alt. Robbin, Robyn)

English, meaning 'bright fame'. Used slightly more often for boys than for girls. Famous Robins include actor Robin Wright Penn and singer Robyn.

Rochelle
(alt. Richelle, Rochel)

French, meaning 'little rock'. Singer and presenter Rochelle Humes featured in S Club 8 and The Saturdays.

Rogue

French, meaning 'beggar'. A character from the *X-Men* comic series.

Rohina
(alt. Rohini)

Sanskrit, meaning 'sandalwood'.

Roisin

Irish Gaelic, meaning 'little rose'. Singer Roisin Murphy was one half of group Moloko before going solo.

Roja

Spanish, meaning 'red-haired lady'. The name also means 'rose' in Tamil.

Rolanda

German, meaning 'renowned land'.

Roma

Italian, meaning 'Rome'. Also the name of an ancient Roman deity, and of a group of nomadic European people.

Romaine
(alt. Romina)

French, meaning 'from Rome'.

Romola
(alt. Romilda, Romily)

Latin, meaning 'Roman woman'. Actor Romola Garai appeared in films including *Atonement* and *Emma*.

Romy

Shortened form of Rosemary, meaning 'dew of the sea', and often the German variation. Actor Romy Rosemont is known for her TV roles in *Prison Break*, *Grey's Anatomy* and *Glee*.

Rona
(alt. Ronia, Ronja, Ronna)

Nordic, meaning 'rough island'. Also the name of two Scottish islands, North Rona and South Rona.

Ronnie
(alt. Roni, Ronni)

English, meaning 'strong counsel'. Impressionist and actor Ronni Ancona has also appeared on TV panel shows.

Roro

Indonesian, meaning 'nobility'. Sometimes used as a nickname for Ro- names (Rosa, Rosalind, etc).

Rosa

Italian, meaning 'rose'. Activist Rosa Parks is credited with being the 'First Lady of American civil rights' after she refused to give up her seat to a white passenger on a bus in 1955.

Rosabel
(alt. Rosabella)

Contraction of Rose and Belle, meaning 'beautiful rose'. Most commonly used in the USA.

Rosalie
(alt. Rosale, Rosalia, Rosalina)

French, meaning 'rose garden'. Actor Andie MacDowell's birth name is Rosalie.

Rosalind
(alt. Rosalinda)

Spanish, meaning 'pretty rose'. A character in Shakespeare's *As You Like It*.

Rosalyn
(alt. Rosaleen, Rosaline, Roselyn)

Contraction of Rose and Lynn, meaning 'pretty rose'. Also a song by The Pretty Things, which was later recorded by David Bowie.

Rosamund
(alt. Rosamond)

German, meaning 'renowned protector'. Famous Rosamunds include actor Rosamund Pike, author Rosamunde Pilcher and the long-time mistress of Henry II, Rosamund Clifford.

Rose

Latin, from the flower of the same name. Famous Roses include actors Rose Byrne and Rose McGowan and the character of Rose DeWitt Bukater from the film *Titanic*.

Roseanne

(alt. Rosana, Rosann, Rosanna, Rosanne, Roseann, Roseanna)

Combination of Rose and Anne, meaning 'graceful rose'.

Rosemary

(alt. Rosemarie; abbrev. Ros, Rosy, Rosie, Romy)

Latin, meaning 'dew of the sea'. Rosemary is the title of several songs. Famous Rosies include actors Rosie O'Donnell and Rosie Perez, and supermodel Rosie Huntington-Whiteley.

Rosita

Spanish, meaning 'rose'. A character in *Sesame Street*.

Rowena

(alt. Rowan)

Welsh, meaning 'slender and fair'. In ancient British mythology, Rowena was a powerful and beautiful seductress.

Roxanne

(alt. Roxana, Roxane, Roxanna; abbrev. Roxie, Roxey, Roxy)

Persian, meaning 'dawn'. A song by The Police. Famous Roxies include the character of Roxie Hart from the musical *Chicago*, inventor Roxey Ann Caplin, and the band Roxy Music.

Rubina

(alt. Rubena)

Hebrew, meaning 'behold, a son'. Also a tropical plant.

Ruby

(alt. Rubi, Rubie)

English, meaning 'red gemstone'. Associated with the comedian Ruby Wax, or the songs 'Ruby Tuesday' by The Rolling Stones and 'Ruby' by Kaiser Chiefs.

Rusty

American, meaning 'red-headed'. Used for girls and, more commonly, boys.

Ruth

(alt. Ruthe, Ruthie)

Hebrew, meaning 'friend and companion'. A prominent figure in the Bible.

Girls' names

Saba
(alt. Sabah)
Greek, meaning 'from Sheba'. Also the name of a small Caribbean island.

Sabina
(alt. Sabine)
Latin, meaning 'from the Sabine tribe'. Sabina was also the name given to certain women of political standing in ancient Rome.

Sabrina
Latin, meaning 'the River Severn'. Also a film starring Audrey Hepburn, and the title character of the sitcom *Sabrina, the Teenage Witch*.

Sadella
American, meaning 'fairytale princess'. More commonly used in the USA.

Sadie
(alt. Sade, Sadye)
Hebrew, meaning 'princess'. Famous Sadies include actor and businesswoman Sadie Frost, actor Sadie Miller and academic pioneer Sadie Tanner Mossell Alexander.

Saffron
(alt. Saffie)
English, from the reddish-yellow spice of the same name. Saffie is a character from ther TV series and films *Absolutely Fabulous*.

Safiyya
(alt. Safiya)
Arabic, meaning 'sincere friend'. Also the name of one of Muhammad's wives.

Sage
(alt. Saga, Saige)
Latin, meaning 'wise and healthy'. Also the name of a herb.

Sahara
Arabic, meaning 'desert'.

Sakura
Japanese, meaning 'cherry blossom'.

Sally
(alt. Sallie)
Hebrew, meaning 'princess'. Famous Sallys include actors Sally Field and Sally Whittaker and athlete Sally Gunnell.

Salma
Arabic, meaning 'peaceful'; Persian, meaning 'sweetheart'. Mexican-American actor Salma Hayek is a star of both film and TV.

Salome
(alt. Salma)
Hebrew, meaning 'peace'. Also found in the Bible.

Samantha
(abbrev. Sam, Sammie, Sammy)
Hebrew, meaning 'told by God'. Famous Samanthas include actors Samantha Morton and Samantha Bond.

Samara
(alt. Samaria, Samira)
Hebrew, meaning 'under God's rule'. Also the name of several places in Russia.

Sanaa
Arabic, meaning 'brilliance'. Also the capital of Yemen.

Sandra
(alt. Saundra; abbrev. Sandi, Sandy)
Shortened form of Alexandra, meaning 'defender of mankind'. Famous Sandras include actor Sandra Bullock, and Sandy is the main female character in the film *Grease*.

Sangeetha
Hindi, meaning 'musical'. Actor Sangeetha Arvind Krish is known in Bollywood simply as Sangeetha.

Sanna
(alt. Saniya, Sanne, Sanni)
Hebrew, meaning 'lily'. Also sometimes used as a shortened version of Susanna.

Santana
(alt. Santina)
Spanish, meaning 'holy'. Usually associated with the (male) guitar legend Carlos Santana.

Saoirse
Irish, meaning 'freedom'. Pronounced 'Ser-sha', Irish-American actor Saoirse Ronan has been nominated for numerous awards.

Sapphire
(alt. Saphira)
Hebrew, meaning 'blue gemstone'. Usually associated with the blue gem popular in jewellery.

Sarah
(alt. Sara, Sarai, Sariah)
Hebrew, meaning 'princess'. Found in the Bible. A particularly popular name in the 1960s.

Sasha
(alt. Sacha, Sascha)

Russian, meaning 'defender of mankind'. Used for both girls and boys. Sasha is one of Barack Obama's daughters.

Saskia
(alt. Saskie)

Dutch, meaning 'the Saxon people'. In Danish the name also means 'valley of light'.

Savannah
(alt. Savanah, Savanna, Savina)

Spanish, meaning 'treeless'. Also one of Queen Elizabeth II's great-grandchildren, Savannah Phillips.

Scarlett
(alt. Scarlet)

English, meaning 'scarlet'. Usually associated with the character of Scarlett O'Hara, from the novel and film Gone with the Wind, or actor Scarlett Johansson.

Scout

French, meaning 'to listen'. The main female character from the classic novel To Kill a Mockingbird, by Harper Lee.

Sedona
(alt. Sedna)

Spanish, from the city of the same name. Also the name of a city in Arizona, USA.

Selah
(alt. Sela)

Hebrew, meaning 'cliff'. Also a phrase used in the Hebrew Bible meaning 'stop and listen'.

Selby

English, meaning 'manor village'.

Selena
(alt. Salena, Salima, Salina, Selene, Selina)

Greek, meaning 'moon goddess'. Famous Selenas include singers Selena Gomez and Selena Quintanilla-Perez (known simply as Selena) and actor Selena Royle.

Selma

German, meaning 'Godly helmet'. Versatile actor Selma Blair has starred in a range of film genres as well as Hollywood hits.

Seneca

Native American, meaning 'from the Seneca tribe'. Also the name of a prominent ancient Roman philosopher, Seneca the Younger.

Sephora

Hebrew, meaning 'bird'; Greek, meaning 'beauty'.

September

Latin, meaning 'seventh month'.

Seraphina
(alt. Serafina, Seraphia, Seraphine)

Hebrew, meaning 'ardent'.
St Serafina was an Italian woman whose illness and suffering contributed to her strong faith.

Seren
Welsh, meaning 'star'.

Serena
(alt. Sarina, Sereana)

Latin, meaning 'tranquil'. Serena Williams has dominated women's tennis in the 21st century.

Serenity
Latin, meaning 'serene'. Also a sci-fi film.

Shania
(alt. Shaina, Shana, Shaniya)

Hebrew, meaning 'beautiful'. Shania Twain is the Canadian country/pop singer-songwriter whose real first name is Eilleen.

Shanice
American, meaning 'from Africa'. Singer Shanice is known for songs including 'I Love Your Smile'.

Shaniqua
(alt. Shanika)

English, adapted from the Swahili word Shanika, meaning 'God is gracious'. More commonly used in the USA.

Shanna
English, meaning 'old'. There is a comic book character called *Shanna the She-Devil* and Shanna Zolman is a professional basketball player.

Shannon
(alt. Shannan, Shanon)

Irish Gaelic, meaning 'old and ancient'. The name is believed to be a reference to Sionna, who was a goddess in ancient Irish mythology.

Shantal
(alt. Shantel, Shantell)

French, meaning 'stone'. Often used as a spelling alternative to Chantal.

Shanti
(alt. Shantih)

Hindi, meaning 'peaceful'. Also mentioned in T.S. Eliot's poem *The Waste Land*.

Sharlene
German, meaning 'man'. Often used as a spelling alternative to Charlene.

Sharon
(alt. Sharen, Sharona, Sharron, Sharyn)

Hebrew, meaning 'a plain'. Famous Sharons include swimmer Sharon Davies, presenter Sharon Osbourne and actor Sharon Stone.

Shasta
American, from the mountain of the same name. Also the name of a Native American tribe.

Shauna
(alt. Shawna)

Irish, meaning 'the Lord is gracious'. More commonly used in the USA.

Shayla
(alt. Shaylie, Shayna, Sheyla)

Irish, meaning 'blind'. Shayla Worley is an American gymnast.

Shea

Irish Gaelic, meaning 'from the fairy fort'. Usually associated with the tree and the nut that goes into creating shea butter.

Sheena

Irish, meaning 'the Lord is gracious'. Singer Sheena Easton rocketed to fame when she featured in an early British reality TV show, *The Big Time*, in the late 1970s.

Sheila
(alt. Shelia)

Irish, meaning 'blind'. Actor Sheila Hancock has had a long and varied career on stage, screen and radio.

Shelby
(alt. Shelba, Shelbie)

Norse, meaning 'willow'. Can also be used as a boys' name.

Shelley
(alt. Shelli, Shellie, Shelly)

English, meaning 'meadow on the ledge'. Famous Shelleys include skeleton athlete Shelley Rudman and actor Shelley Winters.

Shenandoah

Iroquoian (Native American), meaning 'deer'. A river in the state of Virginia, USA.

Sheridan

Irish Gaelic, meaning 'wild man'. Actor Sheridan Smith appeared in *Gavin and Stacey*.

Sherry
(alt. Sheree, Sheri, Sherie, Sherri, Sherrie)

Shortened form of Cheryl or Sheryl, meaning 'man'. Also an alcoholic drink.

Sheryl
(alt. Sherryl)

German, meaning 'man'. Famous Sheryls include singer Sheryl Crow, presenter Sheryl Gascoigne and Sheryl Sandberg, and businesswoman Sheryl Sandberg.

Shiloh

Hebrew, meaning 'his gift'. From the biblical place of the same name, made popular by Angelina Jolie and Brad Pitt's daughter.

Shirley
(alt. Shirlee)

English, meaning 'bright meadow'. Famous Shirleys include singer Dame Shirley Bassey, actor Shirley MacLaine and child star Shirley Temple.

Shivani

Sanskrit, meaning 'wife of Shiva'.

Shola

Arabic, meaning 'energetic'. More commonly a boys' name.

Shona

Irish Gaelic, meaning 'God is gracious'. Also associated with the Shona people of southern Africa.

Shoshana
(alt. Shoshanna)

Hebrew, meaning 'lily'. Made popular by the character of Shoshanna Shapiro in *Girls*.

Shura

Russian, meaning 'man's defender'. In Arabic it also means 'consultation'.

Sian
(alt. Siân, Sianna)

Welsh, meaning 'the Lord is gracious'. Famous Sians include presenters Sian Lloyd and Sian Williams, and actors Sian Phillips and Sian Clifford of *Fleabag*.

Sibyl
(alt. Sybil)

Greek, meaning 'seer and oracle'. Sibyl was a prophetess in ancient Greek mythology.

Sidney
(alt. Sydney)

English, meaning 'wide meadow'. Used for both boys and girls.

Sidonie
(alt. Sidonia, Sidony)

Latin, meaning 'from Sidonia'. Also the name of a French-German princess of the 15th century.

Sienna
(alt. Siena)

Latin, from the city of the same name. Also the name of a type of yellowy-red earth pigment. Sienna Miller is an English model, BAFTA-nominated actor and fashion designer.

Sierra

Spanish, meaning 'saw'.

Siffhi

Hindi, meaning 'spiritual powers'.

Signa
(alt. Signe)

Scandinavian, meaning 'victory'. Also the name of a town in the province of Florence, Italy.

Sigrid

Nordic, meaning 'fair victory'. Sigrid the Haughty was said to have been the wife of Eric the Victorious in ancient Norse mythology.

Siksika

First Nation, meaning 'silken foot'. The Siksika Nation is a tribe in Canada whose name comes from 'silk' and 'foot'.

Silja

Scandinavian, meaning 'blind'.

Simcha

Hebrew, meaning 'joy'.

Simone
(alt. Simona)

Hebrew, meaning 'to hear'. Feminine form of Simon, except in Italy, where Simone is the masculine form of Simon and the female form is Simona. Famous Simones include philosopher Simone de Beauvoir and first female scuba diver, Simone Melchior.

Sinéad

Irish, meaning 'the Lord is gracious'. Used with and without the accent on the 'e'. Famous Sineads include singer Sinéad O'Connor, actor Sinéad Cusack and ice-dancing skater Sinead Kerr.

Siobhan

Irish, meaning 'the Lord is gracious'. Actor Siobhan McKenna is credited with reviving the name in the 20th century.

Siren
(alt. Sirena)

Greek, meaning 'entangler'. Sirens were beautiful and deadly creatures who lured men to their deaths at sea in ancient Greek mythology.

Siria

Spanish, meaning 'glowing'. Often used as a spelling alternative to Syria.

Skye
(alt. Sky, Skylyn)

Scottish, from the large island of the same name in Scotland.

Skyler
(alt. Skyla, Skylar)

Dutch, meaning 'giving shelter'. The name Skyler saw a jump in popularity after the success of the drama series *Breaking Bad*, which featured a main character called Skyler White.

Sloane
(alt. Sloan)

Irish Gaelic, meaning 'man of arms'. Usually associated with Sloane Square in London, after which the Sloane Rangers are named.

Socorro

Spanish, meaning 'to aid'.

Sojourner

English, meaning 'temporary stay'. In the 19th century, civil rights and women's activist Sojourner Truth was known for her phrase 'And ain't I a woman?'

Solana

Spanish, meaning 'sunlight'. The solana is the Spanish word for the side of a mountain or valley where the sun hits.

Solange

French, meaning 'with dignity'. A Christian saint from the ninth century. American singer and actor Solange Knowles is unusual among famous Solanges in that she's not from a French-speaking country.

Soledad

Spanish, meaning 'solitude'.

Soleil
French, meaning 'sun'.

Solveig
Scandinavian, meaning 'woman of the house'.

Sona
Arabic, meaning 'golden one'. Sona MacDonald is an actor of stage and screen.

Sonia
(alt. Sonja, Sonya)
Greek, meaning 'wisdom'. Sonia Rykiel is a French fashion designer. Sonia O'Sullivan was a world-class Irish long-distance runner who won medals at World Championships and Olympics.

Sophia
(alt. Sofia, Sofie, Sophie)
Greek, meaning 'wisdom'. Sophia Loren was actually named Sofia. Italy's most famous actor, she won an Oscar, BAFTA and Golden Globes. Other famous Sophias include film director Sofia Coppola and actors Sofia Vergara and Sophia Myles.

Sophronia
Greek, meaning 'sensible'. Usually associated with the character of Sophronia from the epic poem *Jerusalem Delivered*, by Torquato Tasso.

Soraya
Persian, meaning 'princess'. Queen Soraya Tarzi was the wife of King Amanullah of Afghanistan (reigned 1919–1929).

Sorcha
Irish and Scottish Gaelic, meaning 'bright and shining'. Irish actor Sorcha Cusack has appeared in *Coronation Street* and *Casualty*.

Sorrel
English, from the edible herb of the same name.

Stacey
(alt. Stacie, Stacy)
Greek, meaning 'resurrection'. Famous Staceys include actors Stacey Keibler and Stacey Dash, and presenter Stacey Dooley.

Star
(alt. Starla, Starr)
English, meaning 'star'.

Stella
Latin, meaning 'star'. Leading fashion designer Stella McCartney is known for her ethics and creativity.

Stephanie
(alt. Stefanie, Steffanie, Stephani, Stephania, Stephany, Stephenie)
Greek, meaning 'crowned'. Famous Stephanies include actor Stephanie Beacham, tennis pro Stefanie 'Steffi' Graf and author Stephenie Meyer.

Sue
(alt. Susie, Suzy)

Shortened form of Susan, meaning 'lily'. Famous Sues include comedian Sue Perkins and tennis pro turned TV presenter Sue Barker.

Sukey
(alt. Sukey, Sukie)

Shortened form of Susan, meaning 'lily'. Usually associated with the character of Sukey from the nursery rhyme 'Polly Put the Kettle On'.

Summer

English, from the season of the same name. Famous Summers include opera singer Summer Watson and actor Summer Glau.

Sunday

English, meaning 'the first day'.

Sunny
(alt. Sun)

English, meaning 'of a pleasant temperament'.

Suri

Persian, meaning 'red rose'. Suri Cruise is the daughter of Katie Holmes and Tom Cruise.

Surya

Hindi, from the god of the sun.

Susan
(alt. Susann, Suzan, Suzanne; abbrev. Sue, Susie, Suzy)

Hebrew, meaning 'lily'. Famous Susans include actor Susan Sarandon, singer Susan Boyle and suffragette Susan B. Anthony.

Susannah
(alt. Susana, Susanna, Susanne, Suzanna, Suzanne)

Hebrew, meaning 'lily'. Famous Susannahs include artist Susannah Fiennes and actors Susannah York and Susannah Doyle.

Svea

Swedish, meaning 'of the motherland'.

Svetlana

Russian, meaning 'star'. A popular name in Slavic countries, now starting to spread west. Svetlana Stalin was the daughter of Soviet dictator Josef Stalin.

Swanhild

Saxon, meaning 'battle swan'.

Sylvia
(alt. Silvia, Sylvie)

Latin, meaning 'from the forest'. Famous Sylvias include poet Sylvia Plath, suffragette Sylvia Pankhurst and singer Sylvia Robinson.

T

Girls' names

Tabitha
(alt. Tabatha, Tabetha)

Aramaic, meaning 'gazelle'. A woman raised from the dead by St Peter in the Bible. A very popular name in the USA in the 1970s and '80s, after Tabitha the child witch TV character.

Tahira
Arabic, meaning 'virginal'.

Tai
Chinese, meaning 'big'.

Taima
(alt. Taina, Tayma)

Native American, meaning 'peal of thunder'. Also the name of an oasis in Saudi Arabia.

Tajsa
Polish, meaning 'princess'.

Talia
(alt. Tali)

Hebrew, meaning 'heaven's dew'. Famous Talias include actors Talia Shire and Talia Balsam.

Taliesin
Welsh, meaning 'shining brow'. Usually associated with the Welsh poet Taliesin.

Talise
(alt. Talyse)

Native American, meaning 'lovely water'.

Talitha
Aramaic, meaning 'young girl'. The name is mentioned in the Bible when Jesus raises a child from the dead.

Tallulah
(alt. Taliyah)

Native American, meaning 'leaping water'. Famous Tallulahs include actors Tallulah Bankhead and Tallulah Riley, and the character of club singer Tallulah in the film *Bugsy Malone*.

Tamara
(alt. Tamera)

Hebrew, meaning 'palm tree'. Famous Tamaras include socialite Tamara Ecclestone and actors Tamera Mowry and Tamara Taylor.

Tamatha
(alt. Tametha)

American, meaning 'dear Tammy'. Sometimes used as a spelling alternative to Samantha.

Tamika
(alt. Tameka)

American, meaning 'people'.

Tammy
(alt. Tami, Tammie)

Shortened form of Tamsin, meaning 'twin'. Country singer Tammy Wynette's best-known song is 'Stand by Your Man'.

Tamsin

Hebrew, meaning 'twin'. Sometimes used as a shortened form of Thomasina.

Tanis

Spanish, meaning 'to make famous'.

Tanya
(alt. Tania, Tanya, Tonya)

Shortened form of Tatiana, meaning 'from the Tatius clan'. Dr Tanya Byron is a child psychologist, author and TV presenter on parenting issues.

Tao

Chinese, meaning 'like a peach'. Tao is also the notion of a route or path in Chinese cultures.

Tara
(alt. Tahra, Tarah, Tera)

Irish Gaelic, meaning 'rocky hill'. Famous Taras include actors Tara Fitzgerald and Tara Reid.

Tasha
(alt. Taisha, Tarsha)

Shortened form of Natasha, meaning 'birth day'. Famous Tashas include athlete Tasha Danvers, singer Tasha Thomas and author and illustrator Tasha Tudor.

Tatiana
(alt. Tatyana)

Russian, meaning 'from the Tatius clan'. Famous Tatianas include actor Tatyana Ali, author Tatiana de Rosna and the character of Tatiana Romanova from the James Bond film *From Russia With Love*.

Tatum

English, meaning 'light hearted'. Tatum O'Neal was the youngest person to win a competitive Oscar, picking up the award for *Paper Moon*.

Tawny
(alt. Tawanaa, Tawnee, Tawnya)

English, meaning 'golden brown'. Usually associated with the colour tawny, as used in the descriptive name of the tawny owl.

Taya

Greek, meaning 'poor one'. In several languages the name also means 'princess' or 'goddess'.

Taylor
(alt. Tayler)

English, meaning 'tailor'. Can be used for boys as well as girls. Famous Taylors include singer Taylor Swift and actor Taylor Schilling.

Tea

Greek, meaning 'goddess'. Actor Tea Leoni is known by her middle name, rather than her first name of Elizabeth.

Teagan
(alt. Teague, Tegan)

Irish Gaelic, meaning 'poet'.

Teal

English, from the bird of the same name. Often associated with the bluish-green colour.

Tecla

Greek, meaning 'fame of God'.

Tehile

Hebrew, meaning 'song of praise'.

Temperance

English, meaning 'virtue'.

Tempest

French, meaning 'storm'. Also the title of a Shakespearean play.

Teresa
(alt. Terese, Tereza, Theresa, Therese; abbrev. Terri, Teri, Terrie, Terry)

Greek, meaning 'harvest'. Famous Teresas include nun Mother Teresa, former Prime Minister Theresa May and actor Teresa Graves.

Tessa
(alt. Tess, Tessie)

Shortened form of Teresa, meaning 'harvest'. Tessa Virtue is a Canadian ice dance champion, and javelin thrower Tessa Sanderson represented Great Britain at every Olympics from 1976 to 1996.

Thais

Greek, from the mythological ancient Greek concubine of the same name.

Thalia

Greek, meaning 'blooming'. There are several ancient Greek muses, nymphs and graces who share the name Thalia.

Thandie
(alt. Thana, Thandi)

Arabic, meaning 'thanksgiving'. Thandie Newton is a British film and TV actor.

Names with positive meanings

Allegra – cheerful

Augusta – magnificent

Felicia – lucky

Hilary – cheerful

Lucy – light

Phoebe – radiant

Thalia – flourishing

Yoko – positive

Thea

Greek, meaning 'goddess'. Also a shortened form of Theodora or Dorothea.

Theda

German, meaning 'people'. Theda Bara was one of the silent film era's most prolific and popular actors, appearing in over 40 films.

Thelma

Greek, meaning 'will'. Famous Thelmas include the actor Thelma Barlow, singer Thelma Houston and the film *Thelma and Louise*.

Theodora
(alt. Theodosia)

Greek, meaning 'gift of God'. There are many ancient Roman empresses and other figures named Theodora.

Thisbe

Greek, from the mythological heroine of the same name in the ancient Roman poem *Metamorphoses* by Ovid.

Thomasina
(alt. Thomasin, Thomasine, Thomasyn)

Greek, meaning 'twin'. Singer Tammi Terrell, who was known for her Motown duets with singer Marvin Gaye, was born Thomasina Montgomery.

Thora

Scandinavian, meaning 'Thor's struggle'. Famous Thoras include actors Thora Hird and Thora Birch and the figure of Thora Bogarhjort of ancient Norse mythology.

Tia
(alt. Tiana)

Spanish, meaning 'aunt'. Famous Tias include actor Tia Mowry and the goddess Tia from Native American Haida tribal mythology.

Tiara

Latin, meaning 'jewelled headband'.

Tien

Vietnamese, meaning 'fairy child'.

Tierney

Irish Gaelic, meaning 'Lord'.

Tierra
(alt. Tiera)

Spanish, meaning 'land'. Used most commonly in the USA.

Tiffany
(alt. Tiffani, Tiffanie)

Greek, meaning 'God's appearance'. Famous Tiffanys include the singer Tiffany, socialite Tiffany Trump and the book/film/song *Breakfast at Tiffany's*.

Tiggy
(alt. Tigris)

Irish Gaelic, meaning 'tiger'. Tiggy Legge-Bourke (whose birth name is Alexandra) is known for being a royal nanny to Princes William and Harry.

Tilda

Shortened form of Matilda, meaning 'battle-mighty'. Oscar-winning actor Tilda Swinton's full name is Katherine Matilda.

Tilly
(alt. Tillie)

Shortened form of Matilda, meaning 'battle-mighty'. Has seen a rise in popularity in recent years.

Timothea

Greek, meaning 'honouring God'.

Tina
(alt. Teena, Tena)

Shortened form of Christina, meaning 'anointed Christian'. Famous Tinas include singer Tina Turner, comedian Tina Fey and actor Tina Louise.

Tirion

Welsh, meaning 'kind and gentle'.

Tirzah

Hebrew, meaning 'pleasantness'. Found in the Bible.

Titania

Greek, meaning 'giant'. Also the Fairy Queen in Shakespeare's *A Midsummer Night's Dream*.

Toby
(alt. Tobi)

Hebrew, meaning 'God is good'. More commonly used as a boys' name.

Tomoko

Japanese, meaning 'intelligent'.

Toni
(alt. Tony)

Latin, meaning 'invaluable'. Also a shortened form of Antoinette. Famous Tonis include author Toni Morrison, singer Toni Braxton and choreographer Toni Basil.

Tonia
(alt. Tonja, Tonya)

Russian, meaning 'praiseworthy'.

Topaz

Latin, meaning 'golden gemstone'.

Tori
(alt. Tora, Toria)

Shortened form of Victoria, meaning 'victory'. Singer Tori Amos was born Myra Ellen Amos.

Tova
(alt. Tovah, Tove)

Hebrew, meaning 'good'.

Tracy
(alt. Tracey, Tracie)

Greek, meaning 'harvest'. Famous Tracys include singer Tracy Chapman, artist Tracey Emin and actor Tracey Ullman.

Treva

Welsh, meaning 'homestead'.

Trilby

English, meaning 'vocal trills'.

Trina
(alt. Trena)

Greek, meaning 'pure'. Usually a shortened form of Katrina.

Trinity

Latin, meaning 'triad'. Usually associated with the Christian Holy Trinity. Also the impossibly cool lead female character in *The Matrix*.

Trisha
(alt. Tricia)

Shortened form of Patricia, meaning 'noble'.

Trista

Latin, meaning 'sad'. More commonly used in the USA.

Trixie

Shortened form of Beatrix, meaning 'blessed' or 'voyager'. Also a name used frequently in children's television and film, such as the characters of Trixie the Triceratops in *Toy Story 3* and Trixie the Troublemaker in *LazyTown*.

Trudie
(alt. Trudy, Truye; abbrev. Tru)

Shortened form of Gertrude, meaning 'strength of a spear'. Famous Trudies include actor Trudie Goodwin and producer and actor Trudie Styler.

Tullia

Latin, meaning 'bound for glory'.

Tunder

Hungarian, meaning 'fairy'.

Twyla
(alt. Twila)

American, meaning 'star'.

Tyler
(alt. Tyla)

English, meaning 'tile maker'. More commonly used as a boys' name.

Tyra

Scandinavian, meaning 'Thor's struggle'. Supermodel Tyra Banks is known for her extensive modelling career and is presenter of *America's Got Talent*.

Tzipporah

Hebrew, meaning 'bird'. Used as a spelling alternative to Zipporah.

Girls' names

Udaya
Sanskrit, meaning 'dawn'.

Ula
(alt. Ulla)
Celtic, meaning 'gem of the sea'. Also the name of a Manchu tribe from China.

Ulrika
(alt. Urica)
German, meaning 'power of the wolf'. Swedish Ulrika Jonsson made a TV career in Britain.

Uma
Sanskrit, meaning 'flax'. Actor Uma Thurman is known for her roles in *Pulp Fiction*, *Gattaca* and the *Kill Bill* series.

Una
Latin, meaning 'one'. Famous Unas include enduring British actor Una Stubbs and Irish singer Una Healy of The Saturdays.

Undine
Latin, meaning 'little wave'. Also the name of a water element in alchemy.

Unice
Greek, meaning 'victorious'. A spelling alternative to Eunice.

Unique
Latin, meaning 'only one'.

Unity
English, meaning 'oneness'.

Uriela
(alt. Uriella)
Hebrew, meaning 'angel of light'. Found particularly in German-speaking communities.

Urja
(alt. Urjitha)
Sanskrit, meaning 'energy'.

Ursula
Latin, meaning 'little female bear'. A character in Disney's film *The Little Mermaid*.

Uta
German, meaning 'prospers in battle'.

Girls' names

Vada
German, meaning 'famous ruler'.

Valdis
(alt. Valdiss, Valdys, Valdyss)
Norse, meaning 'goddess of the dead', based on the mythological goddess of the same name.

Valencia
(alt. Valancy, Valarece; abbrev. Vale)
Latin, meaning 'strong and healthy'. Also one of the largest cities in Spain.

Valentina
(alt. Valentine)
Latin, meaning 'strong and healthy'. Valentina Cortese is an Italian actor. Russian Valentina Tereshkova was the first female astronaut, in 1963.

Valerie
(alt. Valarie, Valery, Valorie, Valeria; abbrev. Valia)
Latin, meaning 'to be healthy and strong'. Also a song by The Zutons, which was famously covered by Amy Winehouse. Valia Venitshaya was an actor in the silent film era.

Vandana
Sanskrit, meaning 'worship'. Also the name of a genus of moths.

Vanessa
(alt. Vanesa)
English, from the *Gulliver's Travels* character of the same name. Famous Vanessas include TV presenter Vanessa Feltz and American actor Vanessa Hudgens.

Vanetta
(alt. Vanettah, Vaneta, Vanete, Vanity)
Greek, alternative of Vanessa, meaning 'like a butterfly'.

Vanity
Latin, meaning 'self-obsessed'.

Vashti
Persian, meaning 'beauty'. Also the name of a Persian queen in the Hebrew Bible.

Veda

Sanskrit, meaning 'knowledge and wisdom'. The Vedas are an important set of texts from ancient India.

Vega

Arabic, meaning 'falling vulture'. Also the name of a bright star in the night sky.

Velda

German, meaning 'ruler'. Also the name of a common ancestor named in *The Seven Daughters of Eve*.

Vella

American, meaning 'beautiful'. Also the name of a genus of leafy plants.

Velma

English, meaning 'determined protector'. A character in the *Scooby-Doo* series.

Venice
(alt. Venetia, Venita)

Latin, meaning 'city of canals'. From the city of the same name in Italy.

Venus

Latin, from the ancient Roman goddess of sexuality and fertility. Also the name of the planet.

Vera
(alt. Verla, Verlie)

Slavic, meaning 'faith'. Famous Veras include actor Vera Farmiga, singer Vera Lynn and fashion designer Vera Wang.

Verda
(alt. Verdie)

Latin, meaning 'spring-like'.

Verena

Latin, meaning 'true'. St Verena was a third-century Roman saint who healed the sick.

Verity

Latin, meaning 'truth'.

Verna
(alt. Vernie)

Latin, meaning 'spring green'. Actor Verna Felton was a voice actor for Disney films and productions.

Verona

Latin, shortened form of Veronica. From the city of the same name in Italy.

Veronica
(alt. Verica, Veronique)

Latin, meaning 'true image'. Famous Veronicas include actors Veronica Lake and Veronica Carlson and the protagonist of the *Veronica Mars* series and film.

Veruca

Latin, meaning 'wart'. Usually associated with the character of Veruca Salt from the children's novel *Charlie and the Chocolate Factory*, by Roald Dahl.

Vesta

Latin, from the ancient Roman goddess of the same name, said to be in charge of the hearth, home and family.

Vevina

Scottish, meaning 'pleasant lady'. More commonly used in the USA.

Vicenta

Latin, meaning 'prevailing'. More commonly used in Italian-speaking communities.

Victoria

(abbrev. Vicky, Vicki, Vickie, Vikki, Vix)

Latin, meaning 'victory'. The name became popular during and after the reign of Queen Victoria in the 19th century, and has remained pretty steadfastly popular ever since.

Vida

Spanish, meaning 'life'.

Vidya

Sanskrit, meaning 'knowledge'. Often used in the Hindu faith to refer to learning and knowledge.

Vienna

Latin, from the city of the same name in Austria.

Vigdis

Scandinavian, meaning 'war goddess'. Most commonly used in Icelandic communities.

Vina

(alt. Vena)

Spanish, meaning 'vineyard'.

Viola

Latin, meaning 'violet'. Also a musical instrument like a large violin.

Violet

(alt. Violetta)

Latin, meaning 'purple'. Also a small purple flower of the same name.

Virginia

(alt. Virginie; abbrev. Virgie, Ginny)

Latin, meaning 'maiden'. Famous Virginias include author Virginia Woolf and tennis player Virginia Wade.

Visara

Sanskrit, meaning 'celestial'.

Vita

Latin, meaning 'life'. Often used to refer to the life story of a saint, or their biography.

Vittoria

Variation of Victoria, meaning 'victory'. More commonly used in Italian-speaking communities.

Viva

Latin, meaning 'alive'. Actor Viva was one of Andy Warhol's muses during the 1960s.

Viveca

(alt. Vivica)

Scandinavian, meaning 'war fortress'. Actor Vivica A. Fox is known for her roles in Independence Day, Kill Bill and Soul Food.

Vivian

(alt. Vivien, Vivienne)

Latin, meaning 'lively'. Famous Vivians include actor Vivien Leigh and designer Vivienne Westwood.

Vonda

Czech, meaning 'from the tribe of Vandals'. Singer Vonda Shepard was known for her soft-pop songs and appearances on Ally McBeal.

Girls' names

Waleska
Polish, meaning 'beautiful'. Most commonly used in German-speaking communities.

Wallis
English, meaning 'from Wales'. Famous Wallises include Wallis Simpson, the late Duchess of Windsor, and the singer Wallis Bird.

Walta
Swahili, meaning 'like a shield'. Also feminine form of Walter.

Wanda
(alt. Waneta, Wanita)
Slavic, meaning 'tribe of the vandals'. Princess Wanda was a queen of Poland in the eighth century.

Waneta
(alt. Wanita)
Variation of Wanda, meaning 'tribe of the vandals'. Also the name of an infamous Yanktonai Dakota Native American tribal chief during the 18th and 19th centuries.

Wava
English, meaning 'way'. More commonly used in the USA.

Waveney
Old English, from the river of the same name.

Waverly
Old English, meaning 'meadow of aspens'. Can be used as a girls' name or, more commonly, a boys' name.

Wendy
English, meaning 'friend'. Famous Wendys include actors Wendy Richard and Wendy Hiller and the character of Wendy Darling in Peter Pan.

Wharton
English, meaning 'from the river'.

Whisper
English, meaning 'whisper'.

Whitley
Old English, meaning 'white meadow'.

Whitney

Old English, meaning 'white island'. Singer Whitney Houston was a pop sensation of the 1980s and appeared in the film *The Bodyguard* with Kevin Costner.

Wilda

German, meaning 'willow tree'. More commonly used in Polish-speaking communities.

Wilfreda

English, meaning 'to will peace'. Feminine form of Wilfred.

Wilhelmina

Old German, meaning 'strong-willed warrior'. Many members of the German royal family have been named Wilhelmina.

Willa
(alt. Willene, Willia)

German, meaning 'helmet'. American Willa Cather was a Pulitzer Prize-winning author.

Willow

English, from the tree of the same name. Celebrity children named Willow include Willow Smith (Will Smith's daughter) and Willow Hart (Pink's daughter).

Wilma
(alt. Wilmer)

German, meaning 'protection'. A character from the cartoon *The Flintstones*.

Winifred
(abbrev. Winnie)

Old English, meaning 'holy and blessed'. Famous Winifreds include Winifred Atwell, prison breaker Winifred Herbert, author Winifred Mary Letts and South African activist Winnie Madikizela-Mandela.

Winona
(alt. Wynona)

Sioux Indian, meaning 'first-born daughter'. Actor Winona Ryder is named after the town where she was born, Winona in Minnesota, USA.

Winslow

English, meaning 'friend's hill'.

Winter

English, meaning 'winter'.

Wisteria

English, meaning 'flower'.

Wren

Old English, meaning 'tiny bird'. Often associated with the species of small birds found throughout the world.

Wynda

Scottish, meaning 'of the narrow passage'.

Wynne
(alt. Wynn)

Welsh, meaning 'very blessed'.

Girls' names

Xanadu

A city in Mongolia. Xanadu was the summer capital of Kubla Khan's empire and the inspiration of Samuel Taylor Coleridge's poem *Kubla Khan*. Also a 1980 film starring Olivia Newton-John.

Xanthe

Greek, meaning 'blonde'. Also the name of several characters in ancient Greek mythology.

Xanthippe

Greek, meaning 'nagging'. Also the name of an influential figure in ancient Greek mythology.

Xaverie
(alt. Xaviera)

Spanish, meaning 'the new house'. Feminine form of Xavier.

Xena
(alt. Xenia)

Greek, meaning 'foreigner'. The popularity of this name rose after the success of *Xena: Warrior Princess*.

Ximena

Spanish, meaning 'to hear'. More commonly used in Mexico.

Xiomara

Spanish, meaning 'battle-ready'.

Xiu

Chinese, meaning 'elegant'.

Xochitl

Nahuatl, meaning 'flower'. Queen Xochitl was a legendary queen of the Toltec culture.

Xoey

Variant of Zoe, meaning 'life'. Often used as a spelling variation for Zoe or Zoey.

Xristina

Variation of Christina, meaning 'follower of Christ'. Usually associated with singer Christina Aguilera, who often spells her name Xtina.

Xylia
(alt. Xylina, Xyloma)

Greek, meaning 'from the woods'.

Girls' names

Yadira
Arabic, meaning 'worthy'. More commonly used in Spanish- and Portuguese-speaking communities.

Yael
Hebrew, meaning 'mountain goat'. Found in the Bible.

Yaffa
(alt. Yahaira, Yajaira)
Hebrew, meaning 'lovely'.

Yamilet
Arabic, meaning 'beautiful'. More commonly used in Spanish-speaking communities.

Yana
Hebrew, meaning 'the Lord is gracious'. Also the name of a spiritual practice in Buddhism.

Yanha
Arabic, meaning 'dove-like'.

Yanira
Hawaiian, meaning 'pretty'. Also the name of a character in ancient Greek mythology.

Yareli
Latin, meaning 'golden'. More commonly used in Spanish-speaking communities.

Yaretzi
(alt. Yaritza)
Aztec, meaning 'forever beloved'. More commonly used in the USA.

Yasmin
(alt. Yasmeen, Yasmina)
Persian, meaning 'jasmine flower'. Famous Yasmins include actor Yasmin Paige, model Yasmin le Bon and DJ Yasmin.

Yelena
Greek, meaning 'bright and chosen'. Extremely popular name in Russia and Ukraine.

Yeraldina

Spanish, meaning 'ruled with a spear'.

Yesenia

Arabic, meaning 'flower'. Used as a name in the 1970s for a Spanish-language television production.

Yetta

English, from Henrietta, meaning 'ruler of the house'. Also used in Yiddish-speaking communities.

Yeva

Hebrew variant of Eve, meaning 'life'.

Ylva

Old Norse, meaning 'she wolf'. The name originated in Sweden in the 13th century.

Yoki
(alt. Yoko)

Native American, meaning 'rain'. In Japanese the name also means 'happiness' and 'life force'.

Yolanda
(alt. Yolonda)

Spanish, meaning 'violet flower'. There have been several monarchs of Europe known as Yolanda.

Yoselin

English, meaning 'lovely'. Can also be used as a spelling alternative to Jocelyn.

Yoshiko

Japanese, meaning 'good child'. Princess Yoshiko was the Empress of Japan during the 18th and 19th centuries.

Yovela

Hebrew, meaning 'jubilee'.

Ysabel

English, meaning 'God's promise'. Often used as a spelling alternative to Isabel.

Ysanne

Contraction of Isabel and Anne, meaning 'pledged to God' and 'grace'.

Yuki

Japanese, meaning 'lucky'. Also the name of a popular Japanese singer and songwriter.

Yuliana

Latin, meaning 'youthful'. Often used as a spelling alternative to Giuliana.

Yuridia

Russian, meaning 'farmer'. Singer Yuridia is one of the most popular pop stars in Mexico.

Yusia

Arabic, meaning 'success'.

Yvette
(alt. Yvonne)

French, meaning 'yew'. Famous Yvettes include presenter Yvette Fielding, actor Yvette Nicole Brown and politician Yvette Cooper.

Girls' names

Zafira

Arabic, meaning 'successful'.

Zahara

(alt. Zahava, Zahra, Zayah)
Arabic, meaning 'flowering and shining'. The most famous Zahara is the daughter of Angelina Jolie and Brad Pitt.

Zaida

(alt. Zaide)
Arabic, meaning 'prosperous'. Also a familiar term for grandfather in Yiddish.

Zalika

Swahili, meaning 'well born'. More commonly used in Egypt.

Zaltana

Arabic, meaning 'high mountain'.

Zamia

Greek, meaning 'pine cone'. Also the name of a plant.

Zaneta

(alt. Zanceta, Zanetah, Zanett, Zanetta)
Hebrew, meaning 'a gracious present from God'. More commonly used in Polish and Latvian communities.

Zaniyah

Arabic, meaning 'lily'. Most commonly used in the USA.

Zara

(alt. Zaria, Zariah, Zora)
Arabic, meaning 'radiance'. Famous Zaras include Queen Elizabeth II's granddaughter Zara Tindall, actor Zara Cully and fashion brand Zara.

Zelda

German, meaning 'dark battle'. Usually associated with the Nintendo video game series *The Legend of Zelda* or American novelist Zelda Fitzgerald.

Zelia
(alt. Zella)
Scandinavian, meaning 'sunshine'.

Zelma
German, meaning 'helmet'.
Sometimes used as a spelling
alternative to Thelma.

Zemira
(alt. Zemirah)
Hebrew, meaning 'joyous melody'.
An opera by Francesco Bianchi.

Zena
(alt. Zenia, Zina)
Greek, meaning 'hospitable'.
Usually used as a spelling alternative
to Xena.

Zenaida
Greek, meaning 'the life of Zeus'.
St Zenaida is recognised as one of
the first Christian physicians, during
the second century.

Zenobia
Latin, meaning 'the life of Zeus'.
Queen Zenobia was the leader of the
Palmyrene empire in Syria during
the third century.

Zephyr
Greek, meaning 'the west wind'.

Zetta
Latin, meaning 'seven'. In modern
maths, zetta means 10^{21} (that's
number 1 followed by 21 zeros).

Zia
Arabic, meaning 'light and
splendour'. Musician Zia McCabe is
known for being a founding member
of the band the Dandy Warhols.

Zinaida
Greek, meaning 'belonging to Zeus'.
More commonly used in Russian-
speaking communities.

Zinnia
Latin, meaning 'flower'. Also the
name of a flowering perennial plant.

Zipporah
Hebrew, meaning 'bird'. Zipporah
was one of the wives of Moses in the
Bible.

Zita
(alt. Ziva)
Spanish, meaning 'little girl'. St Zita
is an Italian patron saint of maids and
domestic servants.

Zoë
*(alt. Zoe, Zoi, Zoie, Zoey, Zoeya,
Zoila, Zooey)*
Greek, meaning 'life'. Famous Zoes
include TV and radio presenter
Zoë Ball and actors including Zoë
Wanamaker, Zoe Saldana and Zooey
Deschanel.

Zoraida
Spanish, meaning 'captivating
woman'.

Zorina
Slavic, meaning 'golden'.

Zosia
(alt. Zosima)

Greek, meaning 'wisdom'. Actor Zosia Mamet is known for her roles in *Mad Men*, *Parenthood* and *Girls*.

Zoya

Greek, meaning 'life'. Zoya Kosmodemyanskaya is one of the former Soviet Union's most revered heroines, after fighting for the Russian rebellion during World War II.

Zula

Swahili, meaning 'brilliant'.

Zuleika

Arabic, meaning 'fair and intelligent'. Also the name of Potiphar's wife in the Bible.

Zulma

Arabic, meaning 'peace'.

Zuzana

Hebrew, meaning 'lily'. More commonly used in the Czech and Slovak republics.

Zuzu

Czech, meaning 'flower'. The nickname for one of George Bailey's children in the film *It's A Wonderful Life*.

- Amina →
- Alicia →
- Priya
- ~~Ruya~~
- Anais
- Amber
- ~~Valentina~~
- ~~Fatona~~
- Esme
- Evelyn
- Livia
- Thelma

- ~~Ruya~~

NORA
NOUIA

Farrah
_____

Livia
_____

Maya
_____

Marnie
_____

Priya